The Dawn of Victory – Thank You China

Star Shell Reflections 1918–1919

The Dawn of Victory – Thank You China

Star Shell Reflections 1918–1919

The Illustrated Great War Diaries of Jim Maultsaid

Barbara McClune

Pen & Sword
MILITARY

First published in Great Britain in 2017 by
Pen & Sword Military
an imprint of
Pen & Sword Books Ltd
47 Church Street
Barnsley
South Yorkshire S70 2AS

ISBN 978 1 52671 270 7

Typeset in Ehrhardt by
Mac Style Ltd, Bridlington, East Yorkshire
Printed and bound by Replika Press Pvt. Ltd.

Pen & Sword Books Ltd incorporates the imprints of Pen & Sword
Archaeology, Atlas, Aviation, Battleground, Discovery, Family History,
History, Maritime, Military, Naval, Politics, Railways, Select, Social
History, Transport, True Crime, and Claymore Press, Frontline Books,
Leo Cooper, Praetorian Press, Remember When, Seaforth Publishing
and Wharncliffe.

For a complete list of Pen & Sword titles please contact
PEN & SWORD BOOKS LIMITED
47 Church Street, Barnsley, South Yorkshire, S70 2AS, England
E-mail: enquiries@pen-and-sword.co.uk
Website: www.pen-and-sword.co.uk

STAR SHELL

REFLECTIONS

PART 3

BY JIM MAULTSAID

the CHINESE LABOUR CORPS

Sketches Stories

Photographs

the DAWN of VICTORY

Foreword

This is the third and final volume of Jim Maultsaid's Great War Diaries entitled *Star Shell Reflections*. As his Granddaughter, I do hope that you will enjoy it, and also read the earlier volumes if you have not already.

Please take a moment to pause and reflect on how these books came into be being. How a young man who left school aged thirteen with a passion for sketching decided in 1919 to put together his sketches and stories from the notebooks and drawing pads he carried with him from 1914–1919, during and after the Great War. When starting out his plan was to make a scrapbook, but this turned into five large handwritten diaries.

This was an entirely self-motivated task, which became a labour of love, commitment and passion. He succeeded and excelled in creating a series of remarkable and unique historical records that are invaluable and have stood the test of time for close on a century; I am confident that they will continue to do so.

This particular book is special as he records his time with his much loved but little-known Chinese Labour Corps.

He not only describes their culture and ways, but also tells fascinating stories of their everyday contribution to the war effort, a part of history rarely written about or touched upon.

I am proud to dedicate *Dawn of Victory* to the memory of the 96,000 Chinese Volunteers who served and particularly those who gave their lives during the Great War. I especially have in mind the memory of his own unit, 169 Company Chinese Labour Corps, so proudly declared by my Grandfather as 'The best in France'.

Barbara Anne McClune

Introduction

'Can this really be the end? The end of that adventure started so long ago. How long ago? Five years and three months. Like the waves my thoughts race in currents through my brain. Was I sad? Was I glad? Reader I cannot tell.'

To have lived through these days … lived to look back on them and again bring to the mind the loyal devoted Chinese and white workers who faced such difficulties along with me … and won through.

A glorious page of history was written by these men (East and West) in those days long ago on the lines of communication on the Western Front.

I was fortunate in being attached to a company of a very exceptional type of Chinese. Our boys were young and full of life, as most boys are, and quick to learn. When reading the stories you must not forget these boys were in a strange land thousands of miles from home. The pictures breath the spirit of those hectic days of August 1918 and depict a phase of the Great War seldom, if ever, touched by any of the stories of these days.

I have done my best to set before you our marvellous work that was performed by the CLC and in a small measure hope I have succeeded in giving you an insight into the heart and soul of those great workers of 169 Company.

Let me say – I will never meet men of higher honesty fair dealing, just staunch and true. My regard for the Chinese boy is deep and profound.

In conclusion I'll never forget 169 Company of glorious wonderful boys – I salute you one and all.

Bravo the boys from the land of the dragon, bravo indeed.

Jim Maultsaid

My chums Simpson, Thompson and Forrester gave me a royal reception – even my own skipper, Captain Curtain, unbent a little and looked mighty pleased to have his Ulster officer back once more. 'An' shure, I was delighted myself to get right in amongst them all again – those pals of mine.'

'Return-a-la "tree-bon" la! la!' Broad Chinese smiles spreading over yellow faces the first morning I took up duty again with No. 2 Platoon. My imp of a sergeant almost jumped for joy. I had great trouble in getting rid of his shadow for several days afterwards. 'Why do you follow me around?' I asked him. 'Because I don't want to lose you again,' he replied!

Gone to his Forefathers – strange rites

The burial of a Chinese boy was a strange ceremony in many ways and to us some of the methods did appear rather 'unique'.

'MOVE ON'

Their graveyards were kept apart from the white people and were generally on the side of the hill on rising ground 'to secure repose and drive away evil spirits' and a running stream of water if at all possible was preferred on or near the bottom of the burial ground. The idea of this was, I suppose, to keep the evil spirits on the move? The head of the corpse is always towards the head of the hill and the feet towards the stream. The grave itself was dug around four inches deep, a mound of earth some two feet deep is then piled over the grave 'for security'. But I am moving too fast or putting the horse before the cart. Let me start at the beginning.

The corpse is dressed and handled by his nearest friends. A clean new suit, washed and ironed, is put on the body and it is now all ready for the last journey. Arriving at the burial ground a short halt is called before the actual burial takes place. Forward moves the procession, in silence and reverence. The body is placed in the grave and no service of any kind performed; if there is a service, it was not carried out in France at any of the burials I took part in, so I cannot say or do not know if such takes place. Anyhow the soil is now piled in and a mound some two feet deep is built up.

Stepping forward the nearest of kin places several crumpled newspapers on this mound, strikes a match and sets them alight.

FOR THE RETURN
This is to drive away all evil spirits and give him a new clean start in the life to come. He will not be troubled by these fiends when he comes back.

Next a fresh clean suit neatly folded is placed on the top of the grave; this is his new outfit fresh and clean, all ready for the 'comeback'.

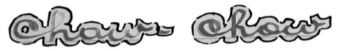

Then apples, oranges and patties (hard white bread rolls made without any yeast are called patties) are set on the mound also; this is for his long journey through space to the new world. He is now well provided for, as you can see, and wants for nothing.

Their belief is that each spirit comes back to this earth and is the living soul of themselves – enters into some of them and still lives. That is to say that 'Wang Chung', now alive and well, contains the spirit perhaps of his great-great-grandfather! Or some ancestor of a long-forgotten generation. Each and every race to their own beliefs.

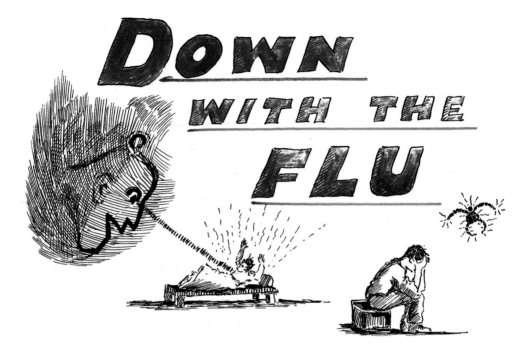

It got me! That 'flu bug. Laid low and unable to do anything for myself, it was a horrible experience indeed.

My boy – poor soul was at his wit's end and never left my side for fear I would die – and truth to tell I hardly cared if I did or not. Winter storms swept around the wooden structure, cold blasts blew from cracks in the walls, and I lay and shivered, and sweated too. Hot, feverish, tossing from side to side it was the worst spell I ever had on Active Service. The doctor gave me several calls and a few doses of medicine and said I had to lie in bed. In fact I could not have got on my feet if I had been offered a million pounds.

What worried me most of all: was it the 'flu I had – or one of those mysterious Chinese diseases? I was scared stiff. This did not help me to get well any sooner. My brother officers shouted through the wooden partition to me each morning and at night, but were forbidden to enter my sick bunk to see me. Quite right too, or the company would have been left in a mess by having no officers for duty. Days were long, and nights longer still. The devotion of that boy of mine was sublime; he was a mother and a nurse to me. I can still picture that little yellow anxious face peering down at me and saying 'plenty good today officer?' I always said 'Yes!'. 'Ding hola.' 'San Gowdy' (meaning – that's good – grand indeed) he muttered, and the face lit up. A wonderful kid!

BACK TO DUTY

A week passes. I recover and shake off the fever. A few days more and I'm back on duty, 'the Lord be praised'. Goodbye the 'flu. Goodbye!

IT will not be out of place at this stage to give you an insight into the real character of the Chinese coolie by picture and a short article.

I was fortunate in being attached to a company of a very exceptional type of Chinese; some of the other companies were indeed poor and of inferior mentality. Our boys were young and full of life – as most boys are – and quick to learn. When reading the stories you must not forget that these boys were in a strange land thousands of miles from home.

SONS of CHINA

THESE boys afforded me a great opportunity to study the ways, and different outlook on life held by them from our western ideas. You will, no doubt, by now have come to the conclusion that I did not miss much; well I set out at the beginning to get at the very bottom of things and view from the Chinese angle such problems that arose from time to time. How I succeeded I can only leave to you to judge.

I never treated them in the 'heavy' or 'overbearing' manner adopted by some Chinese Labour Corps officers. My method was more or less to reason with them as I found they were no fools. They liked a square deal and as a rule give you one in return. What more could you ask? If you made a promise and carried it out you went well up in their estimation. I must say that they always tried to carry out any bargain they made themselves. In fact, I would almost make bold to say that the Chinese in many ways are far more honourable than we white people; this from my own experience.

THIS TYPE WAS RARE IN OUR LOT

YOU will notice how the different types of coolie vary in looks. Our company were more or less all young and nearly all from the same part or province of China. We had an odd one here and there who did not conform to the standard type, but we generally found that these particular boys were from some faraway part of that mighty country and hardly knew what the others were talking about. Of course the various companies differed quite a lot and when I got to know my own lot thoroughly I could pick them out.

Sons of China

A FAVOURITE CROP.

J.M.

On the next page you have some of my sketches, torn from my active service book; nothing better appears in these pages so far as illustrating the varied types mentioned throughout in the stories of the CLC.

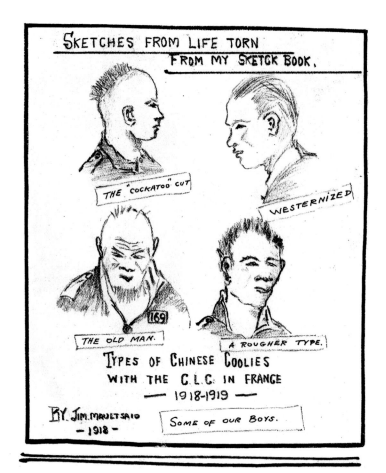

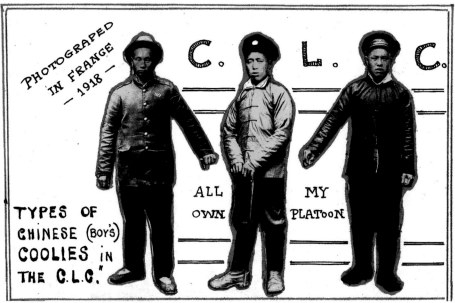

SONS of CHINA.

ON COLD WINTER DAYS.

JIM.MAULTSAID

SONS OF CHINA

MEMENTOES GALORE

Fond of being photographed, I had little difficulty in securing quite a picture gallery of 'mementoes'; most of these are here for your inspection. No doubt they are interesting?

Some of them wondered what I was really playing at when I asked them to stand still for a few minutes as I sketched a rough outline of their features. Put me down as being 'off the top' – not wise? Their varied haircuts amused me thoroughly. Note the clean-cut appearance of the three boys in photograph. No pigtails here! No Sir! The lad on your left wears his workaday suit and the other two have their Sunday best on. The great improvement in their appearance is best compared if you turn back to the story 'Stiltwalkers' in the previous book. This was accomplished under our care and teaching.

"PECULIARITIES"

THE Chinese were for Labour work only. Work!
YOU were 'Ding-how' (good) or 'Ding-by-how' (no good).
WHEN properly handled – great workers indeed.
THEIR friendship gained – your friend always.
THEY expect you to keep your word (promise).
PEACEFUL, quiet fellows. Some had hearts of gold.
GREAT gamblers: good losers; debts paid in full.
WE helped them to save their wages by banking.
THE pay was 1 franc per day (10d/4p) for coolies.
TO hear them defend themselves on trial. A treat.
ALL came to France with pigtails. Few went home with them.
EACH coolie had his service number on a brass band on his wrist.
ON a cold winter's day five or six jackets were worn.
HOT days. Jackets came off one by one. Funny!
RELUCTANT at all times to sell a chum. Fine.
WHEN tried for offences (if found guilty) said so.
IN the art of smuggling they stand supreme.
COOKED rice to perfection. No milk or sugar.
DRANK tea, black tea, no sugar or milk.
A CHINESE feast usually meant some twenty courses.
CHOPSTICKS were brought to France but soon discarded.
ARTFUL fellows in their own way, but honest.
ALWAYS swore by their ancestors. Back – back.
TRADES of all kinds represented in our lot.
WONDERFUL workers! Wonderful boys!
PICKED up French easily. English not so easy.
GREAT adventure this, for them, over in France.
I WISH them rest, and peace, and happiness.

CHINA LAND

JIM MAULTSAID

CHINESE RIVER HOUSE AS PICTURED BY ME, AS THEY SAT AND TOLD ME ABOUT THAT FAR AWAY MAGIC COUNTRY OF THEIRS

CHINA LAND

THE day's work is over. I sometimes took a stroll through the compound and had a chat with the coolies as they sat and smoked, yarned and played cards. Funny little cards they used, long narrow strips of cardboard. Often I was asked about my country: what it was like, what size it was, and many, many questions.

A good full-size map of Ireland helped me to explain. They could hardly believe me when I told them we built the largest vessels in the world – such a small place as Ireland, surely not? And the greatest rope-works, also tobacco works; how I longed for five hundred packets of the Gallagher cigarettes to hand out as an advertisement! And what an advertisement it would have been! And then Irish soldiers – how I praised them! Oh boy!

My chalk came into action and I sketched pictures on the side of the wooden hut. How interested they all were.

Jim Maultsaid.

STRANGE CUSTOMS

Then I took a turn and asked many questions too. Strange to say these boys gave me the impression that they regarded their own 'China – land' as far in advance to our western states in many ways. For example, the Chinese had forgotten more about the art of printing than we would ever learn. And as for silk, why it was made out there thousands of years ago. So there you are! Then many strange customs were explained to me – their different Gods: God of the Sun, the moon, the stars – and their evil spirits too. Oh, it was wonderful to sit and listen to it all, and form the pictures in your mind of their 'China – land'.

HOW my bright boy used up his spare time is illustrated below. This is a sample of his handiwork and was presented to me. Note the regimental numbers he displays. Why he gives three of them I fail to understand – but he makes quite a good attempt at our figures. His own name, I take it, appears on the top of design. I'm afraid he used my inks to make his sketches; he was hard to watch.

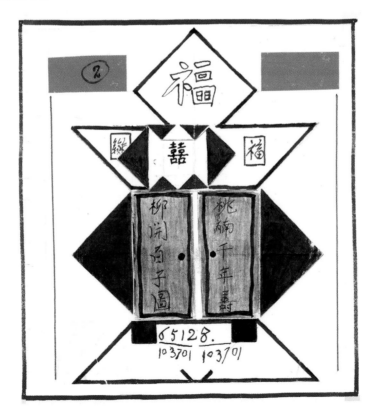

AS SOLDIERS.

A CHINESE FIELD GUN TEAM IN ACTION AGAINST THE JAPANESE.

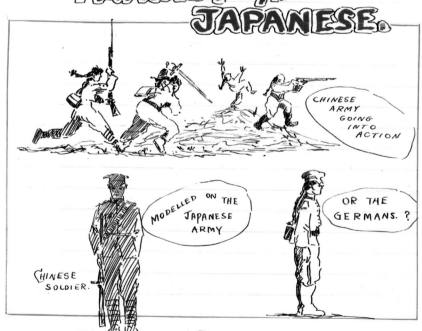

THEIR ARMIES

THEY told me all about their army, or should I say armies. How they fought, lived, and died. It did seem strange to me to listen to them, and compare our army ways with theirs. From all I could gather most of their training was modelled on the German and Japanese methods but, truth to tell, I would not have fancied much the job of leading them into battle. Many brave fellows no doubt … but …

THEIR WOMAN FOLK

Then their womenfolk! From infancy their little feet were put into iron cages of some sort – all screws and bolts – and were never allowed to grow or expand. This custom, I think, has now more or less died out. You can see a picture of a Chinese girl and form your own idea of their beauty. Can they beat ours? This picture was given to me by one of my coolies, as a little gift, and here it is in my book. I cannot tell you much more about Chinese girls as I never had the pleasure of meeting any.

WHIRLWIND WORK

THESE days were mad 'whirlwind' days: work … work … work! We almost drove the Chinese to destruction and ourselves to H★★★. We only stopped short at the 'slave methods', no whips of course, but every art was used in getting the last ounce from those brown bodies. It was a case of every convoy was a 'rush' one. Task and time limit every time. The speed was simply maddening; yet, it had to be done – more and more supplies called for, each day was heavier than the one before. Could we stand up to it – this stupendous rush?

HUNDREDS OF THOUSANDS

Hundreds of thousands. And hundreds of thousands. Again and again. Boxes of petrol. Tins of lubricating oils. Drums of grease. Trucks and trucks, loaded, sealed, shunted out and away up the line – to keep the mighty wheels of war moving.

WE SHIVERED . . . .

Winter blasts blow over the bleak Belgian low lands. Snow. Rain. Sleet. But not a moment's respite for us on the lines of supply and service.

Soaked through and through it mattered not, we had to stick it. Miserable fellows these Chinese boys of ours looked in winter time. Not being used to this kind of weather, it was a severe trial for our Chinese men and in my heart I did indeed feel sorry for them. We could do nothing with the elements and had to 'carry on'.

We shivered. Shivered hard, cursed the war, cursed our fate. And worked harder than ever. Did our troops not depend on us? Of course they did!

WONDERFUL N.C.O.'S

Blessed with wonderful NCOs who were full of ideas and ambition to get the very best out of their platoons, it was a pleasure to give orders knowing they would be carried out to the last detail.

A BOMB HERE . . . .

Here on this page you have a view of one of our petrol dumps, only a small section of course, but enough to give you some idea of 'the works'. Note the tremendous stacks of boxes, and the sections at work, and the convoy train, and the sentries on guard, and the big petrol tank … Dangerous spot during an air raid?

A bomb around here; a case of farewell! No wonder we were sometimes nervous during Jerry's visits! No wonder our Chinese boys flew for dear life. You would have done the same when the Hun man came, with his bombs and aerial torpedoes – AND DEATH!

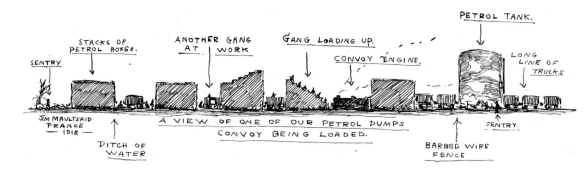

A VIEW OF ONE OF OUR PETROL DUMPS

ACTUAL PHOTOGRAPHS

Here you have an actual picture of one of my squads on loading a truck. Truck to stack, for stock. Notice the old bag each coolie carries over his shoulder. This was to ease the rawness of the end or edge of the box. It was also used for wiping away the sweat and as a kind of head covering sometimes during rainstorms or snow. In fact it acted in many various ways and appeared to be invaluable to the average coolie. Most of them also wore a broad cloth belt that kept their upper and lower garments together in some mysterious manner. Funny fellows – all!

FULL "BATTLE CRY"

Note the loose tins of petrol that have become detached from their boxes. These were gathered and replaced in new boxes – four tins per box. It was a treat to see one of these squads in full 'battle cry' loading up.

..... WINTER BLASTS BLOW — IT MATTERED — WE HAD TO CARRY ON — ....
— NOT —

SONS OF CHINA — IN WHIRLWIND WORK —

Tonight's indent for working parties is larger than ever. 'Where under the sun can we get them from!? Every available coolie on camp duties, every short-term "CB" man (confined to barracks) will have to be raked out for duty tomorrow.' Thousands of cases of petrol required and must be delivered to the ASC Officer Commanding at 6.00pm to make up his train. And we must not fail.

STUPENDOUS FIGURES

What a day! Hectic … mad … rush … hustle … crashing of cases from morn till night.

Even our white sergeants and corporals lend a hand, all to complete our stupendous task. When I tell you that each coolie in my squads had an average of ten to twelve tons to his credit for the day's work, actually carried on his shoulders and back, to and from the stack, and to truck, you have some idea of what these lads accomplished! Some of our labour leaders would collapse if these figures were put before them. Yet what I tell you is true, and if my returns to HQ could only now be produced they would astonish you.

LIKE A FILM

As a matter of fact I was once hauled up for, should I say, 'faking' or 'cooking'? a daily return of work done, but that's a story that will come along later. The strange part about it is, I was wilfully underestimating our work, yet was pulled up for the very opposite. But, as I said before, more later.

……… YEARS AGO ????

Troop trains. Ammunition trains. Red Cross trains. All kinds of trains passed us in scores every day, to and from the battlefields. We wave a greeting to the boys as they sit on the steps of the open doors, their legs hanging out – just as I sat myself years ago, or was it a hundred years ago? The past was like a dream, or a cinematograph film that I was watching. And yet I was on that film myself. Strange!

LOYAL …. DEVOTED …. CHINESE

To have lived through these days, lived to look back on them and again bring to the mind the loyal devoted Chinese and white workers that faced such difficulties along with me. And won through.

WHIRLWIND WORK

On the next page you see me with my head ganger on the right and the old Father of our flock on my left. This is the old gent I told you about in my story '87 not out'. Note the cage containing his pet sparrow. This picture was taken on the petrol depot. You can see

the stacks of petrol behind us and the corner of the filling shed (see the story 'Petrol! Petrol! Petrol!') This ganger was one of the finest and most intelligent Chinese boys I ever met. He held his position from the first days in France until the end.

OUR CHINESE POLICE

NATIVE POLICEMAN.

HEAD CONSTABLE.

SECOND IN COMMAND.

PICKED men all!

Our native Chinese police force were all picked men. Each company had its own police squad to deal with minor offenders etc. I must say as a general rule they carried out all their duties in a first-class manner, but we had to always support them with white NCOs at critical moments. Naturally they were all known to the police, often being related in some way and, of course, orders from a brother or a cousin did not go down too well at times. You understand the position?

Some clever fellows amongst our MP squad. They kept us well posted regarding 'grievances' and unrest in the ranks – a most important thing as it gave us a chance to nip in and 'kill' the trouble, but we had to be very careful as 'spites' were sometimes exploited through the medium of the native police; this required tact and much understanding. You must not imagine that these men came under the heading of spies. Far from it – as a rule they were most loyal to their own and us.

MANY DUTIES

They were held responsible for a clean camp, clean huts, clean cookhouse and general neatness. Lo and behold any slacker they caught! The CB men were also looked after to see that 'fatigue' duties were performed, and all the coolies in the guardroom got the full attention of our MPs.

The head of the police was the head of all our five hundred odd Chinese. A most responsible position.

A SPECIAL gang was picked to deal with oils, drums, cans, canisters, containers, tins, casks, barrels, and large tanks. Anything in the oil line fell to this squad. It was a dirty job, too, but, for all that, these twelve lads grew to love their work and in a short time became experts. You can see them at work in the photographs and my sketches. Each platoon had an oil gang. The platoon officers used to have a bet on their speed, and hold competitions. Mine had their share of the victories, but these trials were sometimes wasteful, as all was sacrificed for speed, speed, speed, so we cut it out.

THE SWORD SWALLOWER

One of my lot was a 'Sandow'. He was the only man I ever knew who could lift a barrel of oil from the ground, get it right on his back and carry it to truck. Strange to say he was also our star turn acrobat and you can read about this fellow in my story 'The Sword swallower'. And by the way he was also an ex-soldier of the Chinese army. Quite an interesting fellow, his influence in the oil gang was immense, yet he was not a ganger. Temperamental and moody he was not altogether fitted for this job. A splendid worker for all that.

RARE CONTRAPTIONS

The appliances used by these boys were remarkable. Crude, homemade, but clever, all to ease their work. Ropes, chains, and planks of wood all played their part in the loading of their cargo. My little sketches make their methods clear to you. No doubt you'll agree they were cute?

Never a drum out in their count.

THE OIL GANG

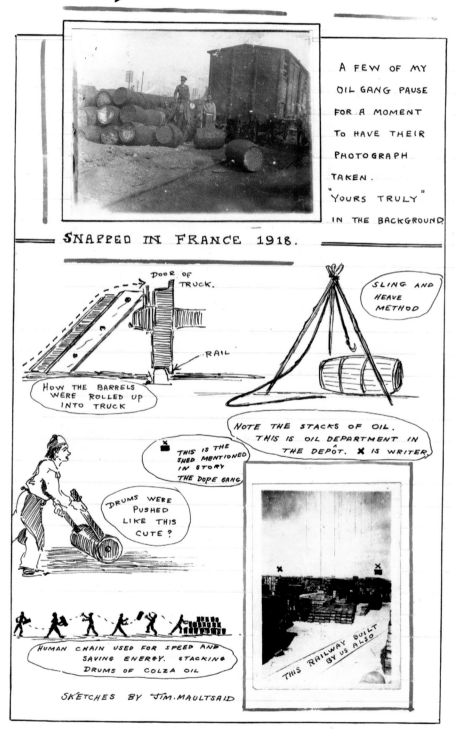

A FEW OF MY OIL GANG PAUSE FOR A MOMENT TO HAVE THEIR PHOTOGRAPH TAKEN. "YOURS TRULY" IN THE BACKGROUND

SNAPPED IN FRANCE 1918.

DOOR OF TRUCK.

RAIL

HOW THE BARRELS WERE ROLLED UP INTO TRUCK

SLING AND HEAVE METHOD

NOTE THE STACKS OF OIL. THIS IS OIL DEPARTMENT IN THE DEPOT. ✗ IS WRITER

THIS IS THE SHED MENTIONED IN STORY THE DOPE GANG

DRUMS WERE PUSHED LIKE THIS CUTE ?

HUMAN CHAIN USED FOR SPEED AND SAVING ENERGY. STACKING DRUMS OF COLZA OIL

THIS RAILWAY BUILT BY US ALSO

SKETCHES BY JIM. MAULTSAID

26

E – Er – San – Sir – woo – five at the time. So many rows. One hundred, two hundred, three hundred, four hundred up! Up! Up! Strange chalk marks on the side of the truck. Try it yourself officer and make sure! But we soon found it was useless work, and left it all to them. And you could have staked your life on the correct amount being in that truck.

"FIREWATER".

When on the methylated spirit job we had to keep our eye on them. Temptation stared them in the face. It was saleable to the French – easy money. It made a good old drink of 'firewater', so we had to watch them carefully. Sometimes a glazed eye, unsteady step, or an uncalled for spirit of joyfulness give us the clue to a drum with a hole made by a large nail. Then investigation commenced. But they were staunch little devils to each other, and it had to be punishment for the whole squad as often as not; one would not give the other away. Against all this, I was proud of my crack oil gang.

WHEN I tell you that this festival occupied two days you'll have some idea of the importance of 'Celestial Moon' celebrations in the eyes of our Chinese boys. For me to try and tell you what it all exactly represented would be an utter impossibility, but I can give you some idea of why it was carried out and by the help of my sketches plus the real photographs – taken by Lieutenant English of 21 Company CLC and presented to me – you will no doubt get a fair idea of the 'two big days'.

FATHER NEPTUNE

Jim Maultsaid 1918

27

100,000 CELEBRATE

ALL work has been suspended throughout the whole Chinese Labour Corps in France. One hundred thousand 'cease work' and the scenes I picture can be multiplied by the hundred – all over Northern France and Belgium – to the celestial Dragon. Strange Gods! And as usual the old dragon is dragged in. Also the moon! Wonderful ideas these Chinese have.

WHAT THE CAMERA CAUGHT ON
DRAGON DAY
THESE PICTURES WERE TAKEN
BY LIEUT ENGLISH 21st cov. C.L.C

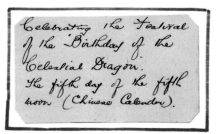

Celebrating the Festival of the 'Birthday' of the Celestial Dragon.
The fifth day of the fifth moon (Chinese Calendar).

MANY weeks of preparation have been spent getting the 'togs', the 'banners', the 'scrolls' and the 'stilts' are ready. Apparently three companies had in this case joined forces, 21, 112th and 169, so we have roughly one thousand five hundred Chinese. Some gathering! What?

THE LORD KNOWS – I DONT.!

The excitement is intense as the orchestra strikes up – the usual wailing noise, and the rattle of tom-toms! Like a spirit coming back from the land of its forefathers! I was transported back – back down the ages as the figures on stilts appeared; marvellous turnouts representing – what? The Lord knows – for I don't! All the colours of the rainbow were worked in somewhere to make a spectacle once witnessed, never forgotten. Various evolutions, dances, high kicking, accompanied by a white and yellow banner on the one side and a blood red flag on the other, goes round and round.

How serious everybody looked. And Father Neptune as I'll call him (you can see him on the first photographs) is fierce looking, but a mighty fine specimen of a man. Note the arms and shoulders – and the bodily strength!

WHAT MY PEN CAUGHT ON DRAGON DAY

THESE PICTURES ARE CUT FROM MY

FIELD SERVICE SKETCH BOOK

CHINESE STILT DANCE ON DRAGON DAY 1st JUNE.

21 COMPANY STAR TURNS

The best part of the day was taken up by these performers. It was a treat to see them all working themselves up into a perfect frenzy. Faster! Faster! And faster! The star turns were all 21 Company men, most of whom came from in and around Shanghai.

29

FINE ARTISTIC WORK

The usual masks of tremendous size and frightful design were much in evidence and some of the artistic work was really a treat. I was more than interested in this section of the programme. Now to me all this conjured up a certain picture and you can see below what formed in my mind. The God of the moon (the Dragon) riding through the heavens. Have I got the idea?

DRAGON DAY — THE FEAST

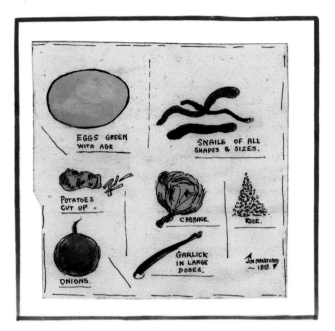

EGGS GREEN WITH AGE

SNAILS OF ALL SHAPES & SIZES.

POTATOES CUT UP

CABBAGE.

RICE.

ONIONS.

GARLICK IN LARGE DOSES.

JIM. MAULTSAID 1919.

WHAT A MIXTURE!

EGGS . SWEETMEATS.
ONIONS. SPICES.
SNAILS .
CABBAGE.
GARLICK .
POTATOES.

COULD YOU FACE IT ?

WHAT A FEAST!

The second day was spent in feasting. What a feast! Again we had to take part. It was not so hard this time as we were getting used to Chinese chow-chow.

THE SCOTCH SERGEANT

I met him, or should I say he met me? Well, anyhow we met! Tattered and torn, he was a pitiful sight. A beard of some two weeks standing was on his lined and weary face. Eyes were dull; he looked a man that had come through the very jaws of death and had now given up all hope. Poor fellow, indeed. The remnants of the kilt hung around his legs and the only fighting kit he possessed was his rifle. 'Well Sergeant, how goes it?' He looked at me, shook his head and saluted. 'It was pure hell, Sir! Pure hell!' I could see at a glance that he was a stray, or lost from his battalion. 'Can I help you old man?' I asked him? 'Well, I don't know, Sir. It's like this. I was the only one left … the only one … and we were seven hundred strong.'

WE MEET BY THE ROADSIDE.

Taking off my water bottle and then dipping into my haversack, I raked out a tin of bully and some hard tack; this I handed to him and said 'sit down'. We sat side-by-side on the side of that old French road. He tackled the food, such as it was, like a wild beast. I sat and looked at him. Was he a deserter, or just lost? 'Now Sergeant, let's hear your story!' He laughed and laughed. Was he mad? Poor fellow!

32

PORTUGUESE LET LOOSE

Marching forward in column of route his battalion were startled and surprised to see little figures hurrying over the skyline and down the road right into them. The Germans – and in a H★★★ of a hurry. Deploy! Like a flash his unit scattered and took all the available cover in battle formation. Closer they came, those grey forms. Then seven hundred rifles spat flame and death. Bang! Bang! Crack! Crack! Crack! Still they came on – on – on.

Somebody yelled it's the Portuguese. And true enough it was, and running like old nick from the trenches. Rifles, equipment all dumped for speed. A breakthrough by Jerry! Good God! Rifle bullets now whizzed overhead. Shells dropped behind and then came closer to crash in the ranks of the Scottish boys. What a mess!

Portuguese soldiers wild-eyed with fear and horror dashing past, and German troops now swarming forward over the rising ground part in pursuit of the 'pork and beans' lot, as he termed them. Ignoring these gentlemen with contempt, as more serious business was now on hand, the Highlanders settled down to stemming the tide of field greys that stormed forward. Open warfare as in the days of August 1914 – open point-blank rifle fire. 'Oh Lord, Sir it was grand! It was simply grand! Brave fellows, those Jerry boys! Forward to some fifty yards of us, and even closer they came … and then … we up and at 'em, charge! Bayonets flash. Rifles are used as clubs. A full-blooded bayonet charge, swaying, cursing, hell for leather, kilts flapping in the breeze. Cries, killings, cursings.'

OVER THE RIDGE CAME THE GERMANS — BACK TO THE AUGUST 1914 DAYS

'Jerry falls back to the crest of the rise. We follow, and walk straight into the furnace. The enemy guns get us and sweep us back – less some hundreds of our pals left dead and dying. Slaughter.'

German reserves press forward, close in, close up. Outnumbered three to one or more, it's a pretty serious job now. The word retreat does not enter the Scotsman's mind. He fights it out. 'Attack, counter-attack. Our boys are falling fast. We are about finished.'

ALL THE WORLD GOES BLACK

All the world goes black, spinning round. Clubbed from the back my friend knows no more. 'How the H★★★ I got here Sir I don't know! Here's the bump on my head.' He shows me a lump the size of a duck egg on his skull as proof of his statement. Hell roast the d★★★ Portuguese. Hell roast them. I'll be going now, Sir!' I direct him to the nearest infantry camp. We shake hands, and I wish him good luck. 'Goodbye Sir! Goodbye!'

The Scotch Sergeant passes on.

At about 7 a.m. on the 9th April, in thick fog which again made observation impossible, the enemy appears to have attacked the left brigade of the 2nd Portuguese Division in strength and to have broken into their trenches. A few minutes afterwards, the area of attack spread south and north. Shortly after 7 a.m. the right brigade of the 40th Division reported that an attack had developed on their front and was being held, but that machine gunners near their right-hand post could see the enemy moving rapidly through the sector to the south of them.

EXTRACT FROM SIR DOUGLA'S HAIGS DISPATCH. THIS SUPPORTS THE STORY TOLD TO ME MONTHS BEFORE BY THAT WEARY WAR STAINED SEG'T. FROM A HIGHLAND REGIMENT. J.MAULTSAID.

FOOTBALL "RED-HOT" OUR FIRST — AND LAST

I WAS PLAYED AT FULL BACK IN FIELD BOOTS.

J.M 1919

A football match that will live in my memory until the final curtain rings down. Football was played, by us, officers, NCOs and men at every opportunity as was the custom throughout the British armies in France and Belgium during the Great War. It dawned on me that perhaps there were enough Chinese boys in my company that would take a keen interest in the game – keen to learn and form a Chinese team on their own. The great idea was put into practice. Night after night I spent in teaching them: how to shoot,

THE COAL-BOYS

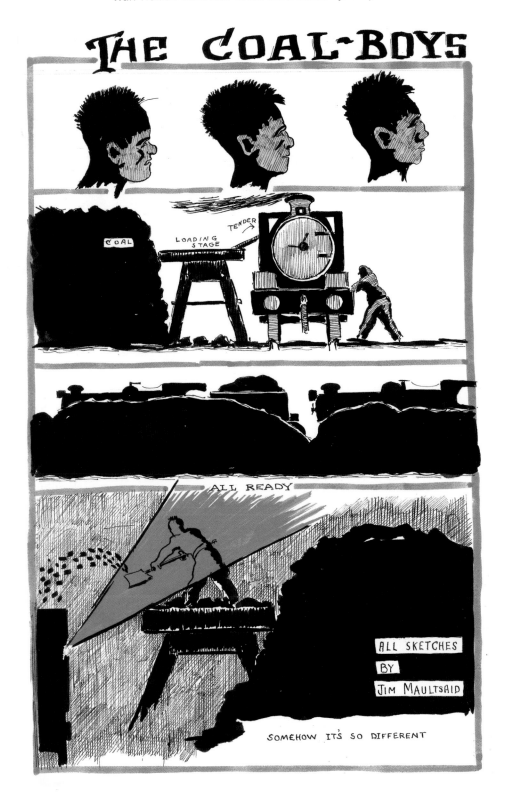

The

COAL-BOYS

The coal gang! Twelve good boys and all splendid workers. They had this work all to themselves. Slept all day and worked during the night hours, coaling the big ROD (Railway Ordnance Department) engines. How hard these little yellow men had to toil too, all during the night hours, filling up the bunkers, getting them ready for the early-morning convoy trains, all ready to pull on and out on their long journeys to and from the various railheads of our supply service.

This was a special gang and was, of course, called the coal gang. Truth to tell, they always looked the part – black as soot and hardly ever clean. Twelve black men, twelve black faces, not Chinese to look at – but black Africans. This bunch did not belong to me, they were part of Forrester's outfit but, of course, I took an interest in them too and had to pay them a visit when on night orderly duty, so can you tell you all about their work, and their little ways.

SOMEHOW its DIFFERENT

Most nights duty commenced in or around the hour of 9.00pm. Picture a long line of huge engines on a side track and a big dump of coal beside them. The stage is the height of the tender. All that is now required is to load up. This work commences. A white NCO, a lance corporal as a rule, is in charge and he gets his orders from the sergeant of the ROD. How many engines are to be coaled up – and when the work is to be finished?

Off go the greatcoats and the usual Chinese undergarments. Shovels are hauled up from a secret hiding place of their own and the glow from the fires shines duly on twelve brown bodies as the night-long job starts. Not much talk or banter on this shift; somehow it's all so different at night, no one around but themselves and a sentry on his lonely night vigil, a black world and so lonely. Each hour seems like two at night, but the work must be done and it is a mighty important piece of work too!

IF WE FAILED !

Imagine no engine for the troop train. No engine for the Red Cross train. Nothing to move the petrol convoy.

Engine missing – no shells!

Missing again – what about bread?

And horror of horrors – how are the poor lads going to be hauled to the ports to catch the 'leave boats'.

Can't you picture all the confusion – if we did not coal the engines?

And we never once failed!

169 Company – never failed.

By a failure on our part we could have caused the boys in the line several days' starvation – and that would never do.

Or failed to support them in a raid – or a reply bombardment by failing in supplying the shells, or … or … all the requirements of modern war.

BURNISHED BODIES

The night is black, jet black, a slight drizzle of rain is falling, the glare from the engine furnace glows in the darkness, casting shadows, red and black shadows, all around. The bodies of the coal gang shine like burnished brass in the glare of the furnace as they shovel like mad, black lumps of coal, in a mad rush to beat time itself. Double work required tonight; the whole system of supply service was working overtime, trying to meet the stupendous demand for more and more convoys. Our armies were fighting now for life and death, trying to hold the Hun back early in 1918, in his last great gamble of the Great War.

BOMBED

Boom! Crash! Boom! Boom! Boom!

JIM. MAULTSAID.

41

The night raiders are on us. Swish! A big bomb hurtles through the sky on its way towards earth and the engines. The red flare has been observed by the raiders – and we received a tremendous shock as the first bomb crashes into the coal stacks to explode with a mighty earsplitting roar, scattering coal everywhere. We dive, under the big engine, and hope for the best. Black, scared faces peer out. It's an awful sensation lying waiting for the next aerial torpedo, and 'Kingdom come' perhaps? Scared? It's a brave heart indeed that would not be…

Crash! Crash! Two more. The engine above us rocks, the ground trembles from the concussion. I hold my breath in suspense – and pray. Our guns now speak. The very heavens seem to be lit up, our barrage is in full swing, the rain now swishes down in torrents, we are safe again as the raiders pass on towards the coast. We crawl out, and work commences once more; our job must be finished at all costs. As a precaution we damp down the red furnace glow, and the silent Chinese shovel for dear life.

MAGNIFICENT

My night orderly report for that night read 'German air raid at XX.XX AM … several bombs fall on coal stacks … raid lasts three minutes … no one killed or injured on the coal gangs … all detailed work carried out in stipulated time … bearing of Chinese and white corporals magnificent'.

Signed J.A.B Maultsaid
Lieutenant
169 Coy CLC
5 April 1918[2]

---

2. The German Spring offensive, Operation MICHAEL, had opened on 21 March and the Allied armies were pushed back as the Germans fought to bring about a negotiated peace before the Allied armies were strengthened by further American divisions.

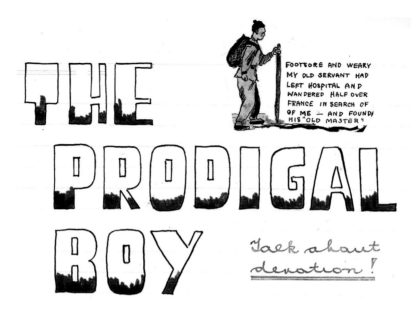

FOOTSORE AND WEARY MY OLD SERVANT HAD LEFT HOSPITAL AND WANDERED HALF OVER FRANCE IN SEARCH OF OF ME — AND FOUND HIS "OLD MASTER"

THE PRODIGAL BOY

Talk about devotion!

Sickness took Wi Ta Ju from me. A sad day for him, poor soul when the MO ordered him away to the Chinese hospital at Noyelles[3] and he lost his master. His eyes were like a hunted animal's, he cried out to me to save him but all the power in the world could not overrule the Medical Officer's report. I was helpless. The big Red Cross van called. He was carried out and placed in it, but he whispered 'me return – a – la Mister Moraside, me return – a –la!' My servant boy since the first day of duty in the CLC, that kid would have cheerfully died for 'his master'. He was my shadow! My yellow shadow.

MONTHS PASS AWAY

Months have passed away. His place has been filled by another youth and I had to teach this boy all over again.

a SHOCK

The shock of my life awaited me one fine evening when I returned to camp and found Wi Ta Ju installed in my wooden shack, calmly polishing a spare pair of field boots, brushes, paste etc., all scattered around, just as if he had never been away.

He was in a deplorable state, all torn and tattered, big red sores on his feet, long hair – in fact a pitiful sight. He stands up and salutes me and says 'return – a – la'. 'So I see old

3. The main cemetery for the Chinese Labour Corps of the British Army is at Noyelles-sur-Somme. There are 842 graves in the carefully-tended cemetery, each marked by a white Portland stone Commonwealth War Graves Commission headstone. Elsewhere on the former Western Front Chinese labourers are buried in about forty different cemeteries.

man,' I gasped! Outside stands boy no. 2 – he flatly refused to return to his platoon – and, of course, I could not have two boys on my servant list. Here was a pretty pickle. All my talk was of no avail. Neither of them would budge.

I took a walk and got the Sergeant of the NCOs' cookhouse squared to take no. 2 off my hands. He agreed to this and Wi Ta Ju took over his duties once more. The little devil was pleased. How did you get back? Here's his story. He deserted from the hospital, set out on the long trail, tramped over half of France, tracing his beloved master from place to place, and at long last after some five weeks on the road found ME.

MY ARTIST FRIEND AGAIN BREAKS OUT.

YOU have here on the pages that follow some more examples of my Chinese boy artist's work. No doubt you will agree with me that he was indeed a real exponent of his art, and all its rare expression. I price these pictures beyond all worldly value from a sentimental standpoint of course as a lasting reminder, to me, of those days gone into the dim past, never again to be recalled except in my memory. Can you wonder at me, as I turn the pages of this book going back to it all, and living over those 'shadow' days, mixing with those rare, strange fellows – life! life! life!, ideas, customs, language all so foreign to us, yet at the bottom of it all just humans, such as ourselves.

REAL CHINESE ART.

FINE WORK?

"Moving"
Pack up—and go!

'169 will move out at 10.00am on the 10th as per instructions from group commander. Officer Commanding Company to make all necessary arrangements.' Hustle and bustle. Each platoon officer looked after his own flock. The Sergeant Major rushed platoon sergeants and the white NCO boys; they in turn (as usual) made the Chinese hop around. The cooks, the police, the sanitary squad all and everybody packed kits and baggage ready to strike the trail. This was our 'hike' journey, back to our footslogging days once more.

All ready! All packed! See our wonderful transport, big Chinese wheelbarrows, hand carts, etc., etc.

I thought it would be funny if I met the 36th (Ulster) Division lads, leading a mob like this! Some fine fun! What a laugh at my squads! Fred Karno's boys Jim? Where did you get them? Oh my hat!

"Fall in"!

A shrill blast on the Sergeant Major's whistle set some five hundred Chinese boys on the move.

'E. Er. San, Sir, Woo One, Two, Three, Four, Five.' Platoon is formed and number off.

'All correct, Sir.' 'Quick march.' A last fond look at our old camp, and we say goodbye for ever, and move out to an unknown fate.

Our style of moving was unlike anything on earth. The ranks were uneven, stragglers everywhere. Enough to break the heart of any old-timer. Yet we covered the ground somehow or other. We bumped, we bored and took up most of the road. Sour looks from passing lorry drivers, blacker looks from an artillery column, as this long-drawn-out crowd of wee yellow men with their big packs made the their way onward. A d*** nuisance muttered an idiot of a captain who passed us in all his glory, leading a white labour battalion; and his own outfit were a sorry looking lot of grade Z men. Truly we were unpopular on the march, but it was not our fault that we were on the highways of France. Blame the big noises down at HQ (Noyelles) for this. Blame anybody – but us.

WE PLOD ALONG

Pat – pat! Pit – a – pat! Not the regulation thud! thud! thud! of the old days here. It's a shuffle – half walk – half dog-trot. As we pass through a small French village the British troops turned out to see us. Broad smiles on every face, and looks of pity. How I read all their thoughts. 'Poor fellows', I can hear them say, 'what a mob!' Looks of amazement from the French inhabitants. What new army was this? Surely we have not come to this. Surely not.

The day drags on, we still move onward. A halt is called and black milkless tea is served out. Not much of a meal, but yet it refreshed us. No band to relieve the monotony, none of the old songs to cheer us up. Just slog along.

The oddness of it all seemed funny to me and several times I had to bring myself back with a jolt, back from my daydreams. I was surprised indeed how the Chinese boys were able to stick the pace; in fact they were covering the ground at a smarter pace than a lot of regular battalions could have done.

MY SHADOW

Keeps on 'shadowing me'. Wi Ta Ju keeps guard. He follows like a sheepdog on my footsteps. A great lad this! He would have followed me to the gates of H★★★ itself. I still can see the perky face, with a smile on it, and the big pack on his back, and another large bundle containing the Lord only knows under his arm.

See old '87 not out' and his cage on the march! See 'little Titch' with a pack twice his own size!

I was amused and greatly interested, you may be sure. The novelty of marching was now wearing off and the reaction setting in. Sore feet started and nothing surprised me more than to see some of our boys hopping along in their socks on the rough uneven roads. Still we plodded on kilo after kilo.

Daylight is going fast. It's going to be some job, night marching with a mob like this. Each lot of three and four caught hands like little children to try and keep together. I hope to goodness we get clear road for the rest of our journey.

AT LAST

We strike our final destination! Leg sore and weary, we land at a very rough wooden camp – our home for the present. 10.00pm from 10.00am in the morning, all day on the highways, but here we were. All hands to the task of sorting things out. Glad indeed were we to stretch ourselves out in our old sleeping bags and forget all our worries. Crash! Bang! What the H★★★ is wrong now?

Earsplitting explosions rent the night air. Jerry again? Yes! Sure enough. Chinese – in all directions – terror stricken. Let them run! Up and out in a few seconds, that old tin hat on any old way, and still half-asleep we curse our fate. What a life! All quiet again. Yes, but what's the bright flare? It's only our cookhouse in flames, unsaveable. It's a roaring furnace now. Dies down. Keep clear. Jerry will come back. But strange to say he did not, and now all that is left is a smouldering ruin. It's a hectic life this!

Peace reigns once more. The rain patters down. I'm weary to death, and crawl into the old bag once more.

A wonderful lot of men, these are boys of ours. Careless, free, reckless and wild. It is quite easy to understand their outlook on life of course. Here today – tomorrow …

A finer lot of fellows could not be found on the Western front – on any front in fact.

LET ME TELL YOU

Let me tell you a little story that will bring home to you their reckless spirit and illustrate their devil-may-care mode of life.

A STORY

It's a winter's night. The rain slashes down on our old corrugated iron hut. The high wind threatens to lift the ramshackle structure, every blast leaving us with the firm conviction that the next one would leave us at the full mercy of the elements as we crouch around that old brazier (made from a big old drum) trying to get some heat into our chilled bones. It's a h★★★ of a night, mumbles Forrester! Just one h★★★of a night! Thump! Crash! Bang! Bang! The tin hut shivers. Jumbled voices outside. We start up and listen. Help! Help! Souls in distress? We rushed to the door and unbolt it. Three waterlogged figures stagger in. Big pools of water form at their feet. Airmen? Yes! Sure enough, and in a bad way. Quick understanding hands whip off the uniforms. We leave them as naked as the day they were born. Blankets are hauled out and wrapped around them. Their hands, and bodies, are massaged. Large doses of strong John Jameson is poured down their throats. Life slowly comes back and then we get their story …

THE CANAL'S VICTIMS.

Out on the spree somewhere these three start out on the return half of their journey in a nice big car. Forgetting, as they usually did, that they were now down on mother earth, the old engine was asked to do some sixty or seventy mph and she tried to do her best. The French roads often run straight as a one-foot rule for kilo after kilo – but the crossroads, or bend, comes sometime.

This small point was overlooked by the driver, and the 'bend' came in the form of the letter T on its side and a canal flowed past on the opposite side. The canal was running high tonight, just level with the road almost, when this big motorcar came crashing along and took the little low-lying ditch like a hunter in full career in the chase. Up and over – a tremendous water spout. Swirling waves, struggling bodies.

"J.J" "LIFE SAVER".

The car sinks like a stone to the bottom of that old canal many feet down. The icy cold water brings our three worthy airmen to their senses. Picture their battle for life miles from anywhere. One strong swimmer, the other two could not swim a stroke. Our modest hero (the swimmer) would not admit any great feat on his part, but his chums admitted he saved their useless lives.

? ON APPROVAL.

The point now was how could the car be replaced? It was the commanding officer's special bus and home they could not go without it. Much talk and planning. At the dawn of day, one of them slipped out on a very mysterious errand – for what?

Our surprise was great when he returned after a long absence at the wheel of a Rolls-Royce car. A replacement he said when we quizzed him. On approval, or scrounged? How he got it we never found out, but I had an idea that some CO at another aerodrome would be 'missing' a 'Rolls-Royce car, 1, in good order', on a certain day. Some strange and wonderful deeds these days? All aboard! Farewells were then exchanged. Many, many thanks for our glorious Chinese breakfast etc., etc., and flight No. X moves off!

And that car is still somewhere in the old French canal. 'La Guerre!'

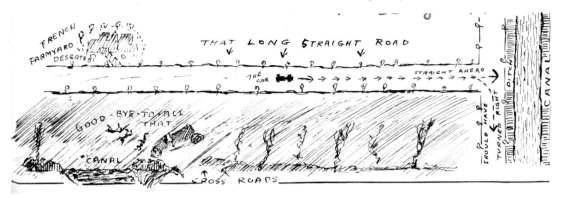

LITTLE TITCH
AND HIS MATE

This was a special job and the squad was 'Little Titch' and sparring partner. What a pair! A splendid pair of workers; between them they could have this particular job in fine style.

NO SOFT WORK

Clean engines! The big ROD monsters pull into their resting places to cool down and await the experts' touch. Covered with a thick coat of grim and rust, it was no soft work I can assure you to tackle these huge powerful engines after several days on the road.

This sideline came about in a peculiar way. I was chatting to an RO officer one day and, as we talked, a big locomotive clanked in just a few yards away. It was an awful state, red rust and dirt. 'That's bad looking,' I remarked, and my friend agreed. Now a sudden inspiration seized me. Here was a job for 'Little Titch' and his chum. 'Say! old man, let me send a couple of my Chinese to polish up your engine – just as a trial.'

He laughed, 'Dammed good, old boy, go ahead and I'll see your boys get the oil and cotton waste they require. Can you do two in a day?' 'Yes! Three if you like!' 'Splendid.' The job was made. Currently I sent for the pocket Sandow and explained the new work. How his eyes shone. 'San gowdy, Officer, San gowdy'. (good! good!) Off go the jackets. Sleeves up, and into battle sail the pair of them. I stand by and give advice. 'Good lads! Keep it up.' Oil was splashed around. Elbow grease in fine style was laid on. Gradually 'she' took on a new and brighter look – and brighter still I made them make 'her'.

53

SHE'S A BEAUTY!

This was a test. I wanted no flaws. She's finished! What a beauty! Hadn't looked like this for years. 'Go and get "plenty big officer",' I next commanded Titch, 'come see a la "Ding hola engine".' Astonishment and pleasure was written all over his face as he gazed on his new thing of beauty.

'Splendid, Maultsaid! Wonderful! The job is yours. Will you take it on?' 'Shure!' 'Stand still a moment.' Out comes a small pocket camera (they were of course not allowed – but) here you can see us standing in front of our first cleaned engine). She looks just fine in her new coat? That railway ordnance officer was wonderfully pleased, and no small wonder. Three of these were all polished up on the first day – and the drivers got a shock on turning up for duty to find their beloved engines all shining bright. 'Just wonderful. Sir! It's a pleasure to think we have such "beauties" to drive.' All thanked me. I just pointed to Titch and his mate. They beamed all over as I passed the good report to them. But the little beggars were tired.

"PLENTY MUCH PUFF-PUFF"

As they became more efficient in their skill, speed got more and more noticeable until it was a work of art with them. How they loved their work – that pair of small brown boys.

Did I not get a shock one day – as an engine puffed slowly past me and a face peered out from the driver's cabin? And the owner of that face – was 'Titch'. 'Come down – you scoundrel' I yelled. He hopped down at once, after shutting off steam and putting the vacuum brake on. 'Me can now plenty much drive big Puff-Puff,' says he. 'Can you indeed! If I catch you at that again I'll put you in the guardroom,' I stormed at him, but I could hardly keep from laughing outright at the thought of him actually learning to drive. Ye gods! What next? For punishment, I told him that four engines per day must now be cleaned – and left them to it.

Never in the history of the ROD were such 'posh' engines sent out on their long journeys to the railhead. The pride of the 'The great Nord' – and the envy of the French.

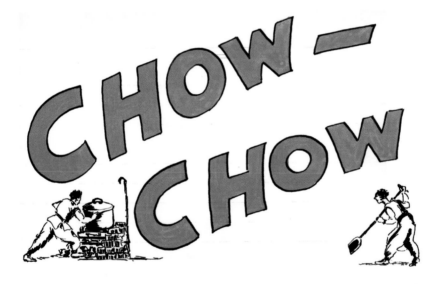

I CANNOT SAY exactly if this word was Chinese, or slang, or just manufactured (as many words were) but be as it may, it was expressive. It meant food – breakfast, dinner, or tea. The Chinese knew it; we knew it and that was all sufficient.

HOMELAND STUFF

Our company cooks were of course Chinese and the food they cooked was as near to their homeland brand as was possible to get from the raw material sent to us, the Chinese Labour Corps.

EARLY DAYS

Early days in the CLC find them using the proverbial chopsticks but gradually this practice died out and our big spoons were used.

Rice of course was the main diet. Cooked to perfection, I often had a plate of it myself. Tea was a regular meal also, but was always sugarless and milkless. I did not cotton to this. Then a kind of small loaf was baked from flour and water – these were called 'patties'. To me they were tasteless, but gave the Chinese boys satisfaction, so of course that was the main thing. Not too much bacon was supplied and the white bread was scarce at times. It was naturally the fighting troops first, then the Labour battalions. And quite right too.

WE WATCHED OUR COOKS

On special occasions they turned out some wonderful dishes – you will find particulars earlier in my history of life in the CLC so I will not repeat it here. Bully beef and potatoes mixed up made a kind of stew (it was always very thin). This was a regular dinner time item. We paid great attention to our cookhouse staff to see that they carried out their work properly. It was important that our workers were well fed – and as a rule they were.

NOTE FOUND IN DIARY BELOW this is what was written

I make no claim.

I loved to talk to the survivors of a battle or strange adventure and in my mind's eye picture all the details given to me by these men, many of whom I chatted with and found terrific materials for sketches and short stories. You will find a sample of these on following pages but, reader, I make no claim to having taken part in these engagements and at the same time I would swear that every word is authentic.

JIM MAULTSAID

GERMAN OR BRITISH?

My attention was attracted to a Hun from the sky, a sky that was rapidly going very dark. Buzz! Buzz! Buzz! Then a break or misfire from the engine. That was a German surely? And yet! Again it breaks out, burr, burr, burr, miss, burr, burr! I guess that fellow is in trouble of some kind, ran my thoughts. I search the heavens for a sight of this lone airman, and fail to trace him. Out for a prowl around I was miles from anywhere and all on my own, so I felt my six-shooter to see if it was in working trim.

She was all correct and loaded up. Good! Slipping the gun back into my big service pocket, I was almost swept off my feet by the swish of a pair of aeroplane wings not ten feet up. Phew! And not a sound. He's done, or coming down, or lost control? I dash over the ditch, jumping the usual dirty stagnant waterlogged bank and follow the direction of the plane. Was this a disabled Hun? I'll have to be more than careful as I knew from experience these German airmen, as a rule fought to the last ditch.

At a jog-trot and bent low as if at the 'advance', I make my way forward. A big black blur on my left front warns me that I'm getting close up. What's that sticking right up into the air? His tail? 'Holy smoke!' Head first into the soft swampy ground.

A thin straight red flare shoots into the blackness – straight up. Fire! The machine is on fire.

Then I get one great shock. Crack, crack, crack. Swishing bullets whizz past me like angry buzzing bees. Zip! Zip! Zip! From past experiences, I flop, straight down, and draw my gun. The fire shoots higher and lights up the scene. I can see the machine now – and it's upside-down position struck me as strange. How could he shoot at me from that position? That settled it. I get up and move rapidly forward. A moan from the figure strapped in the cockpit. A cry, 'Help! Help!' That's a British voice anyhow. 'Coming, old man,' I yell, 'keep steady.' Down on my hands and knees, I crawl beneath the struts and grasp the big broad straps that hold him fast by the shoulders. All his twelve or thirteen stone of humanity is pressing against these d*** straps. I tug. I haul. And sweat. The heat is awful. Frenzied efforts on my part. One of the straps slips, and his big bulk of body falls down on me, almost crushing my life out. But what matters that? Free! He's free! Grasping him by the collar of his leather jacket, I drag or, should I say, slide his body out from the now almost doomed machine. Not a second too soon. Hiss! Crackle! Swish! She's gone!

The flare lit up the darkness for miles around but, thank God, he's safe.

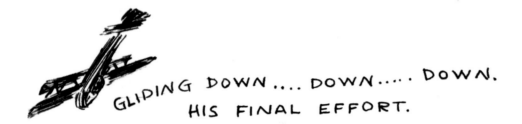

As I steered him back to our camp he told me his story. Chased by a flight of German machines he scudded and scurried, all out, for hours (so it seemed to him) trying to shake them off. Poor soul, he was flying 'blind' and did not have the faintest idea where he was, and I suppose hardly cared. His petrol runs low. He starts to glide. And glides down, down, down. Can't find a landing place, lets the last few drops of 'juice' into the engine. This is the final effort that attracted my notice, then crash!

'Why did you fire your gun?' I asked! 'I did not fire it, it was the heat and the fire that started it going – and it almost shot me to pieces,' his weary voice replied. So we patched up, and duly returned another air-boy inside a few days.

STUPENDOUS

Stupendous events were taking place on the Western Front. All our hard-earned gains on the Somme had been taken from us, not bit by bit, as we had won them, but in big slices. The Hun was now attacking us up in the north also and had made progress there too. Truly our front was in the melting pot. Touch and go! His fresh battalions had been thrown in; these men had been transferred from the now conquered Russian Front and we had to meet a mighty avalanche of men and guns. Critical days! Critical nights.

Our battle line here today. Tomorrow? Miles back.

Our rear guards fought to the last man. Again and again skeleton battalions turned at bay – and perished. Our batteries fired at point-blank range, then blew up the last remaining gun; the gunners had a few snap shots at the advancing field greys then turned and retreated.

EXHAUSTED

The Royal Engineers blew bridges, destroyed dumps of stones, laid delayed-action mines, wrecked railway tracks – all to hinder the enemy. Our infantry were exhausted. It was fight, march, fight. Sleep was almost unknown to these poor fellows. Many fell by the roadside, and of course fell into the hands of 'Jerry'.

No one could help – it was a case of the survival of the fittest 'and the devil take the hindmost'. What a nightmare! And what a deplorable lack of reserves. Where were all the reserve battalions? I'm afraid most of them were at home,[4] until it was almost too late and the Germans within an ace of breaking through to the Channel ports and Paris.

Believe me, it was nearly all over for us during these dark days. I do believe if the enemy had not overstepped his own supply columns (as he did) he would have broken our line. Many were the stories I heard on my travels from French, Belgian, British and refugees of all kinds, young and old.

---

4. They had been kept in Britain on the orders of Prime Minister David Lloyd George who wanted to deny them to the Commander-in-Chief of the BEF, Field Marshal Sir Douglas Haig.

A FUNNY YARN

Here's a rather funny one from a man who still lives and is known to me. 'We were retreating through Ham, on the Somme. The troops are fed up, tired and sore. Down the street we sway and stagger. Propped up against the side wall of the house is an officer of a famous Irish regiment in a bad way from wounds.' My informant is touched at heart. 'I cannot leave him to the enemy close on our heels … but how the H★★★ can I carry him? … I can hardly stand up myself.'

'At the door of a house some yards away stands a child's perambulator, minus the child of course. A godsend … a regular brainstorm grips me. Dropping out I walk across and gather the wounded officer in my arms as best I could and carry him to the perambulator. I lift him up and dump in his blood-soaked body. The springs groaned but bear his weight. Good! Off we go. I push my carriage in front of me. His legs hang over the side. God but it was funny! Or must have been, but I didn't see it then.'

REWARDED ? NOT ME !

And the sequel? 'Coming round to normal that officer cursed me soundly for my pains. How dare I place an officer in this D★★★ position? I let him rave, and kept on pushing, kilo after kilo, pushing the old pram was a great help to me too, it steadied my weary feet. At last I struck an advanced first aid post and delivered "the goods." Rewarded? Not me! I was nearly arrested. He must be cursing yet, and I saved his life. It's a funny war!'

DRAWN BY JIM MAULTSAID
FROM PARTICULARS GIVEN

TO PARIS

YOU will observe from the map on the next page our loss of ground during these first awful days of the big German offensive. Outnumbered by four to one and in places as much as six to one, our troops had not even a a 'dog's chance'. This new sector, some twenty-five miles long, had been taken over from the French about two months before and it was in a bad state. Neglected in fact. Hardly a dug-out or shelter of any kind. No machine-gun emplacements. No strongpoints. Indeed, no nothing! Devoid of dumps, stores, or light railways it was a 'gift' for the modern methods of warfare as a point for attack.

Did the enemy know this and select the sector for this very reason? Sometime before this about 250,000 French troops had gone on strike almost saying 'we fight no more'. This was kept a great secret, but I had heard 'rumblings' of discontent from the French front around about this time. Result! The British army had to take over more of the line, a line that had become dilapidated and neglected – French style!

GENERAL GOUGH was not many days in finding out the state of things when he took over. He cried to GHQ for men and material, and received neither. From prisoners of war and other sources he timed the German attack to the day almost. Yet his advice was ignored for some reason or other. Why they actually took away several of his mounted divisions on 20 March! Think of it! His battalions were all about five hundred or six hundred men (four hundred short in each battalion) and battle-weary already from their battles up north. And yet at home we had hundreds of thousands of fresh young troops. Lloyd George had the 'wind up' in case of a German invasion of England. Ye gods! I'm not going to attempt writing the history of this disaster – that almost lost the war – but shall I tell you a few stories of how our boys fought with their backs to the wall – and saved England, saved France, saved the World from the rule of the 'Hun'.

Glorious and immortal Fifth Army. Irish regiments, of course, occupy the prominent positions in these stories, as my information was from Irish troops.

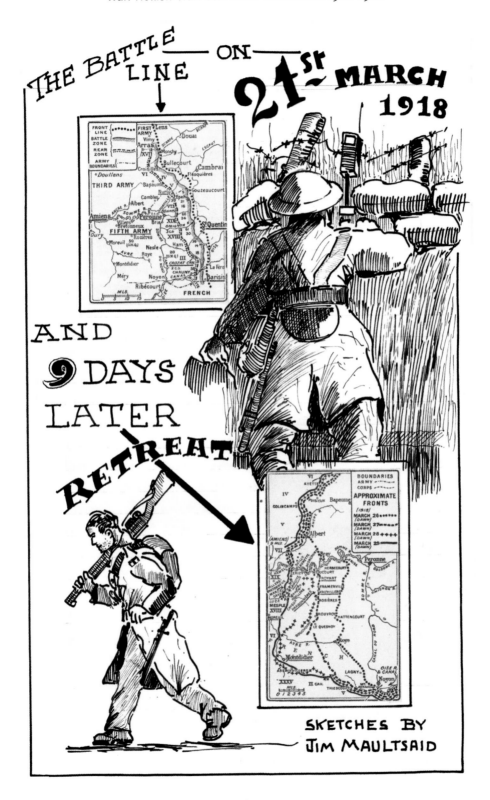

THE BATTLE LINE ON 21ˢᵗ MARCH 1918

AND 9 DAYS LATER RETREAT

SKETCHES BY JIM MAULTSAID

"THE ROYAL IRISH" FIGHT IT OUT.

THE DAWN.

The 2ⁿᵈ Royal Irish Regiment

'Left in the air', isolated in a little village called Lempire, surrounded on all sides by swarms of Germans. Picture this sadly depleted battalion holding out all day long from the break of day until 6.00 in the evening, knowing there was no escape. Ammunition running low. No artillery of any kind. The outlook bleak as could be, and yet those gallant Irishmen from the South fought to the last. Wave after wave of field greys perished against their rapid fire. Still they come, and melt away.

Overwhelming assaults launched every half hour or so could not move them. A fight to the death. Men fall, fall fast, ranks are thinned. Our fire dies down, as few are left to fire. Lance corporals are commanders now. See the wonderful Munster boys on the hill south of Épehy fighting it out. At last the enemy get in amongst them. Surrender? 'That's not the Irish way!' Fierce cruel work by bayonet and club, and the last act of a gallant Irish regiment is played out in the gathering darkness of a March night.

IRISH GRIT

'Yes sir! It was a H***of a night!' A big strapping Munster Fusilier is speaking. Let me tell you his story in a few simple words.

'After fighting all day and half the night we were surrounded, and the order was "Retire". But how? Germans all around us. We could hear them shouting and talking, yet no shooting disturbed the night air. Whispered instructions and we start the great adventure.'

WE RUSH THE BRIDGE.

'Down a little tow-path in single file under the poplars we glided and soon came in sight of a village on the opposite side of the canal (I think it was called Cerisey) but a bridge led across the Somme just here and it was guarded.

Our scouts brought back the news that this was a big open style of bridge and part of it was still on fire, also German troops were on duty on both sides. Our hopes sank to zero. What can we do? It was decided to make a bold venture and march up in columns of "fours" – and when found out – rush the guards. Anything but this tension of keeping quiet and doing nothing. We formed up in silence and marched forward. "Halt! Who goes there?" (In German) My heart is pounding. Our Captain who knew some German replied. A silence like the grave followed, then Crack! Crack! Two bright red flashes stab the darkness. Charge, Boys! A wild Irish cheer and we dash for the bridge. The fierce hell-for-leather attack swept the guard away as the "bhoys" use the bayonet in their dash across.

DOWN A LITTLE TOW-PATH WE GLIDED IN SINGLE FILE.

GERMAN TROOPS ON DUTY BOTH SIDES - OUR HOPES SANK TO ZERO!

A WILD IRISH CHEER!

WE RUSH THE BRIDGE.

SKETCHES BY JIM MAULTSAID

This awful hub-bub brought out swarms of Germans from the village and much firing took place but in the darkness and confusion we dashed into the night – and got up clean away from the spot of trouble. But far from safe yet!

A large tract of swamp stretched before us – and of course we could not go back – so with a never-say-die and a hopeless chance (one in a million), we plunged in. Oh Lord! What a nightmare! The old bogs in Ireland would not have held a candle to this, and then no promise of any security at the end of it. Squashing, squelching, up to the armpits now. Some firm ground, slip into it again, I sure do believe only Irish troops could ever have crossed that ghostly swamp.'

GLORY BE!

'On and on – our hearts sink low. Yet we were free and still alive.

At last firm ground is reached and as a pale moon pops up we see, right in front of us, another bridge! Figures move about, but as yet we are unobserved. Some of our boys fire a shot. That killed any plan making. More shots. We dash forward once more, and every man of that German patrol is killed or died of heart failure on seeing this awful mob dashing towards them.

Across once more all that was now left was "hope". We were exhausted. Come on boys! Just one more effort shouts our platoon officer.

A wood looms up in front of us. Where the h***were we? No one had the slightest idea. The dawn is breaking. Were all our victories to be in vain? As we silently move forward through the trees, each man with his own thoughts, and his rifle at the ready, we are startled. "Halt! Who goes there?" in a very English voice. Never did the English language sound so sweet. "Friends! The Munsters." We had struck the woods around Hamel – and were saved. Glory be to God!'

"THE SKINS"
HOLD UP THE HORDES OF FIELD GREYS FOR OVER 48 HOURS AT FONTAINE-LES-CLERCS

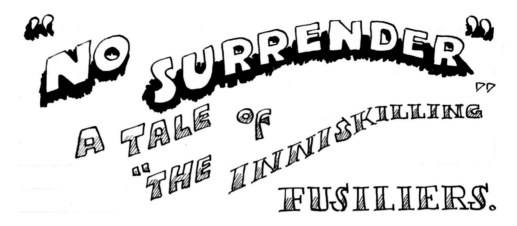

"NO SURRENDER" A TALE OF "THE INNISKILLING FUSILIERS.

VETERANS of scores of battles, this proud regiment, the 1st Battalion Royal Inniskilling Fusiliers, made a stand at Fontaine-lès-Clercs of forty-eight hours on those fateful days 21/22 March that goes down into history as an epic of supreme self-sacrifice unequalled in the long history of British arms.

Pride of Regiment simply radiated from my informant as he told me the story of his chums – how they fought and died – and by the will of Providence he was spared, one of the very few survivors. Spare a few minutes to read and Marvel!

FOG – SHELLS – JERRY

OH AYE! BUT.........

'Mist like a fog bank over the ground. "Jerry" let loose thousands of shells on us, all sizes, including trench mortar oil cans of tremendous bulk. It was an inferno! We could not see ten yards, but knew in half an hour or so "he" was coming.

Our advanced outposts were driven in and we hastily prepared our redoubt (strongpoint) for a siege. The wire was then painfully thin, but the soil was easy to dig and we had thrown up earthworks etc. as best we could. Crash! Flash! Swish – swish. Big shells smash and crash amongst us. Bullets rip and tear through our sketchy sandbags. The mist lifts clear for a moment and we could hardly believe our eyes. Here they come, boys! And sure enough not fifty yards away the familiar steel-hatted enemy with his black pack all complete, in full war paint marching forward on his way to Paris! Oh aye! But not before he passes the "Skins".

A terrific volley crashes out. Every shot a bull's-eye. Oh boy! We could shoot some, our lads – and what a glorious target! The line staggered, hesitated, and collapsed. First round to us. Reserves are hurried up. We could hear them shouting but could not see them now, so kept pumping lead into the mist on our immediate front. Vague forms loom before us. We stand up in our excitement and blaze away. Fighting an invisible foe. And that d*** mist swirling around in clouds. The shelling had now ceased – it was a soldier's battle.'

...... HE HAD TO PASS *THE* SKINS'

'The deep-throated battle cry rises above the din as the enemy troops again sweep forward to the attack. Closer this time. Endless forms fill the gap we blow in their ranks ... thirty, twenty, ten yards, almost at our breastworks. Yes! They were brave, but we shadowed them. As they advanced they shot from the hip and machine guns played havoc with our boys supporting the attackers. Checked again – his last sally had cost him dearly. The dead bodies were heaped in front of us.

Getting a breathing space I glance around. Old chums were gone, just crumpled up in the strangest attitudes. Can they really be dead? Look out boys! Swarming in, those ghostly figures advance once more, and suffered the same fate as their forerunners. One big hulk of an officer gets close up and stands shooting our boys down with an automatic revolver. Jumping the sandbags I dash at him, a scowling face. A bullet wipes my cheek. I plunge the bayonet home, through his stomach. God I'm blood mad!

Hurried preparations for his next move are made. Vacant fire positions are filled by withdrawing our line a little at the sacrifice of our right flank, but it cannot be helped.'

SURROUNDED

'"Hold the line boys! Steady now! Let 'em have hell! Bang! Bang! Bang! Bravo the Skins! "We can bate the whole bloody German army!"

A fair-haired corporal, a son of Tyrone, stands up and defies them, shooting as fast as ever a Lewis gun did. He was the life and soul, and the inspiration of our gallant band. The fourth attack had ended in disaster. The old Skins were holding the key to Paris!

Hour after hour drags past. We thirst for water. "Jerry" launches two more attacks and makes little or no progress. Held as if in a vice.

Night falls and we hold on. As the dawn breaks he comes again, swarms of them, swarming over his own dead to get at us, and we shoot them down. The cry goes up, our right flank "is in the air". Field greys are pouring through the gap. Christ, boys, it's all up now! But worse is to follow. A runner from the battalion on our left brings the news that they were wiped out last night and "Jerry" is through hours ago. Our Irish hearts low as you may well believe, but never thought of surrender.'

7 OF US LEFT. CHARGE!

'Shot at from front, and both flanks we are now a sadly depleted force. The enemy all around us practically, our number was almost up. The Huns came again and again we had crushed over eleven attacks but the next ... would it do us?

All day on the 22nd we fought on. The evening gradually closes in on us, the tide of war has flowed far past us on our flanks.

I count my chums that are left. Seven of us, to fight the next attack, hungry, thirsty, unshaven, dirty, wild-eyed Irishmen… to hold the German army!

Here's the B******* "No Surrender".

Charge boys! A last hoarse cheer and we stagger out to meet our foes. A bayonet charge by seven Irish boys. And we stopped him. Terrific swear words, unprintable language, we stab and parry, lunge and miss. The end, the end. I lose all my companions in that mad awful welter of blood.'

★★★★★★★★★★★★

The teller of this story escaped capture but how he did not tell me.

Let's lift our hats to that wonderful Regiment, the Royal Inniskilling Fusiliers.

LITTLE BLACK DEVILS.

THE STORY OF HOW A BATTALION OF ROYAL IRISH RIFLES
MADE A GLORIOUS STAND IN THE RACECOURSE REDOUBT

THIRTEEN HOURS WE HELD THEM! Nicknamed in one of the German war reports after a hot battle "Little Black Devils," otherwise our Royal Irish rifles, I want to tell you a story of how a battalion of these boys held the Germans for over thirteen hours although completely surrounded and hemmed in on the spot called the Racecourse Redoubt during the March retreat in 1918.

THE AVALANCHE

As part of the 36th (Ulster) Division the 12th Royal Irish Rifles were in the thick of it from the first order of this awful avalanche.

WE WOULD FIGHT

The grey mist sweeps around like a blanket. The bombardment has fallen heavily on the 12th Rifles and their forward outposts have been battered in – disappeared in the mist and brown earth – for ever.

NORTH OF IRELAND MEN

Our main body woke up to the fact that they were completely hemmed in on all sides and it was a case of fight it out or surrender and of course a regiment like the Rifles had only one answer to that – FIGHT.

How they fought too!

'Germans swarmed forward in storm array, and simply melted. Grim, dogged, north of Ireland men stood their ground. Sheets of flame blazed out from our barricades. Clips of cartridges jammed home in the magazine – and each rifle was a machine gun. The d★★★ mist give them a bad time as the targets kept appearing and disappearing in the most aggravating manner.

THE LITTLE SERGEANT

See the little Belfast sergeant who was blown sky high by a big Jack Johnson, his khaki tunic now jet black from grime and powder coaly pick off a German with every shot. Quite exposed above the sandbags he bore a charmed life. He was shooting as if he was on the rifle range at home. God! He was a terror that little sergeant.'

SQUARE FACED........

'Right and left they came, those box-helmeted, square-faced Huns. Three sides now, the pressure is increasing. Our force is being pressed into smaller bounds. The boys are dropping one by one. As the day goes on the enemy gets bolder and bolder although he has already received several sharp lessons. His troops are urged forward to take this strongpoint at any cost. And the cost was terrific indeed, but numbers would eventually succeed? Surely?'

No artillery to help our poor troops. No reserves. No hope!

What the thoughts of these men were is hard to imagine, and the hope of salvation? Nil!

'Steady boys!' Crack! Crack! c –r –a –c –k! Let'em have it. Side by side, shoulder to shoulder, in fact almost back to back now those boys never wavered. But hell, those Jerries are getting daring. Each rush brings them closer.

DARKNESS. DEATH. DISASTER

'The cries, the din of battle wages fiercer. Steel meets steel now at parts of our line. Still we hold the fort, but not for long?

Shadows of evening creep around. Is it morning, noon, or night? The mist, darkness, death, disaster. And those magnificent Ulster troops still battle on. And that black-shirted sergeant still shoots with reckless, daring accuracy by the flare of the lights thrown up by the Hun. That man's spirit still survives and it is typical of his Regiment, those "green and black boys" of Ireland.

The vultures close in. Bombs are now dropping right in the midst of the survivors, but a flicker still flicks "Fight it out my lads," growls the hoarse voice of our little sergeant as he stabs at an enemy who ventured too close and paid the price.

Back to back, almost exhausted shooting, stabbing, and bare fists even. What a battle!

Again and yet again the invaders are thrown out, but return, hand-to-hand. The end can better be imagined than described.'

OVER THEIR BODIES

Another page of history is written. The mist still swirled around. The noise of battle dies down. Only the heart sobs of the dying, only the cries of the wounded, and the mighty foot of the German army tramps over the dead bodies of a glorious band of glorious men on his way to Paris. And the little sergeant???

NO GREATER DEED

★★★★★★★★★★★★★

Several men escaped and swam down the canal for quite a long distance during the night and after many adventures reached our lines to report that their comrades were still fighting it out in the Racecourse Redoubt. This was after thirteen hours of incessant fighting.

From other information, they fought for twenty-four hours on end but were eventually swallowed up. Were these three the only survivors? The history of the Great War contains no deed, or spirit of self-sacrifice to surpass the stand made by these magnificent troops of the Royal Irish Rifles. The front of the 36th (Ulster) Division was never broken.

GENERAL GOUGH in 1917

ONE MORE!

JIM MAULTSAID

HE WAS LEFT ALL ON HIS OWN—TO MEET THE ENEMY.

Surely the strangest story of the world war? Left all on his own, to that utter sense of complete loneliness and the feeling of absolute isolation from all fellow companionship so necessary to us poor humans. What must have been this lone soldier's thoughts?

HE WHO RUNS …

It was during our retirement on the St Quentin front that the CO of a certain battalion decided on a piece of bluff. He would leave his Lewis gunner to cover his 'getaway' and hoodwink the enemy – to give his troops a chance to get out and away. 'He who fights and runs away lives to fight another day.'

YOU MUST STOP

Think of the mixed feelings of that Lewis gunner as his section commander gave him his orders, 'You must stop here for so many hours, let your gun rap every few minutes, and work a big bluff, all on your own. Get me? Battalion orders my son! We leave you at dusk – and retire to ★★★★★★★. When your time is up you can pack your grip and clear out. You may catch up on us … and you may …. Cheerio! Understand your duties?' 'Yes! Sergeant, I understand! Goodbye!'

How his young blood must have run cold. How his young heart must have crashed to his very boots. Into the lions' den? No escape. 'Jerry' was coming, creeping down the old deserted battle-scarred trenches at this very moment – and he had to face him all on his lonesome. Good G★★.

SILENT FIGURES

Crack! Crack! c –r –a –c –k! Crack! Rat – tat –tat –tat. There goes the gun. Silence. Crack! Crack! Rat – tat –tat –tat –tat! Silence. Again burst of gunfire. Silent figures steal out and, like shadows, glide away, leaving the lonely gunner to guard the retreat. Fainter and fainter grows the sound of the bursts of gunfire as distance eats up the ground between the gun and the boys retiring.

INVISIBLE FOES

The silence of night is broken every few minutes as the lone gunner presses the trigger and sweeps his bullets in a wide circle over his front, shooting at an invisible foe. He gazes into black space. How the minutes drag. Far away to his left flank a star shell soars away up into the dark heavens. His gun moves round. Rat –tat –tat –tat. Crash! A shell crashes into the deserted breastworks over and behind him on his right. Rat – tat – tat – tat. He sweeps the muzzle round and 'lets her rip'. The rats scurry past in haste, as always. Never did he feel so friendly to the rats. They were something that really lived in this world of deadness. Rat – tat – tat – tat!
★★★★★★★★★★★★★★

His duty accomplished, that lonely man eventually made his escape and by a stroke of providence managed to find his own lot again. His name or regiment I cannot give. He was a hero of the war!

PATHETIC SCENES AND SIGHTS WERE COMMON DURING THESE DAYS OF STRESS AND SORROW

1914 days were recalled in all their nakedness as crowds of old men, women and children passed down the roads, fleeing before the hated, dreaded Hun (or Boche). It was enough to make one weep as you passed a very old woman pushing an old handcart containing all her belongings and the goat tied to the back, grandfather leading an underfed horse, between the shafts of the big French farm cart, several wideeyed children looking over the side, wondering what it was all about.

UNSEEING EYES

UNCARED FOR

Several cows and sheep wander along in the usual manner, their owners lost or uncaring. Then comes a whole family. The father, a returned crippled war veteran, the mother, poor soul, worried almost to death, carrying a very young baby and four or five more children all holding the mother's skirts. Starved, distracted. Living hopelessness. Pathetic, unseeing eyes, fleeing from 'les Boches'.

WILLING HANDS

Our infantry, our guns, our supply services were greatly hampered by this fleeing mob, yet the boys performed many kind acts as they plodded back. Touched to the very bottoms of their young hearts, our troops extended willing hands and assisted the old souls as best they could down the road to the back areas.

HORROR....DESPAIR....FEAR.

Even the wheelbarrow and the invalid's chair were brought into use in transporting goods and household material. These sights and scenes are long to be remembered – the horror, the despair, and fear.

JIM MAULTSAID.

WHAT DID WE DO?

At the back of these wonderful lads you have read about in the previous pages stood the Labour Corps and not least the Chinese section of this vast organisation. What did we do to help them, I can hear you ask? And I'll now try to tell you a little of our efforts to assist the boys in the line. How we slaved and how we used all our strength – even to the last gasp!

EVERY few hours brought us fresh orders. Orders for petrol for tanks, for motor lorries, for ambulance vans, and the air force. Oils of all sorts wanted at once – always at once – coal for the ROD, stores of all kinds – guns, ammunition, fodder for the horses, blankets, bully beef, biscuits, bags of potatoes, corn equipment – and the thousand-and-one requirements of a modern army. All these were handled by the Chinese Labour Corps. Packed in big trucks or lorries as required for the railhead dump, we slaved from morning light until far into the night – and often during the hours of darkness as well.

EARLY 1918

Often and often our white NCOs threw off their jackets to lend a hand and set an example to the Chinese. All hands to the wheel in a mighty effort to help their chums 'up there'. Never in history did a slave gang work as we worked during those dark days of early 1918 – and never was so much downright honest backbone put into a task. No need to drive: we had them worked up to such a pitch of team spirit that it was a pleasure to see them work.

Readers! It was marvellous! It was wonderful! It was magnificent! No words of mine can give the CLC its full measure of praise for a feat of stupendous magnitude carried out on the lines of communication on the Western Front in 1917-18.

Of course some of the CLC companies were inefficient and lazy, due to the slackness of their officers and NCOs, tending to bring a bad name on a very fine body of men. Not so in 169 Company; we were the finest working outfit in France. All out 100 per cent – yes! This is not boasting – it's fact! And the records bear me out.

OUR DAY

You must pardon me for wondering a little off the main point, but I'll get right back to it now.

Here are a few short sharp sidelights on our working day.

Arrived on the works: the hour is 6.30 on a dreary winter's morning. Snow and sleet cuts us to the bone as our squad sort themselves out without fuss or confusion. It takes a little time to warm them up (I know their style now, and leave them alone for a while) but soon the steady thump! thump! thump! tells me all's well. Petrol boxes are being loaded unto the trucks systematically. All day long, on that cold winter's day, the boys slog on through the snow and slush loading, loading, loading thousands of cases of AA (aircraft petrol). 7.00pm finish! Utterly weary, we crawled back to camp.

SEE THEM GASP !

Six thousand cases wanted! The convoy pulls out at 5.00pm. Each platoon gets the same order and that means twenty-four thousand cases in one day. Give this task to any squad of dockers, or railwaymen, and see them gasp! Every case to be manhandled and a carry of ten to fifteen yards or more – stack to truck. I gather my gangers and give my orders. Start at 6.00am. And I take a risk. 'When you are finished – a – la – you can return – a – la to plenty "chow –chow" and plenty "sleeper".' In simple words, this was piece work. And the result? I was astounded!

FLYING FIGURES

Sweat pours. Much shouting. It was bedlam. Lying figures. The cases simply hurl themselves through space, with an uncanny knack of finding the right spot (experts in action). Jackets have been thrown off one by one and the brown bodies glisten in the dull March sunshine. Gangers curse in their picturesque language. Coolies scurry in hot obedience, and the big iron doors of the French trucks are slammed home one by one each gang is now racing each other (no prize) in open competition, hell for leather!

'MAULTSAID.' A whistle blows, the head ganger runs to me and gasps 'All finish – a – la officer!' I reply, 'Ding – hola – fall in!' And the time was 2.30pm. Great boys! Yes!

Like children they troop back. And Captain Curtain thought it was a strike – until I phoned him the news. 'Maultsaid! You are some lad! Your d*** piecework will break my pure Irish heart.' 'Sorry skipper.' But we have done a fine job.

LOADING CONVOYS

DOWN at the docks CLC boys toiled all day on the quays. Army transports draw in, one by one to the big shed. This, an ammunition train, is rapidly loaded up and the NCO in charge of the convoy gives the order, 'March!'

Next in order comes the food convoy. Another Chinese squad are ready to load the big stacks of bags, containing loaves of bread, cheese and eatables for the troops. Work is well and quickly done. The boys won't be hungry tomorrow anyhow.

LOADING FIELD GUNS

Turn another corner and the eye meets the CLC again in the picture loading – what? Field guns. From food to war! Then you find them further on discharging rolls of barbed wire (that cursed, yet valuable, stuff). For cuteness leave it to the Chinese. Not a hand touches the roll. Working in pairs, an iron rod is passed through the centre hole and both carry it to the stack.

'TANKS'
Now see them hauling one of our big tanks, inch by inch, to its proper parking place.

DID I SAY A REST?

So far as I know, and could see, our CLC boys worked at almost every kind of job of manual labour, saving in manpower some hundred thousand of our fighting troops this 'fatigue'. (No Chinese in my PBJ days, no Sir! That was left to the infantryman – out for a rest? Ye gods!)

TO THE LAST OUNCE
The day's work over, or so we imagined. Rudely shattered dreams. What the h*** is it now?

'Come on Maulty,' shouts Forrester as he shakes me. 'Come on, you son of Ulster – wake up! Here's a G** d***cargo wanted now. Right now.'

Midnight finds No. 2 platoon back on the Depot, not in the best of form, but duty must be done. A rush demand for thousands more of those never-ending petrol boxes means an all-night vigil watching, worrying, coaxing, explaining, and driving the last ounce from the weary brown bodies. Hour after hour we work the long night through to see the shadow of a new day creep across the sky, and hear the dull roar from the guns, and the red, red skyline fading away to melt and merge into the dawn.

GLORIOUS C.L.C.

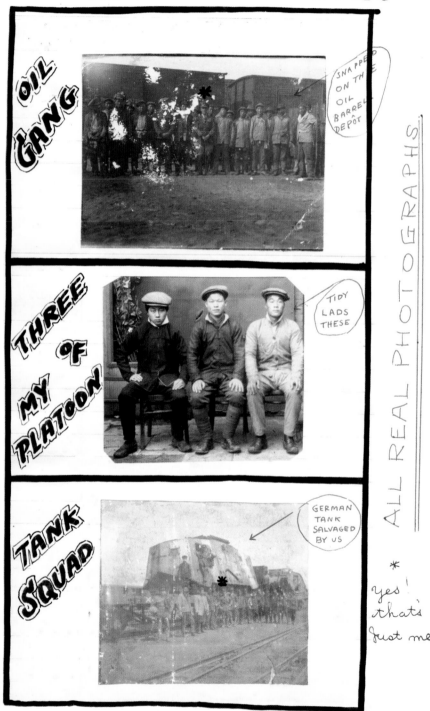

~ GLORIOUS ~ HISTORY

WE manfully played our part in trying to stop the Huns' rush to the ports and Paris.

Days, weeks, months of this never-ending toil. Day and night we stood up to all the demands for more and more of the 'munitions of war'. The bad news drifting back spurred us to great efforts. If we could not fight, we could at least help our fighters, and I have told you enough to convince you that we were 'all out'.

The strain was tremendous. How my platoon stood it, even yet I sit and wonder, and marvel too! Hats off to the Chinese Labour Corps boys of 169 Company, and our white NCOs and our officers. A glorious page of history was written by these men (East and West) in those days of long ago on the lines of communication on the Western Front.

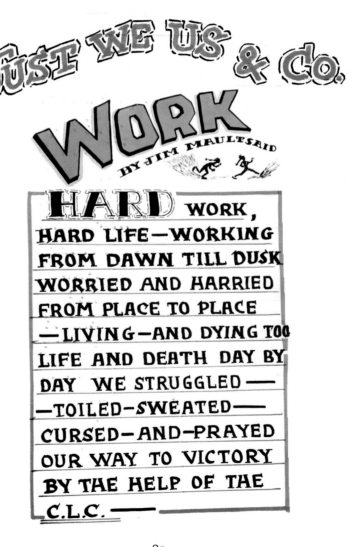

JUST WE US & Co. WORK

BY JIM MAULTSAID

HARD WORK,
HARD LIFE—WORKING
FROM DAWN TILL DUSK
WORRIED AND HARRIED
FROM PLACE TO PLACE
—LIVING—AND DYING TOO
LIFE AND DEATH DAY BY
DAY WE STRUGGLED——
—TOILED—SWEATED——
CURSED—AND—PRAYED
OUR WAY TO VICTORY
BY THE HELP OF THE
C.L.C.——

REAL PHOTOGRAPHS

TYPES OF BOYS YOU HAVE READ ABOUT IN MY STORY "WORK" AND THE ARTICE ENTITLED "AND US"

NOTE..... THE EXTREME YOUTH OF SOME OF THEM.

←A FEW N.C.O's OF THE R.O.D ATTACHED A.S.C. AT REST.

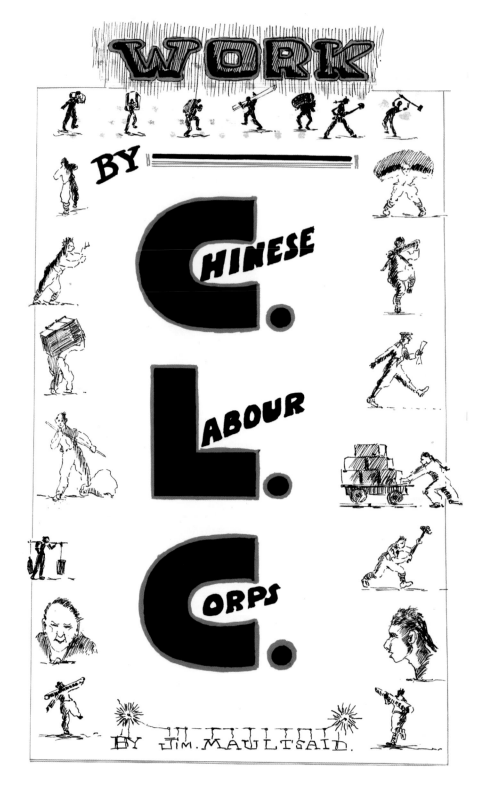

A DAY'S PAY FOR A LETTER! 'CAN YOU BEAT IT?'

When you sit down to write a letter it comes as second nature to do so, not so to the average Chineseman. As a matter of fact about one of our boys out of one hundred could read and write, so you can well imagine how important that 'one' was in this case. Here were five hundred Chinese thousands of miles from home and, of course, the old folks way down had to get news of their loved ones in France. How was it done? Mostly through the medium of a professional letter writer. See the picture of this gentleman, drawn from life, on the opposite page. He is at his work (overtime by the way) which did not in any way clash with his ordinary daily duties.

This fee was usually 1 franc per letter; some long screeds were valued up to 5 francs. Black tablets ground fine made the ink. A long thin brush (not a pen) was used. The paper was then rice paper and in long narrow roles or strips. The characters ran downwards in lines, not crosswise like ours. 'Passed by the censor' always beat me.

THE LETTER WRITER

THE PROFESSIONAL
LETTER WRITER
AT WORK.

BY.J.M.

JIM.MAULTSAID

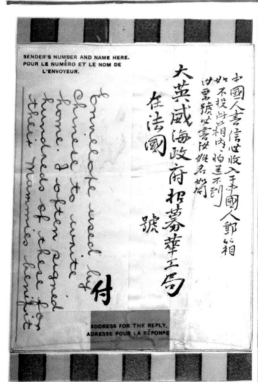

Everyone knows, or should, the inborn love of a gamble in the makeup of the average Chinese. Our outfit were no exception to the rule, and we often had our hands full in trying to keep this craze down, or at least do our best to discourage the practice. We had our share of 'sharpers' or out-and-out gamblers and our biggest worry was trying to protect the mugs or pigeons from falling into the clutches of these gentry.

I have known them to bet on two flies walking up the side of the railway truck.

I knew they often laid odds on the length of the sentence a prisoner would get.

They would put down stakes on the speed of a gang at some work or other.

And bets were laid about the temper their officer would be in – on a certain morning.

Even competitions for spitting would be the excuse for side stakes. In fact they would gamble on almost anything – so there's a little insight into their character.

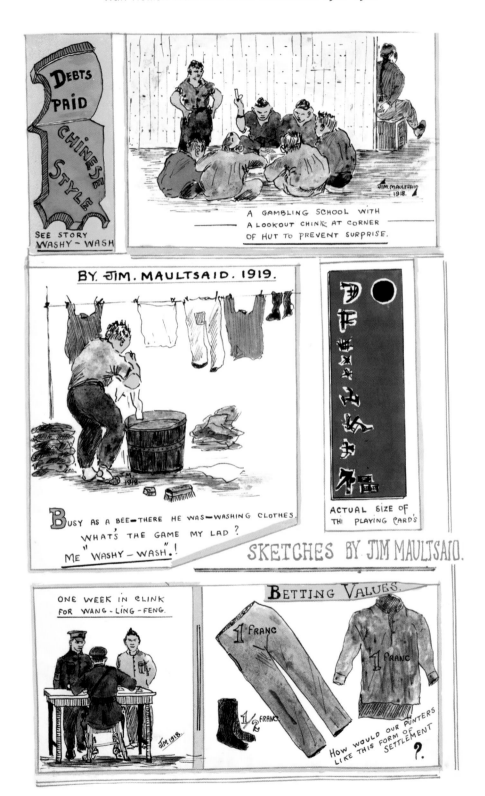

DEBTS PAID CHINESE STYLE

SEE STORY WASHY - WASH

A GAMBLING SCHOOL WITH A LOOKOUT CHINK AT CORNER OF HUT TO PREVENT SURPRISE.

BY. JIM. MAULTSAID. 1919.

BUSY AS A BEE—THERE HE WAS—WASHING CLOTHES. WHAT'S THE GAME MY LAD? ME "WASHY – WASH".!

ACTUAL SIZE OF THI PLAYING CARDS

SKETCHES BY JIM MAULTSAID.

ONE WEEK IN CLINK FOR WANG - LING - FENG.

BETTING VALUES.

1 FRANC

1 FRANC

1/2 FRANC

HOW WOULD OUR PUNTERS LIKE THIS FORM OF SETTLEMENT ?

WANG-LING-FENG

Here's a little story that will amuse you, I'm sure.

One fine morning I missed a youth from his squad and all my enquiries led nowhere, so I hiked back all the way to our camp for a 'look see'. Out and in, round huts I made my way and almost when going to give up the hunt stumbled across his Lordship WangLing Feng, bent over a tub scrubbing away. A line ran from two huts and it was covered with clothes. Beside him was a terrific pile of stuff ready for his attention.

'What's the game my lad?' 'Me washy wash.' 'Oh! Indeed. All that yours?' 'No officer! Boys plenty say me have to washy wash plenty much. Me owe plenty francs.' 'Ah! I see. You were gambling. Come on – tell me it all, or … !'

Bit by bit I got his story. Falling heavily into debt and having no cash to pay, it had been decreed that he had to wash his way out of liquidation. Each pair of pants washed represented a franc, one shirt a franc, pair of socks a half franc etc., etc. He did not sell his chums – but spent a week in 'clink'.

SNAPSHOTS

Some of the old French photographers must have made a fortune from the Chinese lads. When it was discovered that a nice postcard showing a picture of yourself could be had for a franc (a day's pay) there was a regular stampede for the man with the 'wee black box' and you can see some of the results above. Not at all bad looking fellows – some of them. What? Practically everyone in my platoon got an extra copy for his officer and at one time I had hundreds of these mementoes in my possession. How they recall each individual boy to memory! Good lads! Some not so good! And 'Ding by haw' (no good). My own bright bodyguard is marked X. Cute as a fox, he was my 'shadow'. No. 1 was my head Sandow, as fine a fellow as ever I met, white or yellow, and a thorough gentle man. No. 2 was Lieutenant Forrester's boy and No. 6 was Lieutenant Simpson's henchman.

This kid by the way mastered the English language completely before he returned to China. A rare find for some English-speaking business or household in the land of the Dragon.

DADDY AND MAM

Thousands of the postcards were sent home and I had to often write a few words on the back to say how good a boy he was and how happy and well he was. Words of love and words of cheer for the 'daddy' and the 'mammie'. Valuable and treasured in the little far off village, I suppose – even today, especially if the loved one did not return – a – la (as many did not) from the foreign land called France. Sometimes one of these pictures even came in useful as a means of identification for a death by accident or otherwise. The huts were littered with them and a whole side of a wall often plastered over. Photos stared at you from every angle. Rows and rows of them. And not a smile!

This word was a slang term during the Great War. To 'scrounge' in simple everyday language is to steal or take something that did not belong to you. The Chinese to my mind had this business down to a fine art. You will laugh at some of the cute moves employed by them and our counter moves to combat the 'disease'. How we tried to fight it would take a book itself, but I'll illustrate a few examples and leave it at that.

BEATING US

Each coolie was searched every night at the compound gate. At first we found practically nothing but made the discovery later that the 'stuff' was being passed down the ranks from hand to hand as we worked from the top of the squad. The last row left the swag on the ground a few yards in rear and, of course, in the darkness it was overlooked, and then called for later on, or I suppose was picked up by the Chinese guard.

WE COUNTER THEM

Our move against this was to start searching from front and back at the same time and the result was quite a haul on the ground in the centre of the platoon. A big reduction in scrounged goods.

VALUABLE METH

A favourite and valuable item was drums of methylated ('meth') spirits. Our losses were heavy. It was a ready market commodity in certain French circles and many francs passed over for its sale. Mixed with some light wine or other you got a drink with a strong kick, so you can follow the line of value.

An old trick was using a big nail to pierce a hole in a drum through the bottom and place a dixie below to fill up then plug the hole with soft putty, to be removed again when the opportunity arose. Then we captured several that specialised in prowling around the railway trucks on the lookout for a meth truck (they could smell it out actually). Finding a truck, the door was forced open by a crowbar, several drums dropped overboard into the long grass and then collected at night or some convenient time. The trapdoor was actually resealed and, of course, it was always a mystery how several drums were short, no matter how we counted them.

A RARE COCKTAIL!

We had once a cargo quietly doped. About one hundred drums were filled with pure French ditch water on the quiet by our white NCOs, then loaded up, sealed and left in a convenient side track. The truck was actually labelled 'meth'. What a laugh we had some days later when the usual report 'wagon no. 77847 – "meth" 3 drums short'. No trace. That would be a wonderful cocktail from those drums.

WHAT A SHOCK!

I remember a coolie being arrested once by the police on some minor charge and when being searched the Redcaps had a shock when they found a German revolver actually tied to his private parts inside his pants and vest and hanging down. Just think of this idea – and the weight carried!

CLEVER ...... BUT.......

One smart lad we discovered with two flat tin boxes shaped roughly like the soles of boots, neatly strapped on the soles of his heavy ammunition boots, and containing valuable hospital instruments. This arrangement made him several inches taller – and this was his undoing. Clever? But it cost him a month's pay plus thirty days in the clink.

WHOLESALE DRAPERY DEPT.

Another gent took a fancy to a web of cloth and wrapped it very tightly around his body. Unfortunately it made him far too stout and a sharp-eyed sergeant made him disrobe, much to his annoyance and discomfort. He paid the price for his brainwave.

USEFUL PIG-TAILS

During our early days when the long thick pigtails were in vogue, these were used to cover up many secrets. The hair was neatly plaited around the stolen object (usually something long and narrow) then tied with a big bow at the bottom. When the pigtails went so did this hiding place.

"LES CABBAGES".

A tornado in the form of the big Frenchman, his wife, and the whole family of six or seven youngsters once descended on our compound screeching 'la cabbage, la cabbage' or something to that effect. What a mighty uproar. What the h*** was it all about? By many signs and signals, I was entreated to follow them. Now in my mind's eye I could see several dead bodies all laid out, or … but then 'cabbages' could not be dead men, surely? But it must be murder – or something desperate.

PLENTY MUCH STEALER

Some half a mile of walking and the cavalcade arrived at the farm. Leading me out to the back, a garden was pointed out to me. A garden of cabbage stalks – not a single cabbage left. Gone! All gone! 'Finished by your Chinwa, your d*** Chinwa.' Ah! I could see it all now. We were accused of stealing a whole garden of cabbage. Not bad! Come back and search the camp, I ordered. To make a long story short, not a single leaf or a single trace could be found of 'les Cabbages' and I waxed indignant with the Frenchman and ordered him out, or I would have him arrested.

Not for a moment did I suspect my own lot. And yet! The guard was ordered to hustle the 'annoyance' out. Some weeks later a very vile smell arose in or around our camp.

ROW UPON ROW

Days were spent trying to locate the 'gas zone'. Eventually a disused hut was suspected and the door forced. Believe me, or believe me not, there sat row upon row, reaching to the roof the Frenchman's cabbages, rotting. Ye gods! Scrounging on a large scale. I found out later it was an act of revenge for some grievance (imagined or otherwise) and not an act of stealing as no use was made of the haul. Leave it to a Chinese!

AGAINST IT ALL

It must not be inferred from this article that every Chinese boy was a thief or dishonest. Frail and human nature is the same the wide world over; every flock has several black sheep and we had ours. Against all my tales of scrounging, I have scores of lads the souls of honesty and would (and did) trust them with all my worldly possessions, and was never once let down.

"LIKE A TORNADO"

A DAYLIGHT RAIDER

Our troubles from the air up to now had been more or less confined to night visits from 'Jerry' and we did not think he would actually sweep down and give us a taste of his bombs in broad daylight. Of course we had often spotted his 'cameramen' planes high up in the sky taking the all-important pictures of our very important works. As a rule we did not pay a great deal of attention to the gentlemen; they were thousands of feet up, and we had our work to get on with.

ZOOM-ZOOM!

Zurr –zurr –zurr w –h –o –o –m –f! Whoomf! Crash! C –r –a –s –h! Earsplitting – blinding flashes. The very ground rocks and shakes. The shock takes me very breath away as I sway and almost collapse. My first instinct is to dive for cover, but on second thoughts I dismissed the idea and tried to show an example before the Chinese.

Yelling 'Down! Down! Get down,' as I grasped the lie of things and could see the 'Black Hawk' zooming forward hundreds of yards away and rising rapidly. It was his companions I feared, following his footsteps, perhaps several more machines all with their deadly bombs. Huddled figures, scared to death faces, crouched bodies, some on top of each other, lay scattered around, but no more bombs, God be praised!

This was a form of warfare I did not fancy overmuch at any time – and even less now since I had been so badly wounded already. How helpless one feels as the big bombs roar down. What a sigh of relief one breathes as the danger passes by – and by my stars I breathed deeply on this occasion. It was the shock of my life. We had been taken utterly unawares, caught napping if you wish. This lone hawk had swept down from the clouds and given us that 'awful sinking feeling' you read about in a well-known advertising for Oxo. H*** roast him! The b******.

My platoon sergeant finds his speech again as he crawls from beneath a big oil tank. What a covering from bombs!

FOOD FOR TALK

It took us some time to instil confidence in the Chinese boys again and get them properly going at their tasks once more. They talked about this awful day for a long, long time afterwards and I pitied some of the youngsters, for truth to tell it did not do me much good myself. Somehow at the front properly you were on your guard for this kind of thing, but on the lines of communication? Well! It was a shock.

ONLY A MEMORY

The damage done was nil. We had the big holes filled in – and soon it was only a horrible memory.

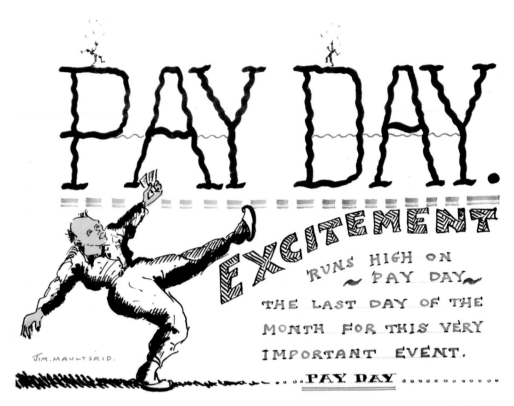

The last day of each month was payday for the coolies and white NCOs. Early in the morning an officer and several NCOs were detailed to report at the nearest French bank and draw the cash in French notes. This sum ran somewhere round about Fr.18,000, so you can see how important this job was. Each man was armed to the teeth with six-shooters and some had service rifles as well. The district we had to traverse was well known as a happy hunting ground for deserters, desperate characters, and tough boys from all the Allied armies in France and Belgium. And a hold-up not was out of the question; hence our precautions – and we could shoot.

'ALL ALLIGHT'
Says Johnnie Chinaman

Having drawn the cash (this was my turn on the pay job) and being well covered from the door of the bank, we sauntered casually out to make an uneventful return journey to camp – all safe and sound.

PAY-OUT
The rolls are carefully re-counted again as the CQMS checks up the pay-sheets and all is ready for the grand pay-out. As a rule we brought the coolies home earlier this day; it was a big job and took hours to complete. Formed up in platoons all is in readiness. I sit behind the cash table.

IDENTIFICATION

'Number Sixteen, seven, eight, five,' chants the CQMS. A coolie steps forward. He salutes me and my platoon sergeant examines his brass wristband. 'Correct, Sir.' CQMS shouts out the amount due – usually Fr.30. I pay over the amount. 'All rights,' sings Johnny Chinaman as he grabs the notes, salutes again and shuffles off.

FIVE HUNDRED PASSED

The same routine is gone through until the five hundred coolies are paid out – then our NCOs.

'THE BANK BOOK'
RICH MEN BACK IN CHINA

During the pay-out a brother officer runs 'the bank'. Each coolie has a bank book of his own and it rests with himself how much he desires to put on deposit. The coolie hands over, say, Fr.20 and his book is then filled in with this amount and the date of entry, also the officer's signature. He examines book and tells the official interpreter he is satisfied. Once a deposit is made there was no withdrawal. Some of these Chinese boys went back home quite rich. It was a wonderful brainwave and saved thousands of them from 'sharks' of all kinds.

18,000 GONE

Piles of notes have gone into thin air. The last man gets squared up and another payday has come and gone. 'All square, Sir!' The CQMS hands over payrolls for my signature as to correctness. A report to the captain, and my work is complete. I'm not sorry; it has been a long day.

LITTLE PARTIES

Little parties and feasts in the old compound tonight. Weird musical instruments chant – and the tom-toms throb. That's tonight – tomorrow … .

FIGHTING DISEASE
WERE WE STARK STARING MAD?

We had always been more careful from the beginning in our sanitary arrangements in 169 Company, but instructions arrived from headquarters about 'how to fight disease'" A new chapter of 'frightfulness' was the result. Each day the cookhouse, the camp – hutments, outhouses, stores, latrines, etc., etc., etc. – had to be carefully inspected. Gallons of disinfectants were poured down drains and sprinkled over floors and in corners. The spray business was taught and used daily. All refuse was packed into tubs and removed.

Blankets were aired in the sun. Huts and sleeping quarters got cleared out each week and thoroughly scoured in disinfectant. Each boy had a bath once a week, his feet and hair duly inspected. Wearing apparel, especially under-vests, had to be washed. Socks – we looked at them and passed along. We taught them how to gargle.

Medical inspections were frequent and suspected cases of disease weeded out. Lectures were given by platoon officers – and only vaguely understood. We even taught them to swat flies. By nature the Chinese man is rather slovenly; that by heavens we taught them something. To his Oriental mind, we must have been stark, staring, raving mad!

"TICKED OFF"

I was called to Area headquarters and practically told I was a 'liar' in my work returns: hard on me, but read the story … .

A message was sent to me to report at the Area Commandant's office at once. What rule had I broken now? My mind worked at high pressure trying to get a line on my offence – but could I? No!

AT THE PORTALS
I knock at the big man's office door. 'Come!' Stepping inside, my hand smartly comes to the salute. 'Please sit down, Maultsaid.'

A LIAR
COMMANDING OFFICER: Clearing his throat, he does not beat about the bush. 'Maultsaid, I do not like your daily work return. In fact I do not credit it. Your figures are faked; no Chinese could do what you say yours are doing. The tonnage is out of all

proportion. In other words you are a *liar*. It must cease at once or you will be sent to a higher court.'

MAULTSAID: I turn pale, gasp for breath – not with fear, but anger. Irish men are renowned for hot tempers, and my Irish blood boiled. 'I'm a liar?' I shouted! 'And so are you, – a d★★★liar.' My commission was forgotten. I did not care a straw for all the generals in the British army at this moment. My beloved Chinese boys were doubted? That was too much for me. Now on my feet, in excitement words flowed from my mouth in torrents – hot burning passionate words.

COMMANDING OFFICER: 'Remember your position. Sit down at once – and calm yourself! Or I'll place you under arrest.'

MAULTSAID: 'You called me a liar. You cannot do that, you had no right to do so, and I retaliated. I'm not sorry. Look here, Sir! Why not try my gangs out? At any time, any hour, any guy you wish, any work you like, as long as you like, against the pick of your Chinese Command. And by my great-great-grandfather (a Chinese oath), they will knock "hell" out of anything you can produce in labour gangs green, red, black or yellow. If they don't, you can have me court-martialled. That's my challenge!'

COMMANDING OFFICER: 'Tall words, Maultsaid! I'll think it over, and deal with you in due course.'

MAULTSAID: 'Please yourself, Sir!'

COMMANDING OFFICER: 'Dismiss! Good day, Maultsaid!'

MAULTSAID: 'Good day, Sir!'

Salute! Dismiss!

I had not many days to wait until my fate was decided through the medium of my 'DUD' gang! On the works a few days after the stormy interview you have already read about I had a surprise visit from the OC Area and his staff. We were going full steam ahead when he called on me. A curt order brought yours truly to his side. 'Come with me, Maultsaid. I want one of your great gangs.' (Did I detect a sneer or was it my hot blood again?) 'Yes,

Sir! Pick it yourself.' 'I fully intend doing so,' he tartly replied. And, snakes alive, he actually picked my duds, after studying them at work for over an hour or so.

My heart sank. Still! I know these scoundrels can rise to glorious heights if they take a notion – but would they? My very honour as an officer and a gentleman in the hands of my worst squad! Imagine my innermost thoughts! A cold sweat breaks out on me as these twelve no-goods passed out from the depot. My platoon sergeant, poor fellow, had almost collapsed; his eyes betrayed his horror and he lost his speech, until the chain-gang had passed out. 'Good G★★, Mister Maultsaid! We are ruined! Ruined.'

"NO PLENTY WORKER – OFFICER FINISH-A-LA!"
MY GANGERS SECRET ADVICE TO HIS SQUAD.

As I was not allowed to witness the test all I can do is repeat the story told me by the ganger in charge of the squad. 'The boys were slow in starting, as you were not there, Officer. Then I told them "plenty worker Mister Morriside (me) will always care for you. No plenty-worker; officer is finish – a – la. No plenty-worker, officer is finish – a – la. Big – big officer [the general] say-so to me, "Ma – mandy", zo (slow work) no bloody good – a – la! Qa – qui – quily (quick work) dig – ding – hola – good – plenty good – a – la. Officer san – san – gowdy. Plenty much bloody good – tri – bon. Come on! Come on! We got the petrol to load – told we had half an hour to do it in (two hours work) and many officers watched us. Boys got hot – got hotter – then went mad. Work! Twenty minutes finished the job. Then another strange gang was brought and we were set to race them.'

"PLENTY GOOD OFFICER"

'Oh Officer, it was easy – we smashed them hollow. You would have been delighted to see the "duds" work – and they kept shouting "plenty – good – officer. Not finished yet! Two gangs (twenty-four coolies" then were brought up, and by my great-great-grandfather, Mister Morriside we beat them all together. Exhausted – the breath run finished – we then sat down and would work no more until our officer was brought.'

WONDERFUL LAD'S ..... THAT DUD SQUAD OF MINE.
WOULD YOU LIKE TO SEE MY CRACK'S SIR!

This is where I came on the scene! A messenger was sent and I reported to my CO. On my way there all kinds of doubts assailed me. *Was it the sack?* Disgraced for life, or congratulations?

'Maultsaid! Wonderful lads! Just wonderful! I humbly apologise and take back all my hard words. Will you shake?' 'Sure!' says I, 'but this is my worst gang. Would you like to see my cracks in action?' His eyes bulged and the looks of doubt and amazement spreading over the faces of the junior officers was to me, amusing. 'Let me get them here and show you the best gang in all France.'

'Talk about work – ah, just do let me demonstrate.' 'Right! Go ahead!' Dashing to the field telephone I rushed an SOS message through for No. 1 Squad – at the double.

ONE OF MANY IN THE 169

Taking full command on arrival I set a tremendous task and gave my crack gang their orders. I then explained to the 'committee' that this was just one squad from 169 – we had dozens as good. Take a pick at any time and try them out. Now wait and see!

EVERY MOVEMENT AN ART
A blast on my whistle and No. 1 dash to their task. I'll make no attempt to describe that 'whirlwind', 'hurricane', 'tornado' scene. It was glorious! Quick as a Flash. Sure as fate! Every movement an art. Two, three, four, five cases of petrol at a time per coolie.

The boxes sailed through space to fall within an inch of the exact spot. The coolies chanted. Sweat became streams running down the lean brown bodies. Faster! Faster! And faster! The pace was terrific. Never shall I see such work again – should I live to be one thousand.

Some days later I was surprised and delighted to get an order to bring one of my gangs to give a demonstration before the representatives of all the other CLC companies in the command. How pleased I was! And I chose No. 2. And I gave over the command to my platoon sergeant. No. 2 felt this big honour keenly – and I knew it was going to be a real class display.

EYES ... EYES ... EYES
Critical eyes, Chinese eyes, white officers, NCOs' eyes – and my own Captain Curtain (proud as could be) all gathered around.

Sergeant Unsworth took charge (this was his special pet squad) and the fireworks commenced. Needless to say, No. 2 excelled themselves, putting up some marvellous figures and a finished display of what Chinese Labour could really do, when properly trained and handled.

The area CO give the assembly a short sharp lecture on how to handle the CLC, pointing out No. 169 Company – Captain Curtain and yours truly – as an example of efficiency.

"FILMED."
HOT WORDS
YOU DOUBT ME?
I BOILED HOT.
SIT DOWN!
I'LL DEAL WITH YOU.
THE BOWED DOWN 2ND LOOT.
RUINED.
I WANT A GANG.
"THE CHAIN GANG" IS PICKED.
MY SERGEANT SAYS GOOD G.....!
NO PLENTY WORKER OFFICER FINISH-A-LA
BOY'S GOT HOT.
CASES SEEMED TO HAVE LEGS
THE BREATH RUN FINISHED.
AND HOTTER.
THE DUDS IN ACTION.
"OH! OFFICER IT WAS EASY."
THEN THEY SAT DOWN
WHERE I COME ON THE SCENE.
WONDERFUL LADS
NO 1 SQUAD ARRIVE AT THE DOUBLE.
I GIVE ORDERS
2. 3. 4. 5 CASES AT A TIME.
MAULTSAID!
LET ME SHOW YOU MY CRACKS!
HERE THEY ARE.
OFF THE MARK.
IN ACTION.
A HURRICANE! A WHIRLWIND!
WE DEMONSTRATED.
A TORNADO!
SWEAT RAN IN TORRENTS.
NEVER SHALL I SEE SUCH WORK.
EYES. EYES. EYES.
REWARD.
I HAD TO STAND MY FOOTING.
SKETCHES! — ALL BY — JIM MAULTSAID
MY CHEST GOES OUT.
IT STANDS OUT IN MY MEMORY.
I STAND HIGH IN THEIR RESPECT.
ALL GOOD THINGS MUST END. BACK TO WORK
"FINIS"

"DEMONSTRAIONS"

This was the first of many displays, or 'demonstrations', by my squads. Each time I sent a different gang, to keep down ill-feeling; even the 'duds' got their chance again, and of course acquitted themselves in fine style. Competition for the big honour was fierce. As a sideline I brought my famous oil gang along one fine day to show their paces in the oil business. 'How to do it' and they could 'do it'.

PROMOTED ⭐⭐ 2 STAR MAN

Shortly after this I was promoted to full Lieutenant and have always had a half suspicion that it was the good work of my little coolies that hastened this 'lift up'.

To my squads I was a bigger man than ever. They placed a lot of respect in rank and, of course, were pleased to see their own officer get 'bigger'. I had to stand my 'footing' over this business. That night stands out in my memory.

The NCOs were not forgotten. And the coolies? I'm afraid they had a soft day (the one following my second star) But all good things must end, so back to reality once more, and on with the work.

CURIOUS FOOTWEAR FASHIONS IN THE C.L.C.

It was really funny to see some of the styles adopted in our company in the footwear department, as well as forms of leg and ankle protection.

COULD YOU?

Could you walk around all day and do your work in slippers cut away at the heel? As in the pictures 9 and 10 on the next page. This was a common turnout. Style No. 3 was the 'posh' turnout when out on a pass. The white part shown is not a sock, but fine white linen wrapped around the feet. Mode No. 11 is really smart and a credit to the CLC. I may add that these feet belong to an officer's boy – and of course he had to be it. Pictures 1 and 6 are short puttees of the cut-down variety. One puttee for both legs and the other used as a body belt. Style No. 2 was a kind of short narrow white band tied up with a tape – useful and common.

Nos 4 and 7 are no styles at all – just careless; untidy and sloppy.

No. 12: note the heavy ammunition boots and long pants. Very serviceable.

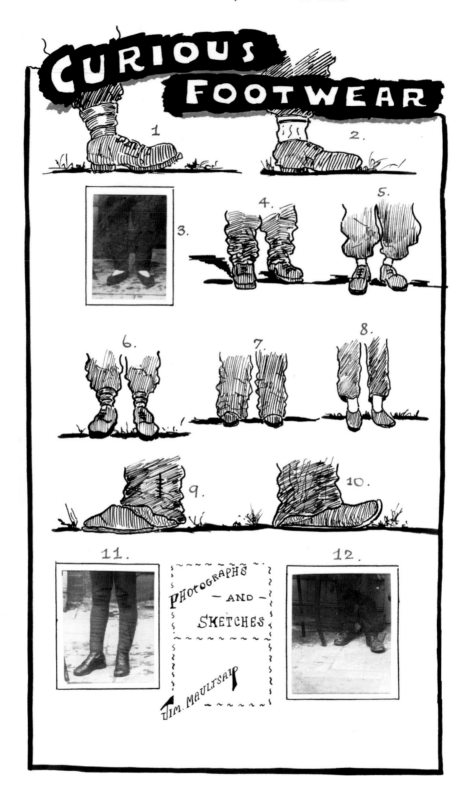

THE SPORTING END.

SEE STORY
LIEUT
"INDIA"

Knowing my weakness for all athletic games you will not be surprised of course to see the above photo of our company football team. These are our NCOs and yours truly in the centre. I sent a line to Linfield FC and we had a ball by return. Where the jerseys came from I cannot now remember – but where there is a will – you know the rest.

GERMAN SPECTATORS

As a team we were far from being skilful but had some great fun in our matches against other companies, depots, detail, Res, etc., etc., etc. Looking back I can well remember our playing several matches in full view of German prisoner-of-war compounds and thousands of very interested Hun spectators watched our efforts from behind barbed wire.

FROM SMALL BEGINNINGS

As a matter of fact these German boys got permission later to form teams in their own compounds and play each other. I have not the slightest doubt it was from the British Tommy that the Germans got the idea of football and today stand very high as a rival to our greatest teams in England.

How a seed grows!

A SPECIAL TRAIN

We even once had a special train (after the war was over) of an engine and two cattle trucks to convey us some thirty-five kilos away to play a match. The ROD supplied the train and also the opposition at the other end and just walloped us about 7 – 0. Not bad!

ROUGH STUFF

Our greatest thrill was a match against the French team of railwaymen. They threw us about like old boots. Wild bull rushes swept us aside and in five minutes or so we were three goals down. Hundreds of French spectators went wild with joy. Rattled? Yes! But we fought back and handed out some 'rough stuff' ourselves. Superior teamwork carried the day and we just 'bunged' ten goals and the result 10–3 for us. A lesson for the French.

A SHOCKING MURDER

POLICE ? BAFFLED.

MURDER! MURDER! MURDER!

This is a chapter I do not like writing as it is a blot on the CLC. At least we were suspected of the crime and I'm sorry to say I agree: all the clues looked like pointing to our Corps.

BURIED TREASURE

An old French lady lived all alone in a farmstead away off the beaten track and rumour had it she was wealthy. That old story of a buried hoard somewhere in the house. All French farmers are supposed to hide their bills and gold, as the banks are not too popular in rural France.

NEVER AGAIN

Poor old soul, she paid the price as her battered body was discovered one day in the kitchen of her home – battered to death and left lying as she had died. It was a sight I do not ever want to look upon again. Everything was in confusion, turned upside down and thrown about just as the murderer (or the murderers) had left it.

WITH PLEASURE
I would have shot him on the spot if I could have done so, but no such luck came my way.

THE STAIN OF CAIN

Our military police, the French police and even bloodhounds all took up the trail, but drew a blank. Parades, questions, cross-examinations were held in all the companies, yet no progress was made in solving the riddle. It was suspected that the Chinese bad man (or men) was the murderer and even the Company he belonged to was suspected, but no definite clue could be brought home.

I have no hesitation in saying that some of the coolies must have known who he was; but a Chinese man does not as a rule split on his fellow countryman, so we were up against a stone wall. Our detectives were baffled and beaten. The old tired body was laid to rest and I'm afraid there is a Chinese man somewhere today with blood on his hands and a sin to answer for to the greatest-great-grandfather of all – the good God himself.

"LIEUTENANT INDIA"

A BUNDLE OF NERVES SHAKE! SHAKE! SHAKE!
WHISKEY
MORNING
NOON AND NIGHT

When I hear discussions on drink and drinking it always brings to mind a character of an officer I knew in my Chinese Labour Corps days. When I think of him (let's call him 'India') it's enough to frighten the life out of me, so far as drink is concerned.

114

THE REMNANTS OF …

He was from an Indian regiment and most of his life had been spent in this country of romance in the service of his King and Country. We nicknamed him 'India' as it was his one and only topic of conversation. At first I put his nerves or 'shakes' down to shellshock. That was my mistake – these shakes were all from the bottle, unfortunately. So far gone was this once fine man (he had been a grand physique) that I never knew him to eat a single meal.

His breakfast was whiskey!

His dinner was whiskey!

And his tea was whiskey!

Supper was the same beverage.

All his pay and allowances were spent on this and cigars or cigarettes. How he always managed to keep up the supply I could never find out. It had almost lost its taste – almost! Think of that! It did not even burn him in the raw – his throat was burnt out and it just tumbled down in a gurgle. His servant boy often said to me, 'Officer plenty much good firewater swallower'. The kid was certainly correct.

"SIMPLY OOZED"

Tremble and shake all day long. A disease now and incurable. Gone beyond redemption. It 'oozed' from his dried-up skin in hot days and he smelled of the stuff from yards away. A living example of the evil of strong drink. And the irony of it all? He was (as usual) a good soul, a man you could have liked.

I have often wondered if poor 'India' ever reached his 'homeland' again. His picture you may see on the left-hand side marked X football team.

STRANGE methods indeed were employed by our boys in trying to catch fish from the canals and streams of France.

PLENTY FISH – A – LA

I was astounded to see them prepare long-handled poles with big prongs on the end. On asking the use these were to be put to, I was informed 'catchy plenty fish – just wait and see!' And I sure did see a lot. Wearing nothing more than a vest reaching to the middle, they

blandly slid into the dirty old canal in pursuit of fish armed with the big long stick, prong downwards. Standing as still as ever any red Indian did, the weapon poised, they would wait for some unsuspecting fish to sail along. Stab! Quick as a flash and as sure as fate that fish came up on the end of the prongs. Whoop of joy! Visions of a fish supper! The excitement is now at fever heat and several French lassies on their way home stop for a few minutes to gaze at this strange scene.

NO BLUSHES

If the coolies were embarrassed I failed to notice it. Of course the 'troops' were mostly underwater, so it was quite all right and no occasion for blushes from the fair French charmers.

LITTLE TITCH

'Little Titch' once tried this form of amusement, but only once – he stepped into a pothole and disappeared. He was fished out immediately and this ended his career as a spears man. No more 'fishy – fish' for a little Titch. They ragged him about this for months afterwards but, little sport that he was, he just smiled!

ENVIED BY THE FRENCH

I must admit they were clever at this and often brought home two or three dozen fair-sized fish of various brands as spoils of war. More than the Frenchmen, with their fishing rods, corks, hooks, bait and the big baskets, caught or would catch in a month of Sundays. Indeed much banter and chaff took place between old Frenchmen and our bright sparks – who got the 'goods'.

"TRACHOMA. A DISEASE of the EYES.

Sweeping through our company, this terrible eye disease gave us a great deal of worry and caused quite a lot of minor 'off-works' for days and weeks at a stretch until we kind of got it subdued.

CHINESE ONLY

It appeared to affect the Chinese only, which was a blessing indeed as we had enough trouble without adding this one to them.

RED SORE EYES

Red sores appeared on the eyelids, the eyes discharged a white kind of matter. One eye affected today and next day the other one. It was a painful malady and for several days left the patient almost blind. Some had it in the milder form and were able to carry on with their work, others were so bad that they had to stay in a darkened room for several days as they could not face daylight. We had to segregate all cases of this disease from their companions and each case had to be reported to our headquarters – on a special form called 'Z' form.

A trachoma company was formed and kept apart at headquarters.

WONDERFUL WORKERS

Of course our own Red Cross Department took steps at once in all cases of signs appearing, these boys having to parade especially several times a day for treatment and good work was done. The boys put in some wonderful work at this period and it was due to them to a great extent that we all got off so lightly compared with other companies. They were great little workers.

WELL WATCHED

We finally mastered the outbreak. We took good care to try and spot any 'comeback' signs amongst the troops by holding inspections every little while taking any boys away for some time from their companions who appeared to be affected. I was extremely hot on my platoon and watched carefully as at this particular time every coolie was worth his weight in gold as a worker.

One thing I found out during my connection with the Chinese they had no love for the Japanese.

JUSTIFIED

Since this story was written it has been more than justified in every word as they have fought several battles (Chinese versus Japanese) and of course the Japanese have had the best of it every time. This was only to be expected as they have all the modern aids to warfare at their command, plus a warlike training dating back I suppose one hundred years or so, but they have not got any more pluck than the Chinese (when up against his yellow brother) but of what use is pluck in these days of bombing from the air, long-range shelling by huge siege guns, etc., etc? Very little indeed!

NO BLOODY – GOOD – A –LA!

Always it was the story of 'plenty much stealer' the Japanese. 'Take our country away, take us. No bloody – good – a – la!' And by heavens it has all come true since 1918. And in my opinion has not yet finished. Personally, I had a kind of admiration, like most of us, for the Japanese at one time, but since my connection with the Chinese that has all gone and now I am inclined to think that this is a nation well worth keeping our eye on. Ask the Americans – or the Australians?

DEEP AS THE ATLANTIC

Johnnie Chinaman used to say 'he is as deep as the Atlantic'. 'A false friend.' No friend at all. If there is a yellow peril, it's here not the Chinese, and I don't think these two nations can, or ever, will unite. The only thing in common is their colour. As for the rest – as far apart as the poles. It's an insult to mistake a Chinese man for a Japanese. They never made any mistake about telling me in very plain language what they thought of the Japanese and you must remember 'the Chinese are the best judges of character in the world'.

When Uncle Sam did really decide to enter the Great War on our side, it was the beginning of the end for Germany. This, to me, was the explanation of the enemy's great effort in March 1918 to destroy the Allied armies before the Americans were in full strength in France. It is history how this terrific attack was eventually held up and strange to say the USA boys (engineers) put some fine work helping us to stem the tide on the Somme front.

YES BOY!

Getting the opportunity to visit the docks on several occasions, I was delighted to see thousands and thousands of lean-faced, strapping fellows representing the mighty USA swarming down the gangways after 3,000 miles and perhaps 4,000 of a journey to help us. Yes! I was proud indeed. I was American-born myself (Darby, Philadelphia, PA) and this was my first view of 'my Army' in the mass. They sure did look good. Yes boy! Just fine! Splendid troops.

"SAY GUY!"

I made it my business to talk to quite a few of them and the usual question was, 'Say guy, where is this little old war being held? Which way?' Thumb jerked backwards was the usual reply, and 'You'll d★★★soon find out all about it – bet your life!'

FUNNY OUTFIT

What funny equipment! Such a rare pack compared to ours. And their rife was interesting, but their canvas leggings were a good thing. I pitied the officers with their stiff collars, not enough freedom here, and their hard-peaked caps – a bit German looking? Then their big slouch hats; these gave way to the British 'tin hat' later.

LISTEN TO THIS

A platoon forms up. The sergeant starts calling the roll, and I got the shock of my life. Here's a sample of the names: Murphy, Donovan, O'Flannaghan, O'Hara, McBride, McTavish, Macintosh, Wilson, Watson, Fritz, Hans, Humbach, Horralacher, O'Sullivan, O'Lafferty, O' Hooligan. What a mixture! Did my ears and eyes deceive me? Or was that the Connaught Rangers? Or the Gordons?

SPLENDID TROOPS

I think the mothers and fathers of these boys were Irish, Scottish, or English. Return of the Mayflower? It was an eye-opener. All the nations of the world were represented here in this battalion of USA youth.

Out for adventure. Veterans of war were sprinkled through their ranks and war ribbons showed up on many khaki shirts and told of battle of bygone days. Bronzed, deep-chested, upstanding fellows, these American infantrymen certainly created a deep impression on me and I knew that 'Jerry' was in for 'hot stuff' in the hand-to-hand business when he ran up against this outfit.

STREAMS OF HUMANITY

As far as the eye could reach it was big troopships, and the never-ending stream of humanity. Men! men! men! Manpower! What chance had the Germans now? Fresh and full of new vitality, these boys would give our war-weary troops new hope, and a new message of victory. I knew it! I felt it! Their moral support even was a victory in itself and their presence in France enough to gladden the hearts of the French – and the Belgians – and the English.

DID NOT WIN the WAR

I know that in later years their writers took far too much credit – and from their films one would be led to believe there was only one army in France and that was Uncle Sam's. This is utter nonsense, of course, as the part their army played was indeed small. Indeed to me it is still a great mystery why it was so small as hundreds of thousands of splendid troops never got the chance to fire a shot, much to their utter disgust, never heard a big gun – and never even got a look at a German except behind barbed wire as a prisoner of war. And there must have been one US soldier for every yard of ground that stretched from the North Sea to Switzerland in France before the end of November 1918.

Those who got the chance to fight fought magnificently as I fully expected they would, but suffered far too much from inexperience and lack of knowledge. They did not listen often to men of experience in the wiles of the wily Hun – and paid dearly for their rashness.

In conclusion I may say that America did NOT win the war – far from it!

My turn for leave came along and I was delighted indeed. A rest from the strain of this life would be a godsend and, of course, the prospect of seeing all my loved ones in the old hometown was alluring. This was my first leave from France. I fretted with excitement as the day loomed near – hoping for no last minute hold-up.

---

5. Poor bloody infantry.

THE POOR "B" INFANTRY

The old quay at Calais looks the same as ever. Bustle, hustle, all is a whirl of Tommies from the battle line in full warpaint, seeming to carry more kit than ever (God help the PBI[5]). Generals, colonels – right down to the second 'Loot' all pushed and elbowed in a friendly light-hearted way.

WHO CAN FORGET ?

Who can ever forget the scene, the feelings, the undercurrent of a subdued excitement held in check as you walk up the gangway of the leave boat? Lord! So near – and yet not 'all clear'.

JACK NEVER SLEEPS

She slides out without fuss. Two greyhound forms loom up on each side of us – our bodyguard. A feeling of security steals over you as this pair of destroyers whips the sea around about us. The British Navy never sleeps. Tommy puts his faith in Jack – and Jack never once failed.

TAKE ME BACK ············

Little space to spare. Every square inch is taken up. Kits are everywhere. Forms fall over each other, but it's taken in good part. Who cares now? 'Take me back to B –L –I –G –H –T –Y.' 'Take me anywhere.' 'Take me over there – I don't care.' The old refrain comes up from the lower deck. We start humming it too. It grows and grows until the whole ship seems to sway to the chorus. Light-hearted Tommies freed from the jaws of hell itself for even a little while pack their troubles in the old kitbag – and forget. Who cares, says the PBI.

DOVER ! HOME !

Dover! The white chalk cliffs of old England loom up. How beautiful they look. Home sweet home! But not half as nice as the old Belfast Lough. Oh dear, no!

EVEN THE MAJOR

Safe! Down the gangways. Tickets are inspected, then a mad scramble for the train; rifles, rucksacks, gas masks are crushed into you, but that's a small matter. Off again! Puff! Puff! Tut – tut – tut – tut, the Southern Railway engine simply groans under her terrific load of war-wearied troops. Everyone is friendly, even the fierce major in the corner turns a friendly eye on the 'young bloods' and swaps cigarettes and yarns like a full blown 'one-star man'.

THE DARK HOLE OF

Dear, dirty, begrimed Victoria station. Black as the dark hole of Calcutta – but oh so friendly! Carriage doors are thrown wide and a surging mob storms the platform. A white sea of faces looms beyond the wooden barriers. Mothers, fathers, sweethearts and wives on the tip-toe of excitement waiting to meet a loved one. Fond embraces. Sobs of joy and pent-up feelings give way. I turn away – not my turn yet.

HAUNTED THE APPROACHES

Out into the street and the usual swarm of 'gay night-birds' accost us in many languages – French, Belgian, Russian and the Lord knows what others. I didn't. These girls haunted the approaches to all railway stations in droves during the Great War. The time was now 2.00 in the morning. An unnatural quietness hangs over this great city of London – not altogether quiet as it never sleeps, but a strangeness. I strike out for the YMCA hutments and manage a shakedown. Off goes the old kit. I throw myself down, and dream the hours away.

YES! SHE'S STILL ON THE LAGAN

Euston! The railhead for 'auld Ireland'. The civilians and soldiers now are about half and half. It's nice to see them again, to listen to their talk and understand it all. I already detect the Belfast tongue and pick up my ears. Yes! She is still on the banks of the Lagan. The corridors are packed. We cramp our limbs into smaller space, happy and contented.

HEYSHAM

Darkened stations, subdued lights are passed. We thunder through the night on our long journey to Heysham. I wake up with the start. Where are we? Red Cap police shout, 'This way for the boat.' I scramble out, grab my outfit and dash on board.

EVEN HERE PRECAUTIONS

Waves lap the sides of our steamer as she glides out into the Irish Sea shrouded in darkness. Even here precautions? No sleep tonight, just a ceaseless walking to and fro. How could you settle down tonight? The dawn breaks over the ocean; searchlight beams from far away sweep across us. Still watched by the Navy? Or is it Donaghadee and the Copelands?

BELFAST !

Larne! Whitehead! Bangor! Hollywood! The island (still silent). All seem to float past, and then Donegall Quay. Belfast! Good old Belfast!

AT 40MPH

It's grand to feel the old cobblestones of the quayside once more beneath your feet. A taxi whirls me homewards via well-remembered thoroughfares. How familiar it all seems again. Up the Lisburn Road at 40mph we speed. Right – turn!

REAL SODA BREAD

Melrose Street – No. 44. Mrs Browne, John, Bertie, and my brothers Ben and Arthur. A glad and joyous welcome! Real soda bread, baked only as Mrs Browne could bake it, real tea. What a spread! How grand it all tasted – and so clean and neat. My! But it's fine to be home – home again in number 44.

'MY SWEETHEART'

I was anxious to see my sweetheart – The girl of my dreams – Jean my Irish Acushla.

Arm in arm stroll we stroll along the Lagan past the first locks, time forgotten, happy in the presence of each other, in our world only. How much was to be told. Lovers' talk, sweet nothings – and the stars look down. War forgotten! Hours like minutes speed away. We kiss – and kiss.

" MY SWEETHEART "

The ten days pass like an express train – down to hours now. I clutch at them like a drowning man. A heavy sorrow grips me. Back again, back to it all. Would I survive – and return?

HOME — BY — JIM MAULTSAID

ON THE WAY TO THE LEAVE BOAT.

THE P.B.I. HAVE MORE KIT THAN EVER.

GOODBYE FRANCE.

WHO CARES NOW?

HOW YOU FELT IN THE LIFE BELT

TROUBLES ALL PACKED IN THE OLD KIT BAG.

DOVER! THE WHITE CLIFFS OF OL ENGLAND, LOOM UP.

THE SOUTHERN RAILWAY ENGINE GROANS UNDER HER TERRIFIC WEIGHT.

DEAR, DIRTY VICTORIA.

HAUNTED THE APPROACHES.

EUSTON

THE RAILHEAD FOR "OULD IRELAND"

THE COPELANDS?

THE ISLAND. NO MISTAKING THIS LANDMARK.

RIGHT TURN INTO MELROSE ST.

AS ONLY MRS BROWNE COULD BAKE IT.

REAL SODA BREAD.

THE DAYS SLIP PAST. 123456789 — HAPPY DAYS —

10 ON WINGS

AND THE STARS TWINKLED

ONE WEEK

RAID FOLLOWS RAID FOR A SOLID WEEK NIGHT AFTER NIGHT HUN FRIGHTFULNESS

TO DEMORALIZE?

BANG

MONDAY NIGHT

Straight into it, I landed. My first night on duty found me taking a hand in trying to repel one of Jerry's air raids, the first of a series that lasted for a solid week, night after night. What a start!

NO USE DENYING

Those troops and civilians residing in and around the Calais district during this week and still alive will long remember this awful spell of Hun frightfulness in 1918.

As part of his big plan for a breakthrough of the reserve lines, railheads, dumps, depots, camps, hospitals, munitions centres, hutments, camps etc., etc. were identified for a fierce and prolonged *strafe* to demoralise us and cause a stoppage in the flow of munitions to the forward positions. Did he succeed?

He did not! But no use denying he wreaked terrific havoc and cost us millions of pounds worth of damage in destruction, not to mention the loss of life.

MY THOUGHTS

The usual German thoroughness brought his night raiders on top of us each night practically at the same hour. We were wise to this and were waiting on him to do our best in the line of a reply.

'THAT'S HIM!'

Crump! C −r −u −m −p! Zirr −zirr −zirr. 'That's him!' The drone of his engines is well known to us. We could tell it a mile away and pick it out from our own nine times out of ten.

Midnight has just gone and we are on duty at the guns. Searchlights are stabbing and sweeping around in the attempt to pick up the enemy. Our big balloons have been hoisted aloft long ago and hang in the air hundreds of feet up, held to earth by wire ropes and devoid of human occupants. What their real value or usefulness was I never found out. The night is not completely dark and visibility is good for us, and the airmen. Good for us – and good for 'Jerry'. My thoughts are far away – back in Belfast – until the first big crash brings me to reality again. Our guns were, up to now silent, but break out in unison and hundreds of shells zip and zoom through the air to burst in the heavens like star rockets thousands of feet up.

TARGETS SCARCE

Never have I heard such a racket in the air. Every week seemed to add to our gun power. Hundreds of guns must now be in action defending our possessions. There seem to be dozens of planes in the air, flying around in circles. Crash! Crash! Crump! C −r −u −m −p! The earth trembles. A dull blaze citywards develops into a wall of fire. Something has caught fire tonight! A bullseye for the Hun. He is now raining bombs and aerial torpedoes down on us in a frantic effort to get rid of his cargo and beat a retreat. It was hot up above.

So far we had not fired a shot. Targets are scarce and far out of range. No luck tonight – for us. The gun crew fret and fidget as they crouched down against the wet sandbags. Poor fellows they were no doubt fed up, but of course so was I. All day on the works and half the night in a gunpit. We were having little or no sleep. Still the boys in the line were a thousand times worse off and I gave them a gentle reminder to this effect.

The guns still thundered! Dull boomings, sharp earsplitting cracks from the French 75s and the drone of our own 6-pounders all joined in splashing the heavens with red-hot metal.

THE BOX BARRAGE

I had heard of the new BOX BARRAGE system of air defence – shooting straight up at no visible target and keeping the Hun on the outside by a sheer wall of gunfire. Was this the game tonight? Sounded and looked d★★★ like it! Not a single round did we get rid of tonight. The all-clear fog horn sounds the dismiss, and the rumble of artillery grows fainter.

The raid is over for the moment. Our machine guns are covered. We crawl out from the pits and slide back like shadows. The hour is 3.00 am.

LIKE A RAINBOW

TUESDAY NIGHT

D★★★them! Out again. We dash for our positions on the canal bank and just get in as the first big bomb drops earthwards. Quite dark tonight and the rain is falling. Half-awake, I grab a Very light and ram it into the pistol as the sergeant yells 'There he is, Sir!' I pulled the trigger and the rocket soars up – up – up – up to burst and spread into a beautiful rainbow far above us. Zurr! zurr! zurr! … zip! zip! Still we cannot see him but can hear him somewhere close. I order the guns to fire by sound and belts of tracer bullets hiss upwards. Blind firing no doubt, but you can never tell your luck.

LIKE AN EARTHQUAKE

Rapid fire now as the sound of his engine gets closer. All four guns full steam ahead. We are all shot in a heap dazed and bewildered as the canal bank sways and trembles. C –R –A –S –H! Like an earthquake at its worst, and we were simply drowned in a water spout. God bless my soul! That bomb struck the water in our canal not far from us. What a narrow shave! And he is gone. The guns bark and roar. We still stand on the alert, but it's practically all over for another night: 2.30am 'close-down'. A splitting headache robs me of any sleep that night.

WEDNESDAY THURSDAY FRIDAY AND SATURDAY

All a repetition of each other. Night after night. Duty – duty – duty. Chinese by day – machine guns by night. And sometimes the 'all clear' did not come through until the dawn. Almost as bad as the front-line trenches back here!

BLACK-CROSS-ITIS

Jerry was playing merry H★★★with our nerves. For nights and nights long afterwards we lay down to rest in our warpaint, one eye open and one ear listening for that hated fog horn. On the rack! The big black cross was on our brain. 'Black cross-it is', a disease! And a

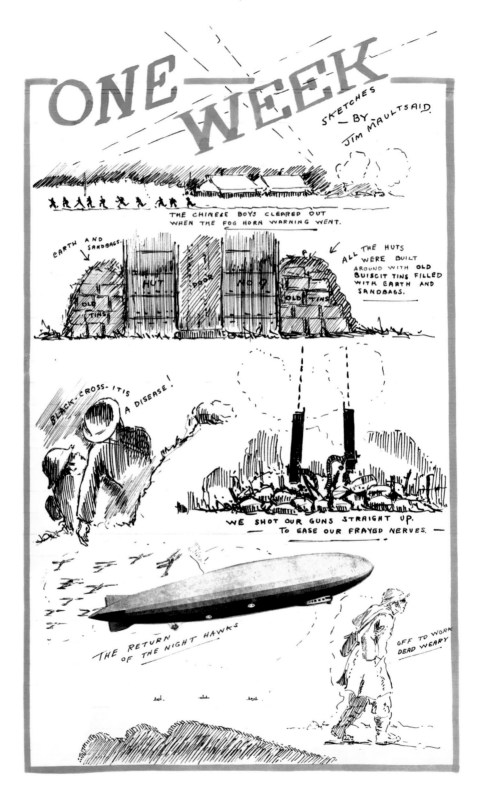

painful one. During the last few nights we take a hand in the barrage business and shot our guns almost straight up also – more to ease our frayed nerves than anything else. Wonderful how soothing a machine gun can be sometimes!

THE RETURN

This spell over, we got a rest from night duty after several false alarms. News came along that the enemy was now turning his attention across to the English shore and colour was lent to this by the early morning drone high up in the heavens coming inwards towards the Belgian coast. The return of the night hawks?

BIG LOSSES

A week long to be remembered. Part of 'Jerry's' last big throw? That cost us in lives, military and civilian, a big total. And material?

Every morning after one of these raids our coolies were out of form and we often had to chase around looking for stray members of our flock. As soon as the fog horn emitted the first blast it was a case of their grabbing a blanket or cover of some sort and dashing off down the highways and byways looking for cover from the fearful German bombs. God help the poor souls; it was a terrible time for them. We had all their hutments sandbagged to prevent injury by flying splinters, but nothing on earth of course would have saved them from a direct hit. Big dugouts were also built, but somehow they preferred the wide-open spaces. These air raids left them unsettled and nervous; their work the next day more or less suffered accordingly.

What mortal man could be otherwise? I have told you in a previous article how it was whispered around that some of the German prisoners in the PoW camps suffered at the hands of the CLC. 'JERRY – NO – BLOODY – GOOD – A – LA.'

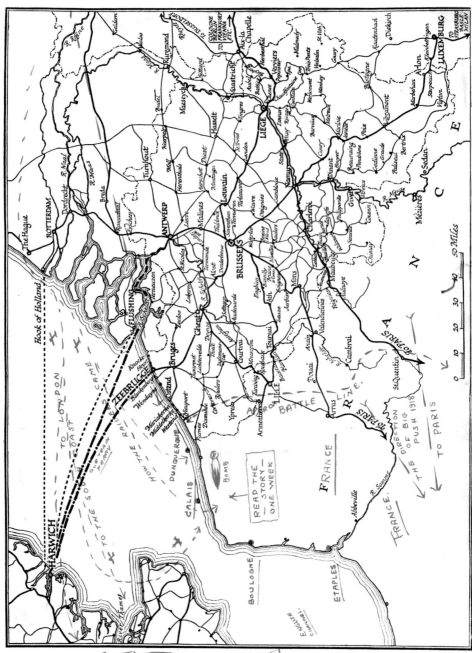

THE TURN of the TIDE
ON the WESTERN front
AUGUST 8th —1918—

the BEGINNING OF THE END
WE STRIKE A HAMMER BLOW

AUGUST THE 8th

1918 was 'the day' – but ours, not the Germans!

The beginning of the end of the Great War, although we did not know it then. Like the enemy we were favoured on this summer's morning with a heavy mist and thousands of our guns smashed out a terrible fire on the Hun defences. The glare lit up our back areas for miles back, the very ground we stood on trembled as if greatly troubled. As the troops and tanks moved forward to battle we stood to our posts on the lines of communication. News of our great and glorious advance came through to us. We jumped with joy, and the French were on the move too! Sweetest news since the beginning of this awful war. Our boys actually cheered as we commenced work on this day. Smiles! Smiles! Smiles! Up went our sleeves.

Life was good again. Now for a bit of our own back! Hurrah!

PLENTY ZO! ZO!

The enemy were turned from the very gates of Amiens – and Paris was fading out! Come on you sons of guns – get into it! Work! Plenty worker! Qui – Qui. German plenty Zo! Zo! (Hurry). Almost finished – a – la! And how they worked! Oh! It was a treat. Records went by the board day after day. The pressure was terrific on supply departments during these hectic days of August, but we did not fail the troops. Not us! Their day was our day. Down the line swarmed thousands of captured German troops; as they passed us our coolies did not forget to rub it in, in real Chinese, and looks of sullen contempt was the only response.

The PoW cages bulged with the new arrivals, their fighting days all over. I was struck by the boyish appearance of many of them – and the old age of others; youth and age, some war-worn, others in brand new uniforms that never seemed to fit them. Not the stamp of the men we met in 1916. Here and there a fine upstanding figure would catch the eye, but not many.

OH! FOR SOME OF THESE TANKS IN 1916

As the good news of our successful attack filtered through, a new spirit of confidence seemed to run through our troops. We quizzed all the wounded as to how the battle was going 'up there' and the reply often was 'We are knocking hell out of him. He's on the run.'

The Aussies and Canadians started the ball rolling in this great battle to be joined by almost every battalion in the British army later on. Our tanks played a marvellous part, clearing the way in many cases for our infantrymen. Oh for a score of these monsters on 1 July 1916. The Ulster Division would have swept on to Berlin – almost! The strange thing about it all was that the divisions engaged were all in the March disaster, worn and tired, yet could turn round and hit back like this! Shades of the Marne once more.

A wonderful fellow, the British Tommy! A black day indeed for Germany! One of the darkest since 1914. What colossal nerve had our own Sir Douglas, and such glorious faith in 'his army'.

The raiding pest was for the moment washed clean out and we got quite a measure of rest and peace to do our very important work. Long hours: from the first glimmer of dawn well into the shades of night we worked and toiled sending up petrol, shells and guns in the order of demand. Days of feverish activity in this month of August as the demand for petrol grew and grew.

142

We must have sent millions of boxes forward to the various dumps and railheads for our armies. And still the cry was more! More! More! All kinds of railway trucks were scraped together and it was nothing strange to see L&NER, L&SWR and GWR all mixed up with the French 'NORD' and Belgian trucks, hauled out by one of our big ROD engines.

My life just hereabouts was all Chinese: petrol, engines and trucks! Work gangs, work reports, sweated coolies, and sweated white overseers. Almost slave drivers – all for the cause! Ten years of energy expended in a few months. Ten years of life rolled into one!

THE REWARD WE PLAYED OUR PART

Hard toil had our boys as lean as greyhounds. Muscles rippled up and down beneath brown-skinned bodies – and the general health of the coolies was at a high pitch.

It was all required to enable us to keep up the strain. Never did discipline and efficiency give better reward. The company was running like a well-oiled machine – well trained and true, an example of what Chinese could do when properly handled. The reward for all our patience and a joy to behold. And the test during these last months of the war was severe; in fact it was almost beyond human endurance. Yet we stood up to it all – and won through! Wonderful Chinese boys! I would not have missed this experience for a ransom, although I almost collapsed under the stress of it all.

At times my wound was on the verge of again breaking out, the old pad and bandages were put on again to help me hold together. Nights I often lay and could get no sleep with the nerves all a jingle and on edge, but I was determined to see it through. Back! Back! Back! Jerry was giving ground day by day. We were fired with a zeal beyond expression.

The black clouds were breaking up and the sun was shining through. Our airmen told us stories of the roads behind enemy lines, all confusion as the Hun turned his back and retreated. Red- white-and-blue-circled planes swept down to add to his troubles, flying low sweeping the roads with machine guns and bombs. The black cross was practically swept from the skies, hounded and harried out of existence by our young devil-may-care flying youth.

The whip hand was ours in the air and we took care they never ran short of 'juice' (petrol). Our tanks never ceased to say chunk! chunk! chunk! Our motor convoy trucks never once failed to whirr for the 'necessary' – thanks to the CLC.

We played our part manfully in this glorious advance, as a supporting arm, no doubt, but very necessary for all that. Bravo! The boys from the land of the Dragon. Bravo! Indeed.

HERE'S A CHARGE BY THE AUSTRALIANS.......
THESE BOYS ARE TYPICAL "DOWN UNER" TROOPS.
THEY LED THE VAN ON AUGUST THE 8th......

RE DRAWN FROM
MY SKETCH BOOK
TYPICAL ANZAC
JIM. MAULTSAID

THE "AUSSIES" KICKED OFF

A WONDERFUL
FELLOW.......
" "
THIS TOMMY
OF OUR'S......
FROM MY SKETCH
.... BOOK...
JIM MAULTSAID.

SUPPLIED THE MOTOR CONVOYS

PETROL DUMP

PETROL

AND THE TANKS

THE LIFE BLOOD OF OUR FLYING SERVICE

EVEN FOR TOMMY TO SIT ON

FOR PUMPING ENGINES

THE EMPTY TINS — WERE — VALUABLE AS WATER CARRIERS — IN THE TRENCHES.

USEFUL AS A CLEANER KILLER OF — PESTS —

ARRANGED — AND — SKETCHED — BY — JIM MAULTSAID.

STARTING FIRES

THE COOK

EDITOR'S NOTE

By Jim Maultsaid

The sketches illustrating this story, 'The Turn of the Tide', are all re-copied from originals as in my war sketchbooks and the originals were sketched in France in 1919, when the noise and the shouting (should I say shooting) had died down. I was on active service for a whole year after the war and had indeed a fine opportunity of doing these little pictures, and took it. My chums kidded me to death, but nights were long and lonesome in 1919, so I passed the long hours at my beloved hobby; it helped to keep me from pining away and soothed my feelings.

The pictures breathe the spirit of those hectic days of August 1918 and depict a phrase of the Great War seldom, or ever, touched by any of the stories of these days. I do hope you have enjoyed my story and my sketches. So far.

'THE HEAVIES'

Boom! Boom! Boom! Flash! Flash! Flash! Thunder and thunder. Heavies in action tonight. Death and destruction somewhere in the German lines. The telegraph boys will be calling with some poor distracted mothers tomorrow.

What a hell of a war. The ground shakes and quivers. Boom! Boom! Boom! Gunners' bodies seem bloody red in the flash of the discharge. Slam! Slam! Slam! Three more monster shells are slammed home. Down the road their brother batteries join in. What a din. Eardrums are shattered. Away on the horizon is a blood-red.glare in the darkness, Hun troops crouching in dug-outs, waiting, waiting, hoping. Zero hour? Official: we attacked at dawn.

Swinging along, splashing, slipping, sliding over the cobblestones of the old French village. Grey skies, rain, rain, rain. Splash! Splash! Splash! Tin hats glistening, groundsheets dripping, sweat rising like the mist over the long column on the march.

Bent backs, sore, weary feet, red, raw shoulders, eyes on the ground, hell roast your g**dammed feet, you b***** fool! Platoon follows platoon. All the same. They shuffle on, ever on. Kilo after kilo ....

But towards the line. The guns rumble, far away to the right. To hell with them. They never cease. I stand in a trance. It all comes back. A tear drops from my eye as the last of the shadows pass into the murk. Eighteen hundred feet.

"THE HEAVIES"

DOWN THE ROAD.....
THEIR BROTHER BATTERIES
JOIN IN.......
HUN TROOPS CROUCH
IN DUG-OUTS
WAITING....WAITING
FOR ZERO HOUR?

JIM. MAULTSAID _ 1918 _ IN FRANCE.

DEATH AND DESTRUCTION
SOMEWHERE IN THE
GERMAN LINES TONIGHT.

TELEGRAPH BOY'S
WILL BE CALLING
TOMORROW!

"THE HEAVIES"
BY - JIM MAULTSAID -

GERMAN
TROOPS
CROUCHING DOWN

EIGHTEEN HUNDRED FEET

BY—Jim Maultsaid

WORK

WORK
SLAVERY.
WORK

PETROL

SHELLS

WORK

DAY

CORN

RAILWAYS

AND
— SKETCHES —
BY. JIM. MAULTSAID

BIG GUNS

NIGHT

AT THE GUNS
NIGHT DUTY.

Would be a better word than work – yes slavery! We slaved – and slaved.

THE DEMAND

Demand from the dumpheads was terrific. They rolled into our headquarters at all hours of the day and most of the night. Always *urgent*. It was petrol, oil, petrol – and petrol. After various sidelines I was back on the petrol department with my crack gangs, back to our old love, work we loved and could do best. Out and out specialists in this branch of labour. No gang of any colour could hold a candle to our 169 lads at this, the loading of petrol.

During these months of August, September, October and November 1918, we were tested and tried to the very uttermost, in fact to the verge of collapse in our efforts to meet all the calls that came down the line for our goods. Never did I see human beings work as we worked those Chinese boys of ours during these months.

20 HOURS DAILY

All I have already written about the marvellous shows we put up pales before our last grand finish in our anxiety to meet the demand.

7,000 – 8,000 – 9,000

The four platoon officers worked twenty-hours per day almost every day. Our white NCOs backed us up to the hilt, often throwing off their tunics and lending a hand at the manual labour end, as an example and to encourage our exhausted coolies. God! It was fierce. Petrol! More and more! Speed! Urgent! At once! 3,000 – 4,000 – 5,000 – 6,000 – 7,000 – 8,000 – 9,000 cases of petrol. Daily – nightly. Can you grasp it?

Even yet I marvel at all the hell-for-leather rush, hustle, 'slam'em in anyhow, anywhere, any angle, nearly – but get'em loaded by hook or by crook.

GENERAL NEWS

You will notice I have not again given you a description of how this petrol was loaded; it is not required in this story as I have already in previous articles and by the numerous sketches demonstrated how it was dealt with, so I'll confine myself to more general news.

5,000
6,000
7,000 8,000
9,000 and
10,000
CASES PER DAY
THE PACE WAS
TERRIBLE

SUPPLIES INCREASE

We were not unduly harried by the Hun raiders at this time; they were far too busy trying to stop our daring pilots, for our boys at this period raided incessantly in ever increasing numbers.

A TERRIFIC TASK

As our line advanced, our lines of communication grew longer; this meant more motor convoys. Our tanks were increasing greatly. The American forces partly depended on our supplies and we helped the Italians even. Then our armies grew and grew, all this to show you why the demand was so great on us. Also add in the tremendous supplies required by our Air Force[6] which had grown to a small army itself – all these branches were crying out for bread (petrol) and the Chinese Labour Corps had to see that that cry was not unheeded – a terrific task.

DAZED –DOPED –STUPID

At times we walked about in a perfect daze, or half-doped for the want of sleep. Some of the coolies were almost stupid, poor fellows, from the physical strain imposed on them. It was not work these days – it was pure SLAVERY.

THROUGH SUNSHINE AND ...

Through sunshine, showers, storms, air raids, hail and snow our task never ceased. Relays of gangs followed each other. Ten hours work, some rest, six or seven hours more, a little sleep, then at it once more. Day was turned into night. Maultsaid in charge. Forrester at the wheel. Thompson in command, or Simpson, or all four at it at the same time. We each had a depot of our own and the 'skipper' watched over us like a father. What a life! Oh what a life!

FADE OUT

Come on boys! 'Qua – qui. Qua – qui. Quicker – quicker. NINE THOUSAND WANTED today.' I gasp at the order. The morning breaks 4.30am. We shiver in the sharp air. A new day begins. Slog, slash, crash, bang, bang, morning drifts into the evening, evening into night. Dazed tired bodies flit about in the gloom.

At last the task is ended. Leaden steps as we drag our wearied bodies homewards. A messenger meets us from HQ. Special order THREE THOUSAND more. My G★★! About turn! We almost pushed them, poor poor boys – too tired to protest, they humbly obeyed. Midnight. One hundred figures crawl along the canal-bank and fade into the gloom.

---

6. The Royal Air Force had been created on 1 April 1918 by the amalgamation of the Royal Naval Air Service and the Royal Flying Corps.

JUST BOYS

I gaze in wonderment at our new troops, just mere lads. Have we really come down to this? And they are to be thrown into the furnace of war, untrained and untried. My eyes opened in amazement as this battalion swarmed down the gangways. Were these Boy Scouts dressed up as soldiers?

POOR TROOPS

Having a spot of work at the docks in Calais it was here that it was brought home to me how hard-pressed the old country was for men. We surely had sunk low in manpower when mere striplings like these were being pushed out to France to meet the Germans.

It struck me as strange indeed as I knew for a fact that we had thousands of fine able bodied men who held the posts as instructors etc. in reserve battalions and cadet training schools, instructional centres and various suchlike organisations. Why not mobilise these men who were athletes of the first order – boxers, footballers, runners – and specialised men of all kinds held by commanding officers as being indispensable. Yet these youths were sacrificed to the 'War God'.

Some of our 'big people' have a sin to answer for in my humble opinion. Then, as the day is drawing to a close, in comes another big convoy and it pours forth such a cargo of poor C.3 men as would have turned a heart of stone to softness.

161

THE HALT – THE LAME!

Old men! Young undersized boys! Underfed looking! Pale faces! The lame – and the blind! What an army! My heart bled for them. Of course we were a young lot in our days – but what a difference. We were volunteers, free as air, out for adventure and trained to the very minute – this was the 14th Royal Irish Rifles YCV, not conscripts like these poor wretches.

ALL HONOUR

Of course you must not misunderstand me. It was downright pity that swept through my blood to think that these young untrained and untried lads were going straight into that HELL up there when we had thousands of A1 men who had never yet heard a shot fired in anger. No wonder my Irish blood boiled over! All honour to the youngsters, they did not let us down but fought the good fight as British Tommies always do, taking their share of glory, and death, just as well as we did. Against this I knew of course that the standard of the German army had also fallen low. Not the men of 1914, 1915 and 1916.

Their fighting days were all over – these warriors who now looked out at us from behind barbed wire. PoW was short for prisoner of war. As these gentlemen rolled in from the battle fronts they were placed in camps surrounded by high barricades of posts and wire with sentry boxes every fifty yards or so apart. The guards were composed of men already wounded or unfit for active service. The prisoners were well treated on our side and fed well too. It was a strange sight to see the different uniforms worn, red, blue, and green. The old stern military training brought them to attention sharply as an officer, British, passes then even on the outside of wire. Some fine-looking fellows and lots just the opposite. Such was the PoW.

A MIGHTY AIR ARMADA PASSES OVERHEAD

One wild Sunday morning in the month of October 1918 a mighty air Armada of British, French, and American planes passed overhead thousands of feet up flying towards the German lines. The drone of the engines brought us all tumbling out from our rough shelters to gaze up in astonishment at this gathering of deadly warbirds battling against a terrific headwind, dark clouds and driving rain to add terror and confusion in the ranks of the retreating Hun. One could not resist a thought of pity for the enemy, but these thoughts passed away as we talked about the gas and the 'flamethrowers' that Jerry had used on us. Our turn now! Flash! Flash! Flash! German anti-aircraft shells are cracking in their midst as we turn away.

ANGRY WASPS

Higher up sweep our planes as these angry wasps sting and whip the heavens in a mad frenzy, but a mere annoyance to the pilots and hardly worth troubling about. As a matter of fact gunfire from the ground as a means of stopping aircraft in the Great War was a complete washout from all I could see and hear. The only defence is machine versus machine, so future generations please note.

FROM 1915 to 1918

The little sketch on the opposite page was sketched that night – it's dull – but so was this day and it portrays the mood of the moment. The very sight of these bombers of ours (this was a raid I take it, on a large scale) passing over the German lines practically unchallenged was a sign in itself of the state into which the enemy air force was now in – almost blind. We had indeed gained the upper hand in the air and, what's more, held it until the end of hostilities. From the days of 'Mad Major' to this! Marvellous, and stupendous!

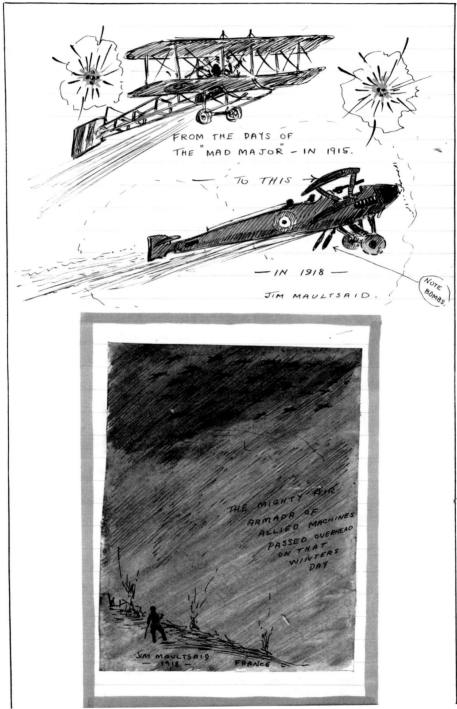

The pace of the past few months was beginning to tell on us. Officers, men, workers, NCOs: all of us were stretched to breaking point. I felt like cracking up but the will to win through was strong and the news from the front line good, so we held together, setting a fine example to our Chinese workers. Night and day we were called to duty; any time – any – it mattered not. Work! Work! Late and early! Onward to the final victory – at any price. No slacking down now. I worked myself to a shadow! Oh Lord! How I worked! Heart and soul I was all out to help the boys. Come on! Come on!

QUICKER

'Qui – qui, quicker! Quicker! Zo !Zo!' Speed, sweat, more speed, we slogged, slogged and slogged. Like the days down on the plantations we drove our Chinese boys to the last gasp – and then more.

PROUD?

Never once did 169 Company CLC fail. Never once did we fail to deliver the goods.

What wonderful fellows those yellow boys were. Workers of the finest quality. How proud of them I was, so proud indeed that I would have pitted them in an open challenge against any labour squad in the world, be they black, brown or white.

Glorious boys those 169 lads! Area Headquarters were astonished at our returns of labour. Nothing was too much for us, no task too big. Captain Curtain (now major) was proud of us – his officers Simpson, Forrester, Thompson and Maultsaid. But we could not stand it much longer. I knew it. I felt it in my bones. But having turned the bend, and now in the straight for HOME, we had to make the last grand effort.

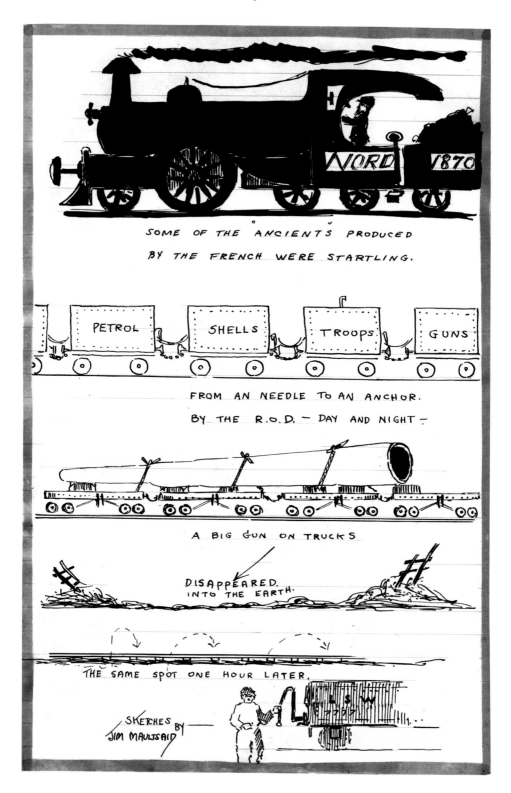

SOME OF THE "ANCIENTS" PRODUCED BY THE FRENCH WERE STARTLING.

FROM AN NEEDLE TO AN ANCHOR. BY THE R.O.D. – DAY AND NIGHT –

A BIG GUN ON TRUCKS

DISAPPEARED. INTO THE EARTH.

THE SAME SPOT ONE HOUR LATER.

SKETCHES BY JIM MAULTSAID

SKETCHES BY JIM MAULTSAID

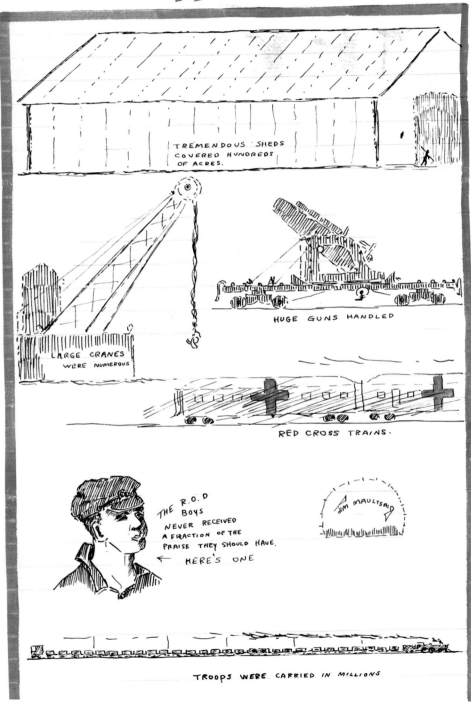

TREMENDOUS SHEDS COVERED HUNDREDS OF ACRES.

HUGE GUNS HANDLED

LARGE CRANES WERE NUMEROUS

RED CROSS TRAINS.

THE R.O.D BOYS NEVER RECEIVED A FRACTION OF THE PRAISE THEY SHOULD HAVE. HERE'S ONE

Jim Maultsaid

TROOPS WERE CARRIED IN MILLIONS

DURING the years 1917 and 1918 marvellous strides were made in our railway communications. A very vast organisation sprang up in a short space of time and took shape in the form of the ROD (Railway Ordnance Department). This department took over all the transport of British war stock from the much overworked French and Belgian lines but, of course, we worked hand in hand with our Allies. Many of the troops will bring to mind how we often cursed the French Railways, but those days passed away and then came our own engines, drivers, etc., etc. Wonderful improvement! Thousands of our best railwaymen came from England: drivers, firemen, shunters, skilled mechanics of all kinds and in a short space of time you might have been sailing along on the Great Western or the Southern almost for all the slight difference you noticed.

The big heavy engines were all specially built and numbered and marked ROD. Thousands of trucks, carriages, Red Cross trains complete, rolling stock of all kinds was brought over and it was no uncommon sight to see a big convoy made up from every known railway company in England – L&NW, GWR, LB&SC, L&SE, etc., etc., and the War Office's specials – ROD.

THINK OF IT

When you think of the coal, waste, spare parts, iron, steel, sleepers, rails and millions of other details required to maintain the special service your mind can only dimly grasp it all. Repair shops of tremendous size and range sprang up overnight as it were and these branches could have almost built an engine themselves. Special trucks were built to carry our big guns, tanks and all odd shipments.

The timetable for convoys and troop trains, also Red Cross trains, were worked out to the second. A very high state of efficiency was maintained indeed and the ROD staff were seldom beaten in any task imposed. Here's an example: a tremendous gun that ran the length of four or five flat trucks just sank out of sight – rails, trucks and all. Into the earth with sucking sound – gone! All gone! This was a pretty fix – no error.

My story has now reached the months of September and October 1918 roughly, and you have read how we all made such supreme efforts in our own way to win the war.

The dark clouds have rolled past. We knew it. We felt it. Somehow the very air breathed something new and sweeter. The air force boys kept telling us 'we have the b★★★★★★★on the run', 'the b★★★★★★ are beaten,' 'got 'em', 'they won't stop until across the Rhine' etc., etc. Such were their expressions of supreme confidence. Of course our airmen were never anything else but confident. Yet somehow there was the ring of truth about this. And then 'Jerry's' raids were getting fewer and fewer. A good sign? And the prisoners of war were getting very numerous. These soldiers as a rule were of inferior type and some downright depressed, telling us that Germany was finished – down and out! Perhaps!

Winning ~ Winning

All the signs indeed looked good. And our troops going back up the line were in great good heart. And the wounded boys coming back give us new heart. Smiling faces – bright smiles for us. 'Guess the old infantry were in grand form smashing the Hun from his never-to-be-taken fortifications in France and Belgium.' Our day had come – so the PBI should surely know.

We were winning – winning – winning all along the line.

The Hun was on the run. And on the run we would keep him. Old folks were already drifting back looking for old home towns, old homesteads that did not exist; the hell of the invader had ground them to dust long, long ago. In my heart I knew and felt the end of this Hell's kitchen was almost in sight.

My thoughts? Hard to fathom even by myself. A terrific desire to get back to my beloved Royal Irish Rifles to lend a final hand in clearing the enemy out and get a little of my own back – revenge? Yet I knew I would have been of very little use in this and resigned myself to the duties on hand and worked as I never worked before. I spared no effort morning, noon or night to further the cause.

And I did not spare my Chinese boys.

The Doom Of Germany.

The gunfire rolls and thunders. The horizon is red.

Jerry is getting a taste of what we got in 1914. The Allies outgunned him. Some of our barrages were awe-inspiring and one thought the end of the world had come – doomsday! But it was the doom of Germany and her associates. News from the Eastern Front was wonderful. Germany's allies had had enough and were collapsing like a pack of cards around her. She would soon be fighting a lone battle – and had not a chance in a million. Doom! Doom! Doom!

Yes, the skies were bright! For us.

She knew her fate I should say around this time and just fought on, for the best terms. Sheer bluff. That did not bluff us. Beaten! All her dreams of world domination shattered. The dreams of a mighty military nation in despair.

Doves of Peace

Old Hindenburg himself, I should say, knew his army could stand very few more of our terrible offensives. When would they crack? And how soon? The tide was rolling in; waves beating down the ramparts – waves of gunfire.

The air was thick with hungry wasps raining down death day and night, never-ending death from the North Sea down to the Alps. No wonder Hindenburg quailed! His armies

OVER BELGIUM

were reeling, smashed right and left. The Eagle's wings fluttered, that proud haughty eagle that strutted over Belgium's bloody fields way back in '14.

Doves of peace were sent out in swarms always to America or via the USA. Mutterings of revolt in the Kaiser's navy. The 'Reds' at work. Yes! Gentlemen, the sign of Doom was in the clouds – for Germany.

WE RULED THE AIR

Never-ending streams of troops, guns, munitions moved towards the line. The red, white and blue circled, swooped and commanded the air, sweeping the sky clear of all opposition. The Blackhawks were paralysed and blinded by swarms of fighters and bombers.

TO THE END.
DOWN THE ROAD.

Don't misunderstand me when I say we were also war-weary after all these four years of bloodshed. Weary to death – but determined to see it through to the bitter end. Very, very few of the veterans of 1914, '15 or '16 were now left. You could have counted them on ten fingers in some of the battalions – yet these grand fellows soldiered on, down that hard, hard road looking for the bend, or should I say the end, of the Road? Many of course came back to it all four and five times after wounds had healed somewhat or illness passed over and took their place in ranks once more, ranks that had changed and changed again until sometimes not a single old timer was there to greet an 'old sweat' up with the last draft. The faces were young – and unfamiliar. Nearly all mere boys.

'THE WRITINGS'
Germany's day as a great nation in the twentieth century was over.
The writing was on 'the wall'.

THE GREAT RETREAT

FROM THE WESTERN FRONT

CRASH!

VICTORY, VICTORY

OUR VICTORY MARCH

Nothing seemed to stop our forward march. Held up here and there at strongpoints for a few hours or so until our heavy guns got up and blew the opposition to kingdom come, at other points our infantry swept through to fair green land, cutting off hundreds of enemy troops that had stayed too long and fell into our net. Day after day our victories were coming through the wires, and via the Royal Air Force, or by the wounded boys.

FORWARD!

We made a point of not throwing any shells into a village or town that was thought to still contain French or Belgian people. This in a way assisted the enemy and they took full advantage of it in many ways. Our plan was to more or less work around these villages storming them from the flanks, then rounding up the survivors or fighting it out in the streets and clears.

Some fierce fighting took place in these places, often over the bodies of civilians who could not resist coming out to meet their saviours at the risk of their lives. Little children and women were often found dead, just lying where they had fallen – victims of the 'God' called war.

Many of these sights were enough to make you weep. Ruined homes – dazed folk wandering amongst the ruins. Starved cattle, sheep, goats and dogs tottered forward to meet our troops all mixed up with Germans surrendering. It was a scene from 'Hell's Inferno' – bloody, indescribable war!

The misery. The fear. The utter abject poverty of it all – pathetic!

MAY THEY BE ······ SPARED ALL THIS

The pictures on the following pages will bring home to you more than thousands of written words my meaning. Study them and ponder – then just go over it all again and say, 'this is war'. May our present generation be spared all this.

BATTALION AFTER

I have gone off the track a little but, pardon me, I'll get right back and tell you my story in my own way ….

Battalion after battalion pressing forward. Frames of heavy, light and medium artillery take up the road. Tanks lumber forward. Convoys of ammunition: wagons of shells, stores, all the requirements of a mighty army on the move – and all going FORWARD. A war of movement again. Our Chinese company are swept from the roadway. We take to the fields – nothing must delay the troops. A Red Cap at the crossroads controls the traffic like a police man at home; he does his job well. Our Chinese get a smile as he gives the salute and directs us on our way. Was it pity or contempt?

The Gordons swing past. How those pipes get you – plaintive, haunting pipes. I almost forgot myself and fell in. Brown knees as the kilts sway, hardened warriors, bronzed weather-beaten faces. Sons of Scotland all, and a credit to their race. Scotland wha - hey! I can see the glens, the valleys, the mountains, the mists o'bonnie Dundee in my mind's eye – and I'm anything but Scotch myself.

181

"THE ROYAL IRISH"

My heart beats – almost stops. The Royal Irish Rifles? Sure as. How I jumped! The chest goes out as I spring to attention and salute the commander on horseback. My own, my very own, Regiment. Oh boy, it was fine to see those Ulster faces pass. What was the band playing? A very popular Ulster tune that had been played down the long years back. How I scanned the ranks for some familiar face or faces, but was sadly disappointed. It was not an Ulster Division battalion and I did not know a single 'old-timer' – but my delight was intense to once again see the Harp and Crown badge on the tin hat (painted green).

I cannot resist the urge for a yarn and fall in alongside a young second lieutenant. We chat about the future and he wishes it all over. Fed up having fought in half-a-dozen battles, I cheer him up by telling him a few more weeks would finish it all (how true my words where, as it was just over a month later that 'ceasefire' was sounded) I did not realise myself we gripped hands and said cheerio and dropping out the last of the close formed ranks clatter passed into the UNKNOWN. Goodbye Irish Rifles!

INTO the UNKNOWN...
CAVALCADE!
TO BATTLE ....

The Sussex, the Staffords, the Lincolns, the Dorsets, Canada, New Zealand, Newfoundland, South Africa, the South Wales Borderers. Then the USA (a small detachment) and a French cavalry squadron. A league of nations past us as we sat this day, jammed, – all moving forward 'to Battle'.

I sat and pondered it all. What chance had Germany? Not one in a million. And our gun power? All sizes, all shapes lumber and lurch past. Horse and tractor. God help the Hun. Men! Shells! Guns! Tanks! Gas! Then more.

A badly battered road was our job. Viewing the damage we made our calculations, gave orders and in no time the work was full blast. Repairs! Make way for the troops. Many jokes were thrown at us as we stand aside and the 'bhoys' tramp on. Interruptions were numerous. A long ragged line of Hun prisoners wander past and I was amused to see their expressions of amazement at our Chinese. Astonishment was writ large on their faces. *Who or what the h★★★★ was this outfit? Was all the world against them?* Such must have been their thoughts.

Then the refugees troubled us, but this time the poor beings were going forward also. What courage – back to look for homes and dwellings already in the dust. We feared a clash with the Germans who had just passed us. Black murderous looks were cast – but it went off quietly and we breathed a sigh of relief. And both lots asked for bread and bully beef. What a war! What a world! Tragedy! Pathos! Despair! Hope! Cavalcade of a century passing before our eyes …

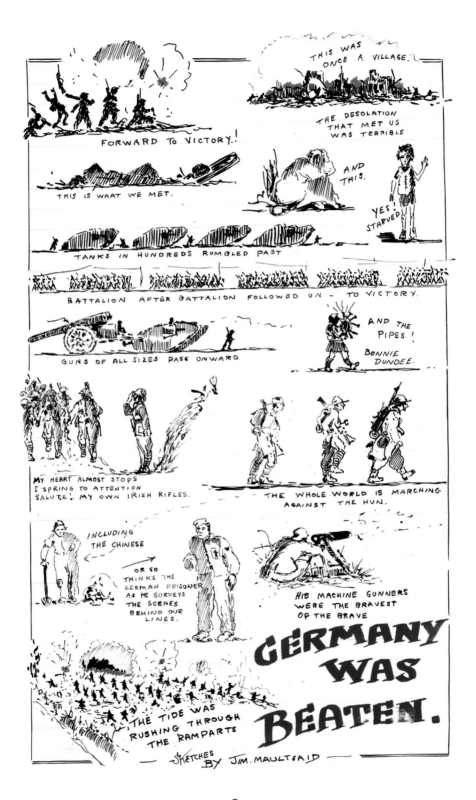

ROLLING THROUGH

Towns and villages that had been in enemy hands for years were falling far behind us. Our troops advancing over the countryside in long thin Indian files – everywhere as far as the eye could see. The Royal Engineers came into their own in this phase of war and had many opportunities for bridge building etc. The weather at this time was cold, wet and miserable. Shelters were scarce, our troops suffered hardship untold, but our morale was high and yet the general opinion was 'Jerry' would stick the winter out.

A trick to delay us was carried out by the cunning foe. They ordered French or Belgian civilians of both sexes out in front of our infantry and knew we would not fire – yet on several occasions confused themselves and could not reform their ranks, falling into our hands as PoWs. Machine gunners only were left to fight us to the end, as rearguards – many brave fellows fell; few indeed surrendered. This section of the German army was the bravest, but the great Hindenburg line was smashed, the tide of khaki, and French blue, was rolling in through the ramparts – like the mighty sea – UNSTOPPABLE!

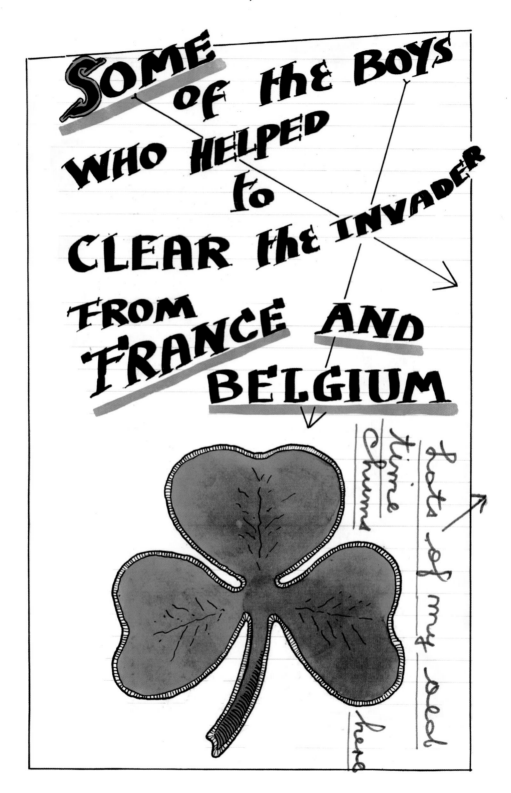

DAILY SKETCH.

THE PREMIER PICTURE PAPER.

THE FIGHTING IRISHMAN'S SLOGAN

Some of the cheery lads of the Ulster Division who, with their comrades of other famous Irish regiments, helped to win Wytschaete the other day. Their slogan is as heartening as their humour is infectious. Gleeful over their wealth of trophies, which comprise every variety of German headgear, and playfully mimicking the Huns who surrendered at the points of their bayonets, they personify the fighting Irishman whose deeds of valour are the Empire's pride.—(Official Photograph.)

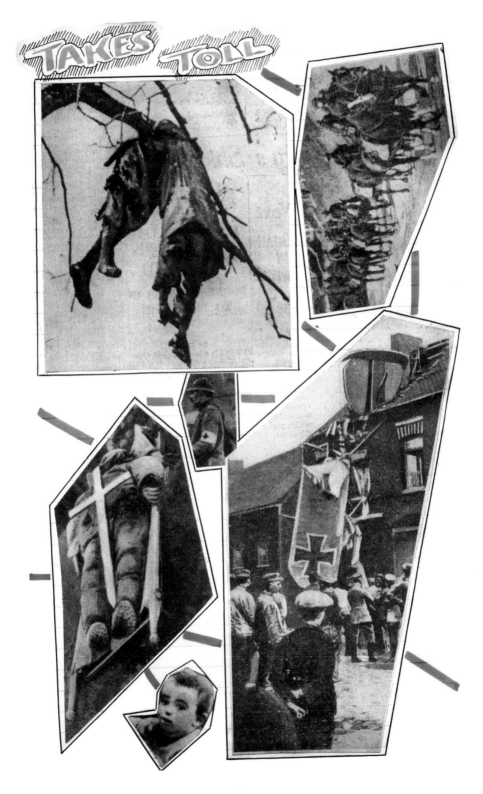

THE FACE
OF WAR
1914-1918

FAREWELL!

TO LONDON

PULLING THEIR WEIGHT

FRENCH POILU AND GERMAN BEARERS.—A French soldier, who has been wounded in the head by a grenade, is carried to hospital by Hun prisoners.   [Exclusive to "The Daily Mail."

OLD MEMORIES Revived

HADN'T BEEN KISSED FOR 40 YEARS

Madamoiselle

WE WILL IN SONG.

EVERYDAY MEMORIES.

With every war is born its songs. At home below, these must be sung to keep one's heart from going out. But there, Tommy must sing, "to keep his pecker up." Foolish songs, they may be, for some of them were flung from Europe, to West during 1914-1918 across a sob in one's heart. To, they were full of memories—and the memories now crowd.

Of the war songs, one can almost say, one can of the old soldier—they never die, they simply fade away. For instance, one would be laughed at today were one to get up on a concert platform and sing "Goodbye Dolly Gray." Yet the song is not dead: it is sunny in the dim background—for everyone who remembers the Boer War remembers the lilt of:—

"Goodbye Dolly, I must leave you,
Tho' it breaks my heart to go,
Something tells me I am needed,
Hark, I hear the bugle calling.
And I can no longer stay.
Goodbye Dolly I must leave you,
Goodbye Dolly Gray."

Another song which did a great amount of good during the Boer War was Kipling's "The absent minded beggar," which ran:—

"When you've shouted 'Rule Britannia,'
when you've sung 'God save the Queen,'
When you've finished killing Kruger with your mouth,
Will you kindly drop a shilling in my little tambourine.
For, a gentleman in khaki ordered South?
He's an absent minded beggar, and his weaknesses are great,
But we and Paul must take him as we find him.
He is out on active service, wiping something off the slate,
And he's left a lot of little things behind him."

Duke's son—cook's son—son of a hundred kings,
Fifty thousand horse and foot, going to Table Bay,
Each of 'em doing his country's work,
And who's to look after things,
Pass the hat for your credit's sake, and pay, pay, pay."

With the Boer War one also associates two fine songs, which have now joined the old soldiers—"Soldiers of the Queen" and "Oh, listen to the Band,"

was the boys' song, sung lustily by poor fellows who began to think they had tasted enough of the war pie:—

"Take me back to dear old Blighty,
Put me on the train for London town,
Take me over there, drop me anywhere,
Liverpool, Leeds or Birmingham, I don't care.

Uol, diddily ivey, hurry me home to Blighty,
Blighty is the place for me."

The "place for me." Poor lads, many of them never saw it again.

If any song ever vied in popularity with "Tipperary," the palm must be given to—
"Pack up your troubles in your old kit bag,
And smile, smile, smile."

It was just the cheery type of song which was hotly required at that time, Tommy also extracted much fun out of a song which declared:—

"Oh, oh, oh, it's a lovely war," and asked,
"What do we want with eggs and ham When we have plum and apple jam?"

Of sentimental types of song, probably "The long, long trail," took the greatest hold on the people, with the greatest of them: "God send you back to me," a song second, and one must not forget a song which many a faithful lassie who was never fated to see "somebody's son'":

"When you come home dear, all will be fair,
Home is not home if you are not there,
You at my heart dear, you at my side,
When your come home at eventide,
God will remember—God will provide."

If there is a lesson to be learnt from the war songs, it is the lesson Kipling tried to teach, its long ago—that once the war is over, Tommy is forgotten, nobody lauds him, nobody sings about him, nobody loves him. The glorious cloak he wore in 1914-1916-1918 fades into a dim back-ground. It is not dead, because when the next war comes along, the cloak will come out for an airing, and Tommy will get a hero again, a hero of song and speech. Kipling was right when he summed it up long ago in two lines:—

"For it's Tommy this, and Tommy that,
and 'Chuck him out—the brute,'
But, it's 'Saviour of his country,' when the guns begin to shoot."

"Sister Susie's sewing shirts for soldiers,
Such skill at sewing shirts our shy young sister Susie shows.
Some soldiers send enquiries saying they'd sooner sleep in thistles,
Than the saucy, soft, short shirts for soldiers Sister Susie sews."

In spite of this mail, Sister Susie carried on her good work. And, while the girls were sewing, they were also encouraging their sweethearts to join up. Perhaps the greatest swinging song of that time was—

"Oh, we don't want to lose you,
But, we think you ought to go,
For your King and your country
Both need you so," etc.

And, more and more lads, donned the khaki and marched off singing cheerily—
"Good-byee, Goodbyee, wipe a tear, baby dear, from your eyes,
Though, its hard to part, I know, I'll be tickled to death to go.
Good-byee, don't sighee, there's a silver lining in the skye.
Bon soir, old thing, Cheerio, Ching Ching, Napoo, toodleoo, good-byee."

The silver lining was rather hard to see just at that time.

In 1915-1916 one began to hear a lot about "Mademoiselle from Armentiers." The chorus, as one knew it at home, ran—
"Mademoiselle from Armentiers, parlee-vous?
Mademoiselle from Armentiers, the same to you,
Mademoiselle from Armentiers hadn't been kissed for 40 years,
Inkey, pinkey, parley vous?

And, the girls at home, beginning to feel a twinge of jealousy for the beautiful Mademoiselle, began to appeal to:—
"Sergeant Brown, Sergeant Brown, keep your eye on Tommy for me
For he might go wrong on the Cont-i-nong,
When he reaches gay Paree,
He'll learn to parlez-vous as they always do, when a French girl they see,
But if my boy Tommy wants to parlez-vous, let him come home and parlez-vous with me."

Round about that time also, the fine song "Keep the home fires burning," began to get a tremendous hold, probably because it appealed to the women folk—
"Tho' the lads are far away, they dream of home,
There's a silver lining, thro' the dark cloud shining,
Turn the dark cloud, inside out till the boys come home."

And, well they did keep the home fires burning, brave yet broken-hearted women!
The Blighty song, on the other hand,

IT WAS A LONG LONG WAY to TIPPERARY BUT

THIS song goes down into history as the song that WON THE WAR!

THE CONNAUGHTS

Naturally the first troops heard singing this famous song were Irish, and of course where there is trouble you'll find an Irishman; his love of a 'faight' is renowned. It is recorded that the Connaught Rangers were the 'bhoys' who introduced this ditty to foreign lands as they swung out from the embarkation sheds and marched forward in 1914 to meet the Hun.

IRISH HEARTS

Soon it was a favourite all over the BEF and the French were quick to grasp its lilting melody. 'T − i − p − p − e − r − a − r − y'; it's − a long way − to go − and it sure was! Somehow or other it was the one song that held its place all through those awful years and was a firmer favourite at the end than the beginning.

Our own battalion sang it, and so did every other mob of old and new armies, right down the years. Exhausted, tired, body and soul almost breaking, that old refrain strikes up and our Irish hearts respond. Sentimental folk we Irish: it struck a chord of deep unexpressed love of country in our hearts and turned our minds eye back to the Emerald Isle. Oh boy! Oh boy! How it gladdened us. Depression fades out, the shadows lighten around us, our burden gets ever so much easier to bear − and we face the kilometres with the new zest. That was the song of songs. And now our lads are nearing that goal we sang about.

HALLOWED GROUND

Without a shadow of doubt old 'Fritzy' was on the run. Memories of the retreat from Mons and the nightmare of March 1918 were stirred in the breasts of old – old in experience only, not in years – warriors as our armies pushed on through desolation and destruction, back through waste, shell-torn ground, ground hallowed by the bodies and the blood of countless hordes of our fellow men: English, Irish, Scotch, Welsh and all the rest. Little crosses, mounds of earth, unburied skeletons marked the scenes of many bitter struggles. Rifles, now rusted, guns twisted and shattered into all shapes, old mess-tins, machine guns silent for ever, barbed wire that had torn many bodies, and bones of many horses met our advancing young soldiers.

Many at first turned sick with the sights and smells but soon became accustomed to all the horror of modern war. Gas still clung to slimy green shell-holes – these often contained unspeakable sights. One I remember well …

STARK HORROR

SKETCHED BY JIM MAULTSAID

It was a very large shell-hole covered all over with slime, and treacherous. Sticking right up out of the green slime was the head of a horse – eyes the size of saucers and stark horror in every line of contour. Perfectly preserved, it was a strange sight indeed. It had died a noble death, like the noble animal it is, man's servant. And it was swollen out of all proportion to its normal size. We gave it a warrior's grave.

DOWN THE STRAIGHT

The work of reconstructing the old battlefields for an advancing army was tremendous. Our first duty was the roads – roads for troops, guns and supplies. We followed up rapidly filling up shell-holes, clearing obstructions, building new bridges clearing the battlefields of all the litter and constructing shelters for our troops. These operations were rendered miserable by the bad weather that always seemed to dog our efforts when on the attack, but nothing now on this earth could check us and progress was rapid as well as effective. The road was long without a doubt, but we were on the straight for HOME and every runner knows that this is the critical time of battle: it's a case of 'now or never', so we put our last ounce into the race and made straight for the WINNING POST.

"The Worlds Drama"

We owed the Germans some old scores – he had fought a great fight. The gong had gone for the last round. He is tottering. One more punch and the victory is ours. Within our grasp!

The cannon roar and thunder down the line. Morning brings renewed activity. Night brings no rest. The world's drama is drawing to a close. The vision in the forwards zones is red – all blood red. The skies are overcast with storm – it does not deter our airmen.

UNDERGROUND

Some of the underground works left by the enemy were marvels of engineering skill. Cement, iron girders and logs of timber used in profusion far below the surface of the ground made these shelters almost gunproof.

Our methods of attack aimed at the cutting off of these points, then calling on the garrison to surrender. Machine guns had cement emplacements a yard thick. Loopholes for riflemen, and even field guns had runaways made of cement. Many of these were built by the Russian prisoners of war, under threat of death. The filth and stench of captured underground caverns was as a rule almost unbearable for our troops. Dead bodies long past burial lay in all corners; human filth of all kinds somewhere else; and things I must not mention. A big time fuse right under several large trench-mortar bombs. Bang! Up goes a death-trap of disease and death.

We learnt a lesson in the art of not interfering with innocent-looking helmets left lying around. Lift one of these – Flash! Smoke and death for several of our boys. A wire across our path. A trip over this – up goes a landmine. More death and horror. He even dug deep pits with spikes at the bottom and covered the top over with grass and earth. Terrible wounds for the unwary Tommies.

GROUND HALLOWED BY THE BLOOD OF COUNTLESS THOUSANDS.

DESOLATION. DESTRUCTION. DEATH.
TORN EARTH. GUNS - AMMUNITION -
UNBURIED BODIES — MET US... SILENT FOR EVER.

GAS FILLED SHELL HOLES.

STILL OUR BOYS PUSHED ON

YOUNG SOLDIERS SICKENED AT THE SIGHTS

WORKING PARTIES FOLLOWED UP

SOME OF THE UNDERGROUND WORKS WERE WONDERFUL.

TRENCH   GROUND LEVEL
EARTH
ELECTRIC LIGHT
BUNKS   AIR TUBE
SLEEPING BUNKS
STORE ROOM   RIFLE RACK   ELECTRIC FAN   SLEEPING BERTHS   MACHINE GUN HOIST.
STEPS TO TRENCH
COOK HOUSE   BOMBS   COMMANDANT   OBSERVATION POST
PASSAGE   AMMUNITION PUMP.   SENTRY.   STAIRS

A DRAWING ILLUSTRATING   CEMENT FLOORS
ONE OF THE UNDERGROUND BARRACKS

MANY FIERCE ENCOUNTERS TOOK PLACE
FOR POSSESSION

ALL SKETCHES
- BY -
JIM. MAULTSAID

THIS

WIRE

TO LIFT THIS
HELMET MEANT   BOMB
BELOW EARTH.

198

ARMOURED CAR ENGAGING ENEMY REARGUARD.

OUR ARMOURED CARS CAME INTO ACTION AGAIN.

A COMMON SIGHT IN THE LINE OF HIS RETREAT. THIS PICTURE WAS PURCHASED IN YPRES 1918.

TREMENDOUS SEIGE GUNS DESERTED.

A STRANGE SIGHT ON THE WESTERN FRONT THE PIGEON VAN.

BACK to OPEN WARFARE AN ADVANCED POST

OUR ARTILLERY BOYS MET AND OVERCAME MANY DIFFICULTIES. — FIGHTING THE MUD. —

AS OUR ARMIES PUSHED FORWARD SO DID THE FRENCH.

AND OUR AMERICAN BOYS KEPT PACE

THE GERMAN REARGUARD LEFT TO WATCH OUR TROOPS..... OFTEN HIS LAST STAND FOR THE FATHERLAND.

ALL PICTURES — BY — JIM MAULTSAID

CULTURE

All the arts of inhuman warfare and jungle warfare were practised by the retreating foe. Yet it availed him nothing. Every one of these traps spurred our lads to greater deeds and the desire for another crack at the d★★★ Hun. He paid for it all, in full and plenty.

Onward! Advance! Towns and villages by the dozen were falling into our hands daily. The inhabitants did not wait for our troops; they came out to meet them, and went mad with joy, but often hindered us, as well as walking into enemy shellfire and perishing in the very hour of deliverance. They were often shot down by German snipers from the back – or machine-gun fire turned on them, mowing the poor souls down like sheaves of corn.

Modern war by a cultured nation! And they wanted to force this creed down the throats of all the nations on earth – but thank God did NOT SUCCEED.

THE ROAD WAS LONG YES! 4 YEARS LONG

The road to Tipperary had been a long one, rough, hostile, strewn with tears of millions, wounds, blindness, sickness, and death. Stark horror, for man and beast. Lungs torn asunder by gas – bodies rent in twain by red hot metal. Jagged gaping wounds – all to satisfy the war-crazed Hun and his allies.

Almost four years long, this road was a rough one for us – we had suffered many terrible disasters on land and sea and in the air. But that saying by a famous foreign diplomat many years ago 'England only wins one battle in any war, and that is THE LAST' was again coming true. We were nearing the end of the road.

The song of The Connaught Rangers in 1914 was to be finished in 1918 – victory was in the very air itself. Did our airmen not sweep some forty enemy planes from the skies in a single day? They did! Blinded and battered – he staggers back – by the same routes as he swaggered forward in August 1914. Our joy was supreme. Reports by cavalry patrols on several fronts were to the effect that they could not find touch with the enemy.

This gives the reader some idea of the speed he was retreating at on certain fronts. Our air force even went out in relays and harried his troops on the March, sweeping down like hawks to machine-gun and bomb the weary troops. Gunners deserted the guns and rode away. Heavy batteries hardly took time to blow up their huge pieces before turning tail. Dumps of shells and ammunition were exploded; terrific fires raged far behind the enemy lines leading up the sky for miles around all night long.

Old French villages were fired in anger and spite. His retreat was marked, in fact blazed, all the way from Amiens in fire and blackened ashes. It will take many, many years to heal the marks of destruction left by the Hun in his retreat.

I came across several of his attempts at imitating our tanks and was astounded at the crude efforts made by such a reputed engineer as the German – at his engine of war. Big, ugly, and cumbersome, they fell far behind ours.[7]

AWAY BACK ......

As this book is not a history of the Great War, and my objective in this story has been attained by giving you a rough idea of what our troops met and conquered during our last big drive on the Western Front in the last few months of war, I'll bring this article to a close and give you a few of my black-and-white sketches depicting the story of the last stand of a mighty military nation that tried to rule the world – and failed.

ASK THE FRENCH

I can hear those Connaught Ranger bhoys singing 'Tipperary' away back in '14, in their deep melodious Irish voices. I can hear our boys in 1915, 1916, 1917 – and 1918 singing that self-same song – the song that won the war. Yes! Won the war! Ask the French. Ask the Belgian. Or ask the Germans. Some, alas far too many, brave Irish lads never saw Tipperary again – were never fated to set foot on their beloved Irish soil or feast their eyes on the grass that is green –oh so green.

BUT THEIR SONG LIVES

---

7. Initially the Germans did not think that tanks were practical and when they did finally decide to produce their own the end result was, as described here, a huge lumbering monster, the A7V, which only saw service from March to October 1918 and in limited numbers. Only twenty were built by the end of the war. Although the Germans did use captured British and French tanks, they never had more than sixty tanks in operation.

Q ships, harmless in appearance but armed to the teeth, aided British naval supremacy

The French Bleriot, with bicycle wheels and 50 h.p. engine, was an early R.F.C. aircraft

Submarines sank 15 million tons of shipping. This is the D5, Britain's answer to the U-boat

British riflemen rest as they prepare for a fighting retreat. Left: German reinforcements move off from Brussels for the front. But the sweeping victory they expected was not to be theirs.

SOME WONDERFUL PICTURES HERE.

The Zeppelin was the early air terror weapon, but its vulnerability led to its replacement

NOVEMBER 1918

E.C.

YOU HAVE HERE
DESCRIBED !!!!!! BY JIM MAULTSAID
A SUPERHUMAN
FEAT PERFORMED
BY the C.L.C. IN LOADING
ONE OF OUR LAST
WAR CARGO'S !!!!! (ALMOST)
ALTHOUGH WE
DID NOT KNOW IT

LITTLE CREDIT FOR C.L.C.

THIS last effort of ours, to my mind, ranks as a feat worthy of special notice. As I have pointed out again and again, we the Chinese Labour Corps did not get a fraction of the credit due to us in our effort to win the war, but I have done my best to set before you the marvellous work that was performed by the CLC and in a small measure hope I have succeeded in giving you an insight into the heart and soul of those great workers of 169 Company. Officered by men who knew what was wanted, coaxed by NCOs who could get the last ounce out of them and kept up to concert pitch by selected Chinese overseers, or gangers, this company of ours was a shining example of what Chinese Labour could, and did, do. If all the force of one hundred thousand Chinese in France had been handled like ours, the work done would have been multiplied many times over. I never blamed the Chinese themselves for inefficiency – but always put the blame on the officers and NCOs. They were quick to note slackness and take advantage of that. Some of the companies were almost a disgrace and almost useless.

"DING – HOLA" OFFICER!

Eleven thousand cases wanted today – and the date was 2 November 1918. 'Special.' 'Must not fail.' I almost collapsed. Could we do it? Not a question of could we, but we must. I read my orders again in the light of a dull November morning at that hour of 5.00 and the cold sleet falls on the field order, the storm shakes the big French truck we shelter behind, my NCOs and me. As I read the order out I can see my gangers look at each other but in their oriental way not a muscle of the face moved. 'Ding – hola, Officer!' ('Very good, Sir we understand.')

They salute and run to their various gangs. 'A h*** of an order,' I add, to the four or five sergeants and corporals; but nothing for it – this is the price of fame. 'Get them into get – h***-for-leather. Dismiss!'

At this pace we'll last about another fortnight or three weeks – and then collapse. I was practically done myself with the tremendous strain of the past few months and I felt I was breaking under it. The wound received in 1916 was troubling me terribly this winter and I did not get an hour's sleep many nights from cold and exposure – yet I was dead tired and done out. The sore shoulder throbbed and throbbed, no matter how I twisted. Then we were soaked to the skin with rain, mud and snow – all day long – and often all night long as well. No place to dry yourself; your clothes dried on your body, but enough of this.

CRASH!

Bang! Crash! Smash and smash! It's the cases falling into the trucks. Like a barrage of artillery. The nose of a big ROD engine pushes its way in through the storm of sleet and

BY JIM MAULTSAID

ALL MY IRISH BLARNEY BROUGHT INTO ACTION.

FASTER THAN EVER. THEY BATTLE ON.

THE WESTERN FRONT BLAZES UP THE GUN FIRE IS TERRIFIC.

NIGHT HAS FALLEN

A STRANGE SCENE – FIGURES SCURRY THROUGH THE NIGHT.

19 HOURS OF THIS YE GOD'S!

MY PLATOON SERGEANT REPORTS 1,000 MORE TO GO.

BELIEVE ME OR NOT I COUNTED EVERYONE OF THOSE LAST THOUSAND CASES.

WE PUT THE BROWN BODIES IN A TRUCK

THEIR BURNDEN SEEMED TO GET HEAVIER AS THE NIGHT WORE ON

THE LAST BOX WAS LITERALLY SHOT INTO THE BIG FRENCH TRUCK THE LAST OF ELEVEN THOUSAND CASES THE LAST... THE LAST........ THE LAST.

OUR JOURNEY HOME THAT NIGHT WAS A NIGHTMARE.

snow hauling some seventy or eighty empty trucks alongside the petrol stacks, keeping us supplied with empties to be filled with our precious cargo.

As our advance was now continuous the lines of supply grew longer and longer – hence the demand for such a staggering amount of petrol. Four tins into each case – eleven thousand cases – and then four of our platoons all on the same task somewhere near us. Just work it out – for one day's output by one company of CLC, 'somewhere in France'. 44,000 CASES! 176,000 TINS!

BIG SNOWFLAKES

The morning wears on. The blood has lost its sluggish movement, warms up, and the boys are quite happy now. Quick, easy, graceful, as they slide and slip over the mud almost six inches deep. Some carry two, some three and some four. Gangs keep an eagle eye on other gangs. The snow is now falling in big flakes. It's funny to see the forms going and coming through the snowflakes, but not so cold as it was.

I blow my whistle. Fall out for some tea. And believe me I was very thankful to share a black tin of tea without sugar or milk with my gangers. No smoking allowed, a strict order – very dangerous amongst all this explosive material. The break is over. Full steam ahead once more. I check up on trucks already loaded, do some rapid calculations and was far from satisfied. Yet the coolies are toiling hard – very hard indeed. This is going to be a stupendous job. The snow is getting heavier and making our task twice as hard. Conditions underfoot are vile – slush, snow and mud all rolled into one. The feet of the coolies are all covered with sacking; it helps a lot, but becomes a drag to some and they kick it off in disgust.

EVENING falls early and the darkness adds to our difficulties. No lights are allowed as they might attract some Hun raider from the skies to blow us all to 'land of our forefathers' (Chinese heaven), so our workers work blindly in the dark. Accustomed to this by now, but this snowstorm makes it a thousand times worse. Battling against these conditions all day was telling its story and the poor souls are becoming exhausted. I made the arrangements for special tea and patties. This extra meal put new strength into tired bodies. Did they not appreciate my thoughtfulness and repay me a hundred times over? They did! Smash! Smash! Smash!

Blurred forms scurry through the night, not a single shirker in the whole outfit. God be praised; how they worked and slaved.

ALL FOR ME ....YES ME!

Truck follows truck; completed, sealed and checked – all ready for some distance railhead, but our task is far from finished.

IRISH BLARNEY

TRUTH to tell the task was beyond us and should never have been attempted, but no turning back now. The night hours creep on. I visit each gang giving words of cheer to each, using all my natural gifts of Irish blarney, telling them we would soon all be back home with the old folks. 'German man' was beaten: 'the plenty run,' 'surrender plenty much,' 'plenty petrol – German bombs finish – a – la!' 'British boys dying for us,' – young boys like themselves. 'Big general says "169 Ding – hola" and me say Tri –bon.'

Lord! How it freezes now. Cold, cold – oh so cold. I shiver in my boots. The snow stops. The world in all its whiteness looks wonderful. Boom! Boom! The Western Front is ablaze. The glare shines up to heaven itself. We can hear the dull roar of the heavies and see the gun flashes. Back goes my thoughts – up there! A new resolve forms itself in my brain. We will finish this cargo or die in our frozen tracks.

'Fall out!' I gather all my mud-stained warriors around me in the moonlight.

POOR BROWN BODIES

Two thousand to go! 'Two thousand more and finish – a – la! I'll get you all double rations. Back to work now. Let's see what 169 can do!' Almost midnight and we have been at it since 6.00 this morning. Almost nineteen hours! Ye gods! Some of the weakest have collapsed already and the poor brown bodies put in a truck, covered up with sacks to keep the heat in them until we finish.

Slavery if you will. I could have dropped down in the snow myself. My head reeled, my body was exhausted but we must, yes we must, fight on. Movements are slower as numbed fingers grasp frozen boxes and hurl them into position. One thousand and then good night. Reader, believe me or not, I counted every one of those last 'one thousand cases' and sighed the deepest sigh of my life as the last of the forty-four thousand was slammed home.

The journey home to our rough wooden shacks that night was one long nightmare. We carried half a dozen frozen forms across rough pieces of timber, some unconscious and some frost-bitten.

11,000, 11,000 ...
My last duty that hectic night was the supervising of the special supper, paid for by myself, then seeing every coolie in bed – the placing of the cripples in our Red Cross hut – and then throwing myself down to catch a few fleeting moments of sleep, but sleep I did not. Too tired even to sleep. Can you beat it? Who could cast a finger of scorn at the CLC? Our task was completed – at a price!

At heart I was proud of my boys. My brother officers struggled home at various hours after me all with the same tale of hardships suffered by their squads, but each and all finished the allotted task. Our Captain Curtain had a kind word for us all. He was, I know, intensely proud of his officers and his company of Chinese. He phoned headquarters to report the completion of the day's work, and said we would never again attempt such a colossal, outrageous order, even if it meant court-martial for him. 11,000 cases. 11,000 cases. 11,000 cases. 11,000 cases. MY BRAIN BURNS. I TOSS AND TURN!

TOO TIRED TO SLEEP

IN A WORLD OF WHITENESS the chinese at rest. 2 a.m.

SWEEPING the SKIES

STORY AND SKETCHES
★ BY JIM MAULTSAID. ★

THE ALLIES TAKE COMMAND of the AIR IN the LAST MONTH OF THE GREAT WAR ON the WESTERN FRONT.

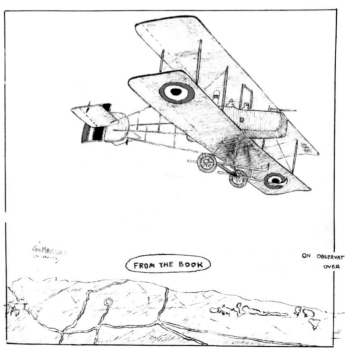

FROM THE BOOK

ON OBSERVAT OVER

THE FLYING "CRATES" OF EARLY DAYS

Here's a picture from the little book. Note the tremendous difference in this craft from the latter days. Carthorse versus Thoroughbred? Stupendous advancement in four years. Almost unbelievable. I sketched them at every opportunity.

WE had made terrific strides in aviation since 1914, and during the last month of warfare on the Western Front completely dominated the air. All honour to the brave pioneers of the early days in 1914 and '15. These men went up to fight a foe in mere skeleton machines put together with bamboo and canvas, without protection of any kind and armed with rifles and revolvers only.

Just think of it! Our air boys of '17 and '18 really knew nothing about hardships compared to these fellows – yet the same spirit of adventure was handed down the years. One thing I always noticed, and that was that the German airman took good care to let us fight most of the air battles over his own lines. He let us do the attacking ten times out of twelve. This was in a sense very cute. Imagine engine trouble ten kilos behind his lines for one of our boys; not much hope of him trying to glide home. No! He was down to the lion's den every time. Then in the very early days his machines were far, far swifter than ours and we were up against it; in fact he was far advanced compared to us and it took us a few years to get level in speed and equipment.

BRAVE FELLOWS

As a rule the enemy flew in squadrons and did not go in for the 'lone flights' of our fighters. Rarely if ever did he operate singlehanded; they waited for us in numbers and made many a sweep from the clouds thousands of feet up; down, down, down – five or six to one. Some terrible dramas were enacted during these moments and it was awful to watch one red–white–and–blue boy battling against half a dozen or so black hawks. Our McCuddens, our Balls, our Mannock' and our Bishops fought many of these fights and did not come off second best by any means.[8]

---

8. James McCudden VC, Albert Ball VC, Edward Mannock VC and Billy Bishop VC were all air 'aces' of the First World War. Mannock was Irish and McCudden, although usually described as English, was the son of a Scottish soldier and his Irish wife. Billy Bishop was Canadian.

215

I don't mean to say the Germans had no brave airmen either. That would be untrue; they had indeed some very marvellous flyers who accounted for scores of our machines. The code in the skies appeared to be much more honoured by both sides than it did on the ground floor. Brave men who could appreciate bravery from the other side? I myself witnessed on several occasions one or the other breaking off a combat when they knew some fighter was doomed and did not go in to land the finishing blow – the laws of nature and gravitation would do that. Like a wounded bird he would come to earth, either in flames or in pieces. What a death! What agony of mind! I never had any desire to be an airman. Mother earth was good enough for me.

BRIGHT JAZZY

As the years passed vast improvements became apparent. Machines got faster and faster. Bright colours, jazzy all reds, stripes, rainbow designs, zipped and roared through the heavens. I was often amused at the numerous 'lucky mascot' paintings on our planes. Hands, skulls, crossed wings, squares, circles and fancy fantastic drawings all adorned these modern implements of war. One fellow I remember actually had a picture of his best girl – or was it some popular actress? – painted on the side of his single-seater. These airmen had an outlook on life as far apart as the poles from us. They lived in a world of their own, away up in the clouds, but seldom talked 'shop' to us, when resting. Always full of life and pep, they lived one day at a time, and sometimes one hour. Here today – tomorrow!

Lost … never heard off again. Patrol duty 6:30am … did not return. No witnesses – no anything, but his name on the death roll of his squadron that night, and perhaps a mere lad, as most of them were. Somewhere in the German lines a tangled heap of spars and twisted wires and the charred remains of what had once been a fine upstanding boy. The price of war!

COULD NOT FACE US

You will have read quite a few of my stories about the war in the air as you read through these volumes so I confine myself to the last grand finish in November 1918 in this article.

........THE SKY BIRD....

We practically swept the Hun from the sky during this period. Our planes out-sped them, out-gunned them, out-fought them, out-bombed them and outnumbered them. And if it had not been for the very bad weather plus bad visibility I don't think a single German machine would, or could, have even got into the air.

We raided their aerodromes day and night, smashed hangars and ruined their getaway stretches of ground with bombs. Their retreating troops were harried to the verge of insanity. Their gunners were scattered to the four winds, and their infantry in the trenches gunned unmercifully. Dumps of ammunition were bombed, railheads had a hectic time. Even trains did not escape. Down swept the sky bird with a load of death. Crash! Flames!

Horror! Then the big Handley-Page bombers took up the running at night to carry over thousands of bombs and drop them in selected spots. Even German towns got a little bit of war brought to their own doorstep during these weeks.

Just a few 'pills' of culture come back to roost? In my mind they did not get half enough but it sure would have been God help them if they had not surrendered when they did from all I could hear and see.

A GREAT MISTAKE

This is not revengeful talk, but I always thought they did not get a fraction of their own 'sauce' that should have been meted out to them. We suffered four years of h★★★ and missed giving them a dose of their own medicine. While we did not blow Berlin to blazes beats me!

Can you imagine them missing Paris and London if the tables had been reversed? Not on your life! They would have laid both cities in ruins without a shadow of doubt – to stamp the Prussian heel on us. Of course I do think that if the 'ceasefire' had not sounded when it did our plans were laid for terrific aerial bombardment and awful nights of terror for many German towns.

THE HEAVENS HUMMED

Hundreds of thousands of air pictures were taken by our photographic planes. These machines were usually protected by several of our fighters. Every yard of the German lines must have been snapped; these pictures were pieced together and some wonderful maps prepared. The art of bluff was employed by us to a great extent in this way. Hundreds of dummy tanks made of wood and long telegraph poles laid over a pair of big gun wheels made a fine snap for Jerry, and looked the part from the air.

Smokescreens were laid to cover over our advancing troops. Small-arms ammunition, bags of food, rockets etc., etc. were often dropped to isolated points. During his retreat the enemy used aeroplanes as rear-guards to sweep down on our boys and machine-gun them, but very often never returned.

The last few days of war found us sending out scores of squadrons. In fact, the air was thick with our planes and, to show the state of helplessness the Hun had fallen to, little or no opposition met these planes of ours. They raided and worried the retreating armies playing merry h★★★ with his troops. His air-eyes were blinded.

STUDY the SKETCHES

His raids on our dumps and railheads ended. His days were over in the air. No more did the big black bombers worry us; they were far too busy looking after the remnants of their beaten army. And the French, the Belgians, the Americans! All full steam ahead chasing him back to the Rhine, but our British effort far outstripped anything attempted by our allies and the number of our machines must have been at least five to one against our allies.

217

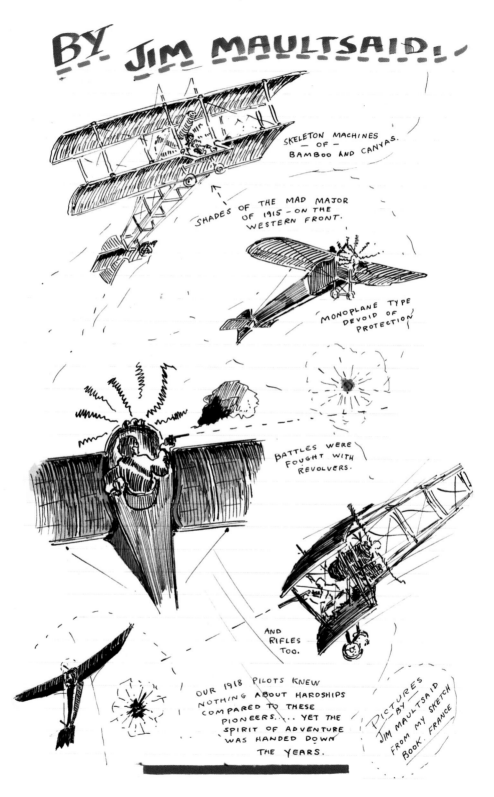

BY JIM MAULTSAID.

SKELETON MACHINES — OF — BAMBOO AND CANVAS.

SHADES OF THE MAD MAJOR OF 1915 — ON THE WESTERN FRONT.

MONOPLANE TYPE DEVOID OF PROTECTION

BATTLES WERE FOUGHT WITH REVOLVERS.

AND RIFLES TOO.

OUR 1918 PILOTS KNEW NOTHING ABOUT HARDSHIPS COMPARED TO THESE PIONEERS... YET THE SPIRIT OF ADVENTURE WAS HANDED DOWN THE YEARS.

PICTURES BY JIM MAULTSAID FROM MY SKETCH BOOK. FRANCE

MANY OF OUR LONE FIGHTERS FOUND THEMSELVES MIXED UP IN A MAZE OF 5 OR 6 BLACK HAWKS

I HAVE WITNESSED THEM BREAK OFF A FIGHT WHEN SOME ENEMY WAS DOOMED.

AS THE YEARS PASSED SPEED'S INCREASED.

THE ENEMY HUNTED IN SQUADRONS.

SOME OF THE DESIGNS WERE FANTASTIC

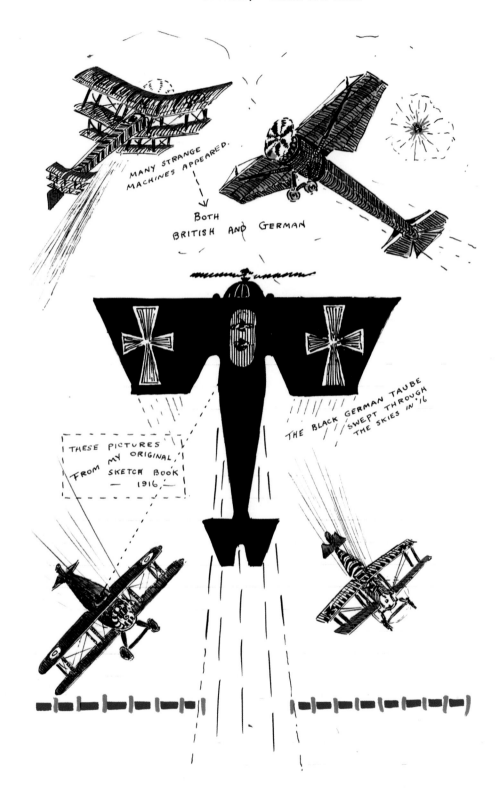

220

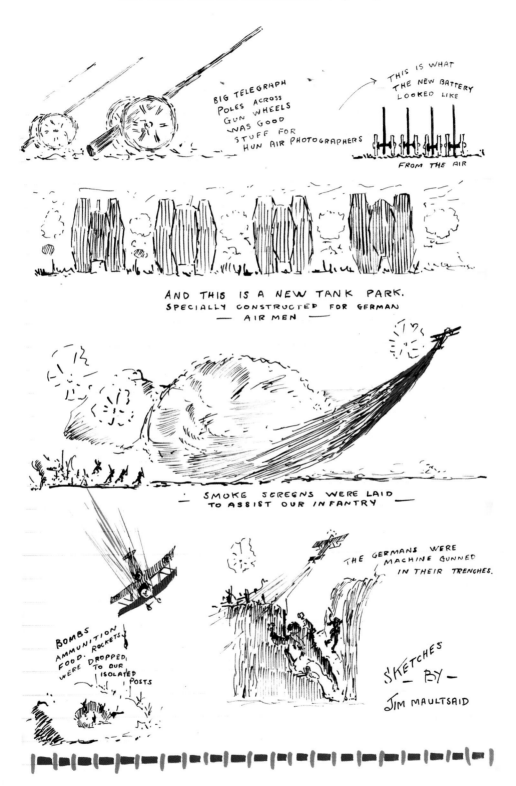

BIG TELEGRAPH POLES ACROSS GUN WHEELS WAS GOOD STUFF FOR HUN AIR PHOTOGRAPHERS

THIS IS WHAT THE NEW BATTERY LOOKED LIKE

FROM THE AIR

AND THIS IS A NEW TANK PARK.
SPECIALLY CONSTRUCTED FOR GERMAN
— AIR MEN —

SMOKE SCREENS WERE LAID
TO ASSIST OUR INFANTRY

BOMBS AMMUNITION ROCKETS FOOD. WERE DROPPED TO OUR ISOLATED POSTS

THE GERMANS WERE MACHINE GUNNED IN THEIR TRENCHES.

SKETCHES BY —
JIM MAULTSAID

Strange to say our last big cargo of the war was AA petrol, or the 'juice' as we called it for our fighting aeroplanes. You will read about this express order in my next story – our last great hustle to win the war. I had many fine opportunities of seeing our airmen in action, and behind the line as well, so you will find my little sketches more than interesting at the end of this article. Many of these I have in my sketchbook and some of them are reproduced here.

●●●●●●●●●●●●FINIS●●●●●●●●●

The skies were swept clean in 1918. As in the past old England won the last round – by a knockout victory. Goodbye to the Black Cross.

I WAS THERE WHEN HE FELL

A thin line of black smoke far, far up in the bright blue sky. It turns red, flashing towards earth at 200, 300, 400 mph to doom! It's a Hun! God! What a sight – the death dive. 'We brought down ….'

The admiration of the PBI was intense for our wonderful 'air birds'. How I often gazed up in suspense and beating heart to watch a dogfight far up in the clouds, to marvel at the skill and crazy antics of this new mode of war and often thought 'all airmen must be mad!'

SHOT DOWN

JIM MAULTSAID

This picture almost speaks for itself in portraying the end of Germany as an air power. Down! Down! Down to destruction! His fighting eyes blinded by the Allies.

At different periods during the Great War the enemy often led us in this new science of fighting in the air and caused us many anxious times, but our youthful airmen were never surpassed for bravery or daredevil flying by any German flying man. The reader must understand that practically every aerial battle on the Western Front was fought over the enemy lines. A tremendous advantage.

A BOLT FROM THE BLUE

JIM MAULTSAID

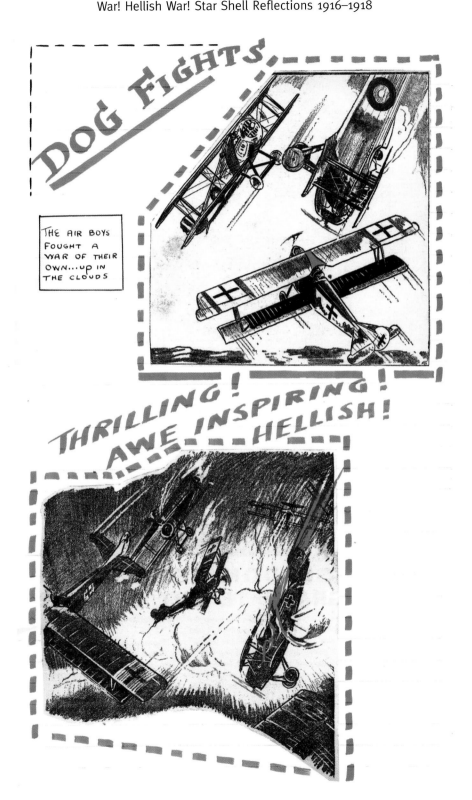

COLONEL
RICHARD MULOCK, R.F.C.
WAS THE COMMANDER OF A
STARTLING PROPOSED AIR-RAID
THAT NEVER HAPPENED — THE
GREAT RAID UPON BERLIN.
THIS RAID WAS SCHEDULED FOR
NOVEMBER 15TH, BUT ON
NOVEMBER 11TH, THE
ARMISTICE WAS
SIGNED.

3 DAYS LATE
WHAT A PITY!

Yes, what a pity! Hundreds of thousands of Germans to this day almost think they WON THE WAR.

Almost! When I look back and think of the horror, the destruction, the poor bodies destroyed by German aircraft and their terrible bombs, I often thought we did not hit their cities and civilian population half hard enough – to bring it home to them and teach them a much needed lesson. We fought too fairly.

FOR BERLIN

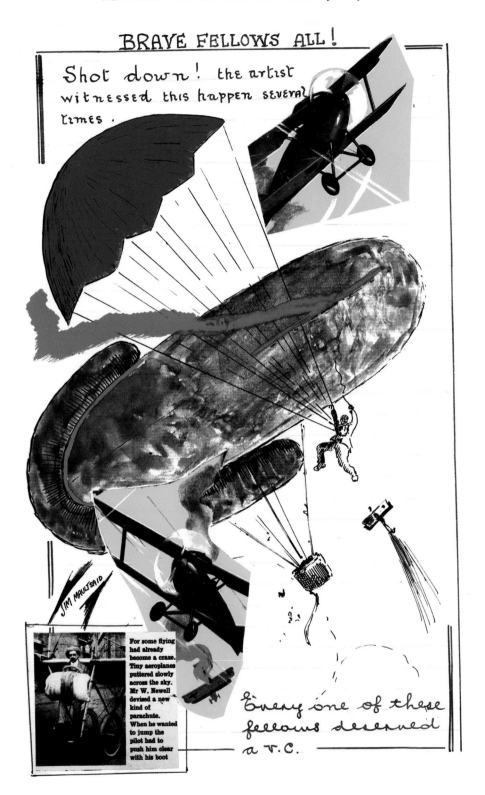

BRAVE FELLOWS ALL!

Shot down! the artist witnessed this happen several times.

JIM MAULTSAID

For some flying had already become a craze. Tiny aeroplanes puttered slowly across the sky. Mr W. Newell devised a new kind of parachute. When he wanted to jump the pilot had to push him clear with his boot

Every one of these fellows deserved a V.C.

227

Of course this picture is drawn from my own imagination, but you can picture the German troops reeling back before the sledgehammer blows the allies, especially the 'despised' British army, back, back to Berlin in 1918.

NOVEMBER 10th 1918

'Special order Maultsaid!' The skipper reaches me a slip of paper and my eyes bulge as I read it. It's a peach of a job for AA (aeroplane juice). Are our airmen going dotty? As I salute I pocket the order and wearily make my way to the rough 'shakedown' to get a few hours' sleep before dawn. The dawn of what? Rumours had come over the waves (mysterious waves) hinting at an early armistice.

AROUND the CORNER

Jerry was beaten! The Germans wanted peace at any price! Surrender on any terms! But then we had heard this so often that it did not impress us much; in fact it did not impress us at all. The day we had talked about, joked about, sang songs about, and all the rest, at our elbow! And we did not, could not, believe – can you blame us? And yet I knew the end was around the corner. All the signs pointed that way. Yet over in Ireland when out route marching and you asked the countrymen how far so and so was, it was just round the corner – and that was usually about five good Irish miles. So – !

It's a dark, dreary, drizzling morning. 5.00am parade. Mud, slush, rain; all is gloom and darkness as we set up a steady plodding pace away out to our dump. Folks at home will be turning over for a little more sleep; only the milk boys and the bakers will be stirring. Queer, the thoughts that race through your mind. But then it's a queer world at the moment. All is madness, death, wounds – or … .

THE DAWN PATROL

Zur! Zur! Zur! The dawn patrol is on its way. We cannot see them – but the work of many propellers reaches our ears from the black heavens above. 11 November 1918! Their last patrol – and they did not know it – nor did we!

I blow my whistle and the toil begins. The clash of boxes is in full swing. Darkness is still with us; the dawn of day is not yet. Our task is a very big one indeed and special instructions to my sergeants and gangers make it clear that this cargo MUST, simply MUST, be ready in time. No shirking; all must work and work like merry h★★★. It would be disastrous if we failed our Air Force – but we never failed yet.

'Get into it boys' Qui – Qui. (Hurry up).' Feet slither through the slush. Bodies heave and sway as the cases are pitched into the trucks. The coolies are warming up. This always took time we discovered, so we allowed for it. The light of another day is now struggling to show us that it really will be daylight soon and not midnight. Truck after truck is completed. Everything is moving well. I sit down on a petrol box and rest.

"LITTLE TITCH"

Wham! Slam! Slam! Slam! The morning cup of tea (Chinese style – no milk and no sugar) is over and fifteen minutes rest allowed. I was glad to sip a few mouthfuls of this black tea as it warmed you up as well as helping to remove that 'sinking feeling' in the pit of my stomach that developed from the want of a square meal in the early, early morning.

'Come on boys into it!' My whistle shrilled out the starting blast. Slam! Slam! Slam!

The Dawn Patrol

JIM. MAULTSAID.

FROM A ROUGH SKETCH.

A glorious, hectic, h★★★-for-leather spirit grips them. Crash! Crash! Crash! I can hear that sound yet – from a distance it sounded like a bombardment. Boom. Boom. Boom. But it's just 169 Company Chinese Labour Corps wound up.

10:55am. 'Wanted on the phone Mister Maultsaid!' A sergeant dashes up, all out of breath. His eyes are sparkling. 'What the h★★★ ?' 'Hurry, Sir. It's the skipper wants you.' 'Hello! Hello!' 'Yes! This is Maultsaid. What's that you say, Sir? Say it again. Good G★★!!! What?'

SURRENDER

hand shakes. The end of it all? Great joy is in my heart. And yet I was not convinced. 'Are you quite sure, Skipper?' 'Sure as H★★★! Maultsaid.' His Irish voice booms over the wire, 'I tell you, my fine b'hoy, it's all over. THE WAR IS OVER. Yes! 'Jerry surrendered at 11.00am, licked to H★★★! Oh! Boy! Oh! Boy!' 'What am I to do, Skipper?' 'Do whatever the blazes you like, you son of Oirland.' His voice dropped into a real Irish old-time brogue when he was excited. The buzzer buzzed, burned up and he was gone.

Like one demented, I dashed up the depot shouting 'The war is over boys. Old Fritz has caved in – like a pack of cards.' NCOs crowded round, and gazed at me in amazement. What their thoughts were was hard to fathom. 'Yes! It's true – quite true.' The smiles were wonderful. Home – visions of the old life once more. Wives, mothers, sweethearts, kiddies – and all the rest. Glorious visions. Handshakes – handclasps; we shake again and again and wish each other all the best.

"LA BOCHE NAPOO"

The Chinese? I had forgotten all about them. Then that awful silence dawned on me. I shout, 'Jerry man finish – a – la! No more fighter fight! Plenty finish! Napoo!' More beaming faces and, I suppose, visions of China? 'Work – a – la finish today! – Zo! Quick march – home to chow chow.' And they were turned as never before to their camp without a single white officer in charge, or even lance corporal.

Dipping into my wallet I find a couple of 100 Franc bills and gave them to the sergeant. 'Go and have a drink, boys, just to celebrate.' Did they go? It was several days later when some of them turned up. Did we care? Not us! Why worry now? I hurried out, down the railway line to the roadway. No fixed plan in my mind. Here comes a motor lorry. A Yankee bus full of troops heading where? 'Jump in, Sir.' I hop in amongst the Doughboys.[9] They all tumble over each other to wring my hands. All ranks represented here – but who cares about rank now?

ALL THE NATIONS

The old bus sways and rocks on springs. We must be doing over 50mph. On! On! Black exhaust smoke pours out behind us as we screech onward in a ride of hectic memory. Through villages, hamlets and wayside lanes we thunder. Old French folks shout and wave their arms in great excitement. We yelled back. Flags of the French, Belgians, Americans, old England are waved at us. Like a mad thing, this load of humanity is hurled from side to side. Was the driver drunk mad? How long or how far we travelled I cannot tell – but eventually we slowed down on the outskirts of a large town. Where was this? The old French signboard said Calais. Good!

Hundreds and hundreds of soldiers and civilians now made a traffic jam. So we hopped it, and mixed with the crowd. Arms interlaced with men of all nations in the world, or so it seemed to me, we danced away down the main street of Calais. What a sight!

In the square a ring-o-roses dance was in progress. Did I see a general dance around? I did!

TOMMY TOPS THE BILL

Red Caps, brass hats – anything from a general down to the humble private. Arm in arm. Young girls, grandmothers, children all in the ring. I was kissed at least fifty times by all

---

9. The nickname applied to US infantry soldiers until the Second World War when 'GI' became the norm. 'Doughboy' may refer to the dough cakes that formed part of the US soldier's diet in the nineteenth century and the name can be traced back to the US-Mexican War of 1846-48. However, it was in use earlier in the British Army, during the Peninsular War, and in Nelson's Navy.

sorts of French and Belgian womenfolk, and men as well. 'Bon English Ah! la! la!' 'Tra – bon Englandtarre.' 'Bon soldat.' Songs were sung – English, French and Yankee – but when someone started the Tipperary refrain the roar must have shaken the housetops. Everyone knew it. Everyone sang the song that surely won the war: 'It's a long way to go …' but we have got there RIGHT NOW!

Bottles of wine – red wine – were showered on the troops – all free. The French people got so excited that half of them did not know what they were doing. How they hugged the British Tommy, wrapped their flags around us and kissed flag and all. Every Tommy was a hero that day – and what a day! To the end of the chapter I'll never forget. Drunk with excitement, frenzy if you will, the hours pass like minutes. On! On! With the dance.

LONG LIVE ENGLAND

A dance of victory, a dance of freedom. 'La Boche' finished. Napoo! Napoo! Hurrah! Hurrah!

The freedom of the town was ours. Was it the Lord Mayor that they hoisted on the top of a beer barrel? I'm blessed if I know; but he commanded silence, got it, and made a dramatic speech of which I knew very little but caught odd words of praise for England (a tremendous cheer) America (more terrific cheering) and then his own beloved France. We sang all the national anthems and a band that sprang from nowhere crashed out. Something caused the big drum to slip down; a big fat French man was pushed into it and what cries of fun rent the air. All was taken in good heart. Who could be sad or sullen today?

A little mite of ten summers took my hand. I lifted her up, and she throws her little arms around my neck, then gives me a little baby kiss. Her little brother tacks himself onto my belt. Here I am with two kiddies – a boy and a girl – and what am I to do with them? They were lost in the crowd, and I was at loss too, but would not desert them until I found their mammy or daddy. Suffice it to say I had them for over two hours before we bumped into a distracted mother. I parted with my badge as a souvenir. What a story the little folk told their mother. She blessed me – not once but many times for such kind and loving care over 'les enfants'.

SWAYING HUMANITY

Swaying humanity; backwards, forwards, jostled, sang, danced. Caps were exchanged, hats for top hats. American sausers crowned many flashing French lassies. French blue on British lads. All mixed up. Even that Chinese had arrived in town by some means and took part in the rejoicings. Some wild man shot his six-shooter off into the air – all six shots – and caused a commotion for a few seconds. 'The Wild West' – shooting up the burgh! He was disarmed.

Evening shadows fall, merge into night, but the mad world of pent-up feelings has not yet abated. In fact it is rowdier than ever. Some of the troops are now beyond control almost, as the wine has gone to their head – or maybe it's the excitement?

THE END OF the DAY

I had been invited to drink dozens of times but did not accept – it had no attraction for me.

Tired out, weary to the point of collapse, I begged a lift on an old French farm-cart that was passing outward bound from Calais about midnight to somewhere up the road and was helped up over the big wheel to fall into a load of hay and sink gratefully down. I must have fallen asleep as it was with a start, plus bones that ached, that I opened my eyes to find myself wrapped up in a rough horse-rug – still in the hay – but no movement. Where the h★★★ was I now? Creeping out, I was astonished to find the horse gone, the cart at rest, in the middle of the usual French farmyard. I step out to thank my friend and he meets me on the threshold of his kitchen door. My thanks were waved aside and I was brought into the house. The good wife was astounded to find I was 'l'officier Anglais' and bustled around in a flurry of activity to place a fine breakfast on the table all for me. How I enjoyed that meal – my first since the previous morning. That old couple would not hear of any reward or thanks so I cut a badge from my coat and took a small photograph out of my pocket and passed these over as a 'Memento'. Tears of gratitude gathered in their eyes – then I got up to say farewell.

BON VOYAGE!

Both took me in their arms and embraced me. 'Bon voyage, officer, bon voyage, long live England!' I had to be up and moving – so I salute and stride out. The fresh breeze stirred my blood as I stepped merrily out on my journey of return – and yet my direction must have been of the foggiest as I got a shock when I hailed a motor lorry of ours and had a yarn with the driver who convinced me I was going the wrong way. So I ended up by stepping up beside him and going in the very opposite direction with him.

No need to bore you with the many and various false trails I followed before I struck camp again – that afternoon. Done up! But a glorious welcome from all my brother officers who thought I had been lost – strayed – or died. I'm afraid most of the troops had what is called a bad head after the day before and were trying to get rid of it, in the usual manner by having 'some more' firewater. I was not in trouble with this complaint, so I left them all to it.

AUG '14 WAR! WAR! WAR!

Utterly exhausted I crawl into my old sleeping bag without shedding a single garment, or even my heavy field boots. My Chinese boy hovers around all smiles and sympathy for his 'own officer'. As my head touches the ground and fast asleep, the dreams come – dreams – dreams.

MY DREAM

August '14. War! War! War!

The call to arms. Right. Right. Form – Fours. Squad, Halt! Tramp, tramp, tramp. Canvas tents. Huts.Billets. Finner camp… Randalstown. Bramshott. Seaforde. Bordon. Bands playing. Southampton. le Havre. Rain. Mud. Mud.

Marching in the slush. Strange sights. Desolation. Trenches. Snow. Sleet. Rain. Mud. Barbed wire. Rats and rats. Ration parties. Wiring parties. Bombing parties. Slush. Mud like glue. Dam it. Sunshine. Sweat. Rifles. Bayonets. Machine guns.

SHADOWS PASS.......

Patrol duties. No man's land.

Star shells. Rockets. Flares. Bombardments. Wounds. Death. Midnight burials. Old chums missing. More horror. Faces and forms flit past. Lieutenant Wedgewood. Lieutenant Monard. Captain Willis. Lieutenant Robb. Lieutenant Walker. Penman. Lorimer. Savage. Kelly. Rogers. Rooney. Sergeant Kelly. Quarter Master Powell. Mitchell. Dixie kid. Reid. Porky Black. Stanley Black. Lindsay.

Platoons. Battalions. Regiments pass on. '15 dies out. Swamps. Caves. Chalk. Forests. Trenches. Guns, Guns, Guns. Aeroplanes. Air battles. Bombs. Dive boys. Railways crash! Crash! Crash! Crash!.C −r −u −m–p! Big Black Berthas. Choking fumes. Gas masks. Summers days. 1 July '16. Red Dawn. Roaring hell. Raining shells. Bayonets gleam.

Advance! Into the jaws of – Shooting – Clubbing – Stabbing. Mad frenzy. Dripping blood. Blood. Blood. Death masks. Inferno. Whirling hell.

BRAVERY! DESPAIR!

Come on the Rifles, the Skins, the Faughs! Glory be! No surrender! Forward boys! Bravery. Despair. Demented cries. Surrender? No D★★★. Fear. Hold on. Hold on.

Evening shadows. Gun flashes. Cornered like rats. Fight it out, the Ulsters. Star shells. Potted helmets. Prussian curses. Red–hot rifles. Surrender! Never a thought. Smash! Hell! Down! Down! Down! to the uttermost depths. Hours of blankness. Crawling. Dead. Dying. Red blood. Pain. Suffering. Injections. Stretchers. Red Cross vans. Field hospitals. Doctors. Anxious-faced sisters. Angels of kindness. Clean white sheets.

Loving care. Sea waves lapping the sides of big transport. Home and loved ones. The year fades away. 1917 into focus. Reserve battalions. Old friends. Gradual return of new life. New health. New interest. Drafts for the front again. Medical boards. Cambridge. London. Belfast. France again. Boom! Boom!

RETREAT! RETREAT!

Zurr! Zurr! Zurr! Fokkers. S –w –i –s –h! Yellow faces. Why have the boys turned yellow? Is it a new poison gas? Chinese. Petrol. Petrol. Petrol. Ammunition trains. Convoys. Whirr! Whirr! Whirr! Black-crossed ships flashing in the sky. Searchlight beams. Crash! Sunshine. Shadows. Sorrow. Sadness. Duties. Day and night. 1918 looms up!

Dark depressing days. March. Retreat. Retreat. Retreat. Backs to the wall. Fighting it out. The Somme. Arras. Ypres. Petrol. Ammunition. Guns. Planes. Men. Men. Men. Petrol boxes float past. In millions. Stacks. Dumps. Sweated coolies. Slave driven. Exhaustion. On! On! All for the troops.

Death from the heavens. Tortured bodies. Gaping wounds. Sickness. Disease. Eternity. Never-ending. Still on Down the Road.. Captain Curtain, Simpson, Forrester, Thompson. The wild men. Nightmare. Cavalcade of years gone past.

I STARE INTO SPACE

All mixed up in coloured lights. Tracer bullets. Lewis guns. Flashing shells. Bombs! bombs! Cold sweat. Feverish sweat. I shiver. Start. Wake up.

Am I dreaming? Is it real? 'Hell Jim boy – the b***** war ended yesterday!' 'What year is this?' '1918!' 'And the date?' 'The 12th.' Yes! Yes! I jump up, drop into an old chair made from a biscuit box and stare into space…

It's all over. No more death. No more wounds. No more destruction. My life is spared. Why was I spared. I say a prayer, thanking the Great Good God for all his mercy. God was merciful to me. Five years of my young life gone. But what years!!! I would not have missed it all. For worlds. What pals. What a glorious chums! The bravery. Self-sacrifice. And the mighty Hun was crushed. Trampled down. And the glorious RIGHT triumphed over MIGHT, smashing a nightmare, after years of agony.

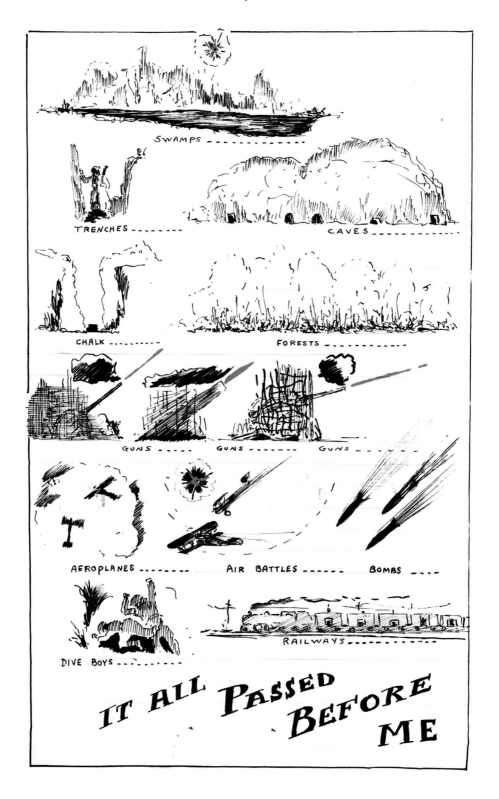

YES!

FROM JACK KANE'S SCRAP BOOK.

Captain J. V. HYNDMAN
Chichester Park, Belfast), died of wounds,
Y.C.V.'s.

Lce.-Cpl. R. BOTHWELL
Y.C.V.'s), formerly of War-
nocks, Ltd., Royal Avenue,
killed.

Private W. LORIMER,
14th Batt. Royal Irish Rifles (Y.C.V's), whose
death is reported from France. He was a
son of Private W. Lorimer, 113 Cosgrave
Street, and his wife lives at 106 Mountcollyer
Avenue, Belfast.

Lieut. J. L. WALKER,
on of Mr. F. M. Walker, Helen's Bay
formerly of Courtrai), the first officer of the
Y.C.V.'s to fall in action.

Captain S. WILLIS,
Coleraine (Y.C.V.'s), missing

Sergeant CARL PENMAN,
14th Batt. Royal Irish Rifles (Young Citizen
Volunteers), killed in action on March 15.
Deceased was 19 years of age, and his widowed
mother resides at 5 Craig's Terrace, Belfast.

Lieutenant R. RENWICK,
Belfast (Y.C.V's), wounded.

Lieut. VICTOR H. ROBB,
Kirk-Bruighean, Fortwilliam Park, Belfast
(Y.C.V.'s), wounded.

Sec.-Lieut. R. V. GRACEY,
Helen's Bay (Y.C.V.'s), missing

I SEE THEM ALL.

WHAT AN ADVANCED DRESSING STATION LOOKS LIKE AFTER A BATTLE.—Here our wounded are being tended with all the skill and rapidity possible near the battlefield itself. These "stretcher cases" are here prepared for regular hospital treatment further behind the lines. German prisoners help. [*Official Photograph.*]

CRUMP -------- BIG BLACK BERTHA'S -- -- -- -- -- -

CHOKING FUMES ---- GAS ----- MASKS -- -- -- -- --

— *NO MORE GAS* —

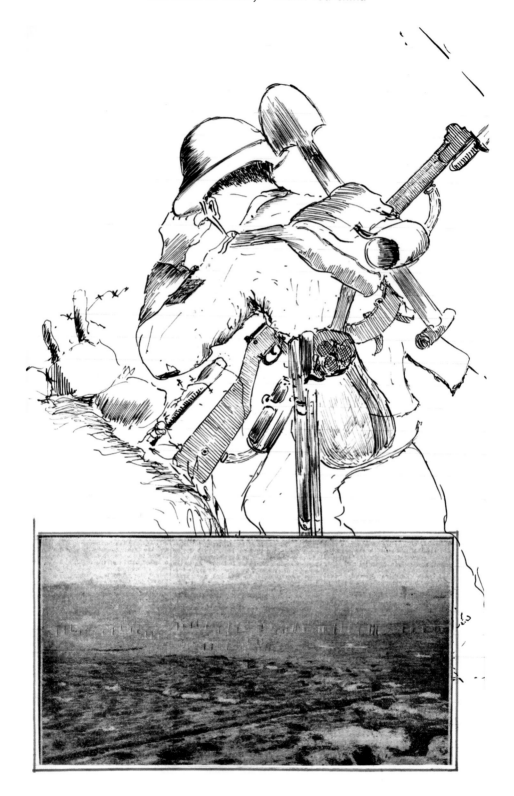

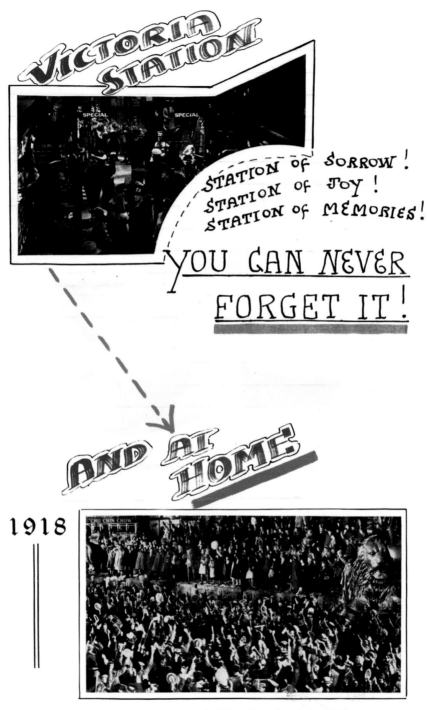

VICTORIA STATION

STATION of SORROW!
STATION of JOY!
STATION of MEMORIES!

YOU CAN NEVER FORGET IT!

AND AT HOME

1918

—*And then November 11th, 1918 . . . .*
Sirens at home . . . . Silence on the battle-
fronts . . . . London mad with a joy transcend-
ing heaviest sorrows.

251

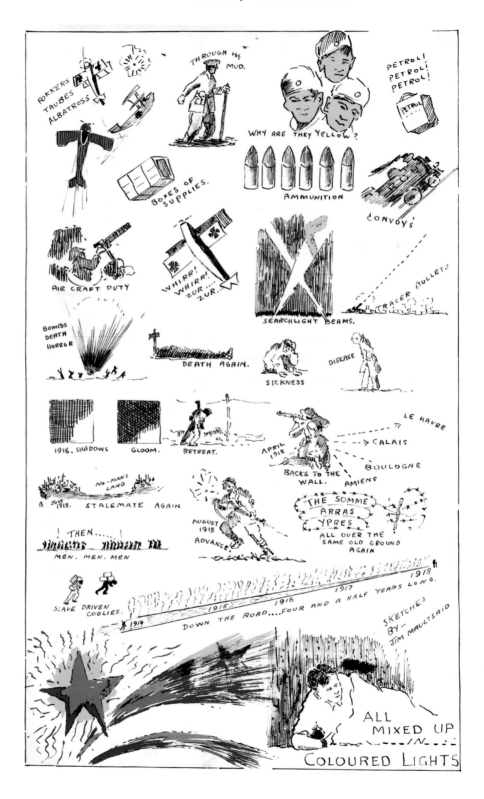

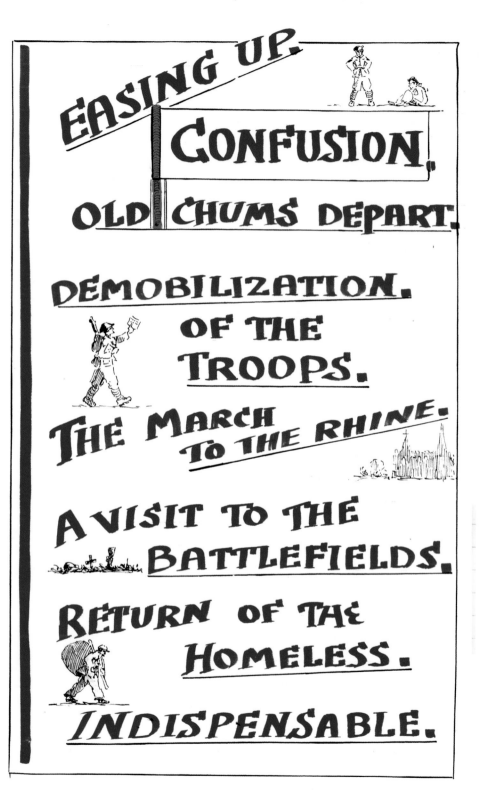

EASING UP.

CONFUSION.

OLD CHUMS DEPART.

DEMOBILIZATION. OF THE TROOPS.

THE MARCH TO THE RHINE.

A VISIT TO THE BATTLEFIELDS.

RETURN OF THE HOMELESS.

INDISPENSABLE.

LIFE

was now easier, or should I say we took it easier. No hustle or bustle. The Chinese fell off very badly in their working output and, to tell the honest truth, I had not the heart to speed them up as after all we had 'horsed' them to the point of exhaustion and I considered they were more than entitled to a 'break' – and took care they got it. Do not in any way misunderstand me as I made them do a fair honest day's work – but no more.

WHAT A MESS RETAINED

What a mess things where in when 'ceasefire' sounded! All was confusion. One part of our army was going to the Rhine – and the rest wanted home. So did I, but no home for me. In a few weeks my fate was in some mysterious way decided in a communication for our captain marked 'Confidential and Secret.' Maultsaid must be retained as 'indispensable' (ye gods!).

This was my fate. How long was this to last? I was annoyed to say the least of it as my thoughts were to get home and try to get a job, or the old job back if my firm would have a wanderer, and as 1914 got first preference (I was one of these) you can well understand my feelings to see my brother officers and NCOs get demobbed and yours truly left in France. Why was I to be retained? Sorry, I cannot answer; but I think it was my complete understanding of the Chinese boy as a worker, my almost full control of their language, and my ability to get the best out of them, if you will pardon this boast. Be it as it may, I was chosen and, as you read on, you will see I had to serve the full sentence of one long year (1919) on foreign soil.

In fact I was there to say goodbye to every single original officer, sergeant and corporal who served with 169 Company, so I ask you! In fact I was in command of the company at different times for several months – O/C 169 Company CLC, Lieutenant J. Maultsaid, acting Captain!

MY HEART BLED

Reader – this is a period hard to describe. So much of life flowed past. In the first few months of 1919 I met people representing almost all the nations in the WORLD. Going home, or trying to! Lost and strayed. Our boys coming back. Germans, Russians, Poles, Jews, Belgians, Italians, Swedish, Indians; yellow, brown and black boys. 'Down-under boys. Boys from the ice belts. The USA lads, north and south. All turning wearily to the homeland. Then the poor souls searching for loved ones who never were found in many cases.

Looking for homes, blasted to the skies by the Hun shells and bombs many years ago. Yet they searched and searched in vain. I saw it all, 'the Aftermath of War'. I helped to feed the starved ones, I helped to comfort the weary ones. My heart bled. I cursed the Hun. I do not intend nor I do not attempt to record a fraction of these sights or scenes that are ever mirrored on my brain. You will only get flashes in the pages that follow – flashes of 'the passing show'.

The stage of 1919 in France. How I would have loved to march to the Rhine! But it was not for me. So I bade them cheerio and envied them.

WARS AFTERMATH

A desire possessed me to go and see the old battlefields. And I went. Leave was easily obtained. I made my way to that godforsaken spot YPRES and I spent many days wandering around this gloomy place: St Jean, Poelcapelle, Zillebeke, Hill 60, Hellfire corner, Wyschaete, Passchendaele, Pilckem, Merkem, Dickebusch, etc., etc.

Then on to Ostend, Zeebrugge, Dixmude – Poperinghe, Dunkirk. The barbed wire was thick on the promenade, the big twisted guns in their turrets, the underground searchlights and all the rest. The picture postcards shown at the end of this article were secured in Ypres itself on this trip and will give you some idea of how the war left this place. It was sad, also dreary, in these dull November days of 1919. I had a most uncanny feeling in Ypres: as if the place was haunted; the 'ghosts' of countless legions hovered over 'hell's Inferno'.

ALL QUIET !

All was so quiet. The shuffle of leaden feet: down to the edge of our old front line, looking for timber and galvanised iron to try and build a shack of some kind to keep out winter blasts from famished bodies, I was glad to see the end of it – and travel on. Up and over the ridge. How did our boys hold Ypres? Looking down at it from the old German positions it was a death trap. Every yard of it was under fire. Was it not madness after all, trying to hold such a place? I think it was! Did sentiment play a part in our operations?

The effect on the French and Belgian people might have been disastrous, and yet did this balance our terrible losses? I don't think so, and shall never be convinced otherwise. We should have let it go and picked our position a little further back.

WANDERING'S

My wanderings over for the moment, I returned to my Chinese and spent quite a lot of my spare time writing up my notes and sketching my sketches; you have them all before you.

WASTE.

The stores of war material on hands after the war was simply stupendous. Millions of shells, guns, ammunition, miles and miles of stacks of foodstuffs, miles of sheds and miles of everything required to keep a war going for many years. And the waste? It was heartbreaking. Waste and decay set in as the months went past and our authorities seemed to be in a muddle about what to do with it. I would honestly say we lost millions – and millions of our 'wait and see' policy. Hundreds of thousands of cases of tinned food, jam, biscuits, meal and flour rotted in the ground. Bags of oats, packs of hay turned green and stank from exposure. It was WASTE! WASTE! WASTE! It almost broke my heart to see it. I felt like writing to the *Daily Mail* or the *Daily Express* exposing it all but knew I would have been up for a court martial and I did not want that after coming right through it all with a clean sheet.

You may ask what my remedy was? Well! Here it is

MY PLAN

1. We should have sold it all at bargain prices to the French and Belgians who would have been delighted to buy, I know, and let them dispose of it in their own way, allowing us to clear out. This I believe was what the Americans did do. And very wise too!
2. (a) Send out skilled, or unskilled, labour workers in battalions to remove the stores.
   (b) Given us the power to employ French civilians in our areas as labour workers.
   (c) Put our mind to the business and not dilly-dally; organise and ship home at once.
   (d) Poor use was made of the infantrymen who were not eligible to be demobbed.
   (e) In point of fact we failed badly in the disposal of our perishable war stores. In my mind very badly indeed – and I was on the spot.

Of course our Chinese boys were employed in many of these 'disposal' jobs, but were far from sufficient to cope with it. Again I knew that all the ships were wanted to take our troops home; and the one and only sensible move would have been to sell to the French. We did not do it – and lost MILLIONS!

TONS OF RUBBISH

The pages that follow will tell you briefly how we wandered from place to place doing the rag-picking act. Clearing up. Mopping up. Sorting out. Trying to straighten out the mess.

A BLUNDER

On top of all our own stores came the rubbish sent down by the Germans as part of the price demanded by the Allies in goods such as railway engines, trucks, stores etc. This in my humble opinion was a terrible blunder on our part. It would have been no loss and a grand riddance; we could have very well done without it, believe me.

Everywhere you turned was rows and rows of guns. Heaps of aeroplanes. Limbers, wagons, harness, hospital beds, tents, machine guns, shells, iron huts, shovels, picks, bundles of bags, stacks of petrol, tinned meat, equipment and rifles, horses and mules, engines, machinery, boots, greatcoats.

Anything and everything from a needle to an anchor. The litter and the waste from a world war! All was confusion – utter and complete!

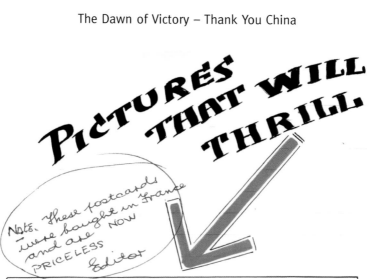

PICTURES THAT WILL THRILL

Note. These postcards were bought in France and are NOW PRICELESS — Editor

Ruines d'Ypres 1914-18
The ruins at Ypres
Eglise des Sœurs de la Sainte-Famille et rue Gustave de Stuers.
Church of the nuns of the Holy Family and Gustave de Stuers streetr

Ruines d'Ypres 1914-18 Place de la Gare et boulevard Malon.
The ruins at Ypres Station place and boulevard Malon

THE HOMELESS BUILT SHACKS FROM THE WRECKAGE OF WAR.

SEARCHING FOR THE OLD HOME

THEY SCOURED THE BATTLEFIELDS FOR BUILDING MATERIAL.

STRANGE FIGURES FLITTED DOWN OUR OLD TRENCHES

THE SCENE OF DESOLATION WAS COMPLETE.

AND STOOD ON HILL 60.

I STOOD IN THE TRENCHES AGAIN.

AND SKETCHED THE RUINS OF YPRES FROM THE OLD HUN FRONT LINE.

YPRES

SKETCHES BY JIM MAULTSAID

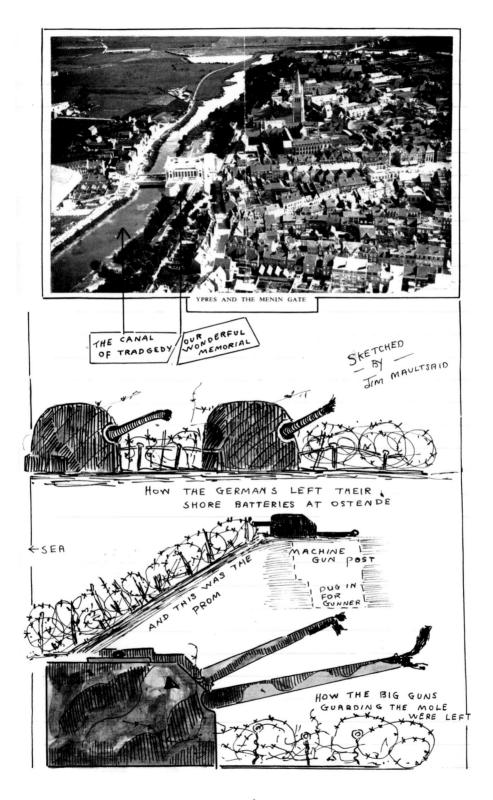

YPRES AND THE MENIN GATE

THE CANAL OF TRADGEDY

OUR WONDERFUL MEMORIAL

SKETCHED BY JIM MAULTSAID

HOW THE GERMANS LEFT THEIR SHORE BATTERIES AT OSTENDE

←SEA

AND THIS WAS THE PROM

MACHINE GUN POST

DUG IN FOR GUNNER

HOW THE BIG GUNS GUARDING THE MOLE WERE LEFT

LIFE FLOWED PAST

ALL THE NATIONS of the WORLD!

264

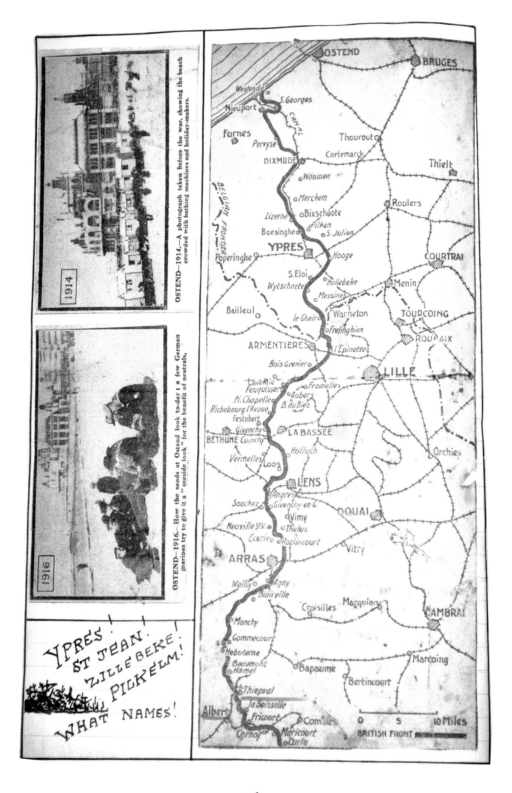

OSTEND—1914.—A photograph taken before the war, showing the beach crowded with bathing-machines and holiday-makers.

OSTEND—1916.— How the sands at Ostend look to-day : a few German marines try to give it a "seaside look" for the benefit of neutrals,

YPRES! ST JEAN! ZILLEBEKE! PILKEM! WHAT NAMES!

SKETCH FROM THE BOOK.

JIM MAULTSAID.

THIS IS AN EXAMPLE OF WHAT ARRIVED AS PART OF GERMANY'S WAR DEBT TO THE ALLIES. MY ARTICLE IS WELL NAMED? NOW READ THE STORY.

266

"THE BERLIN EXPRESS"

first real surprise I got shortly after the Armistice was a big German train pulling in to the ROD depot one fine day. To say the least of it the engine was ancient and some of the rolling stock not far in advance of it. I was again surprised when the driver spoke to me and touched his cap. Of course I did not understand him but could see at a glance that both he and his fireman were German, and both were starving. I gave orders for bread, cheese and tea, much to the astonishment of several French soldiers and some civilians standing around. Never did I see such eating. The food disappeared. Looks of pleasure, much saluting and signs of great pleasure for a square meal from the two Germans. It gave me some pleasure too; after all the war was over now.

THE END OF THE BERLIN EXPRESS

Crowds gathered in a short time and great interest was taken in the first fruits of victory. Some wag labelled the engine 'The Berlin Express' in large white letters, a very neat one. Dusk had fallen and I left the sightseers to it all, including some of my own bright Chinese.

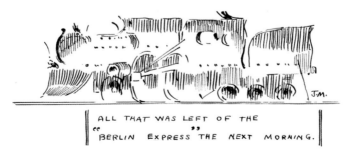

ALL THAT WAS LEFT OF THE "BERLIN" EXPRESS THE NEXT MORNING.

"VANISHED"

Next morning I got the shock of my life when I again viewed 'the train'. It was a complete skeleton, stripped of all spare parts, in fact practically nothing left but the boiler and driving wheels of the engine. How some of the parts were carried away beats me but they had simply vanished into thin air. The allies would not get much cash value from this consignment; the troops had the best of it I'm afraid.

"SOUVENIR" OFFICER PLENTY MUCH..

"PLENTY MUCH!"

Shock number 2! My boy slides up to me that afternoon all ready to make a confession (I could read him like a book by now). 'Plenty big German engine – down at depot. Yes! Plenty much souvenir, Officer – Oh! Boy has 'San-gowdy' one for Officer' (san-gowdy is Chinese for a good). 'Have you?' A hand comes from his back and out of the seat of his wide breeches is produced a plate with a fine German eagle printed on it. He had spent half the night screwing it off the front of the engine, all for his own officer. Leave it to the Chinese! I admonished him in no uncertain manner but had a good laugh to myself; my plate was the envy of the mess.

MY LAST RACE

SPORTS DAY

To keep us from feeling lonely a big sports day was suggested. The OC of the area asked me to do a poster for the occasion. This was my first since Cambridge days and I turned out a real beauty sketched on a big sheet of canvas, all the colours of the rainbow. He was simply delighted. I had to borrow some colours from my Chinese artist and he also helped me to fill in the lettering and the big sketch of a runner.

"RUNNING YET"

JIM MAULTSAID

It was a fine piece of work. I took care to see that my Chinese artist got his fair share of the praise from the major. Between us we delivered the 'goods'; that was that.

My next job was OC sports, work after my own heart, and how I enjoyed the fun of it all! I racked my brains for an all-round programme. The usual flat events were easy but some fun must also be provided, so I included a mule race for officers, a greasy-pole pillow fight, a special brand of obstacle race, etc., etc.

The band had a band race and I even included one for the French civilians, so the chart was set fair for a full day's fun. Now the prize money had as usual to be found from the officers and we had to dip very deeply indeed, but it was all for a good cause and no grumbles. No trouble at all in finding a big flat field and less in squaring the French owner. He would do anything he could for the British troops, and he kept his word. He even had the grass cut for us and the ground rolled. What more could he do?

THE CHARGE OF THE LIGHT BRIGADE!

The day dawns, bright and fair. Our luck is in. The kick-off is at 11.00am morning session. Crowds of troops (all nationalities) flock in and flocks of French and Belgian folk roll up. The gun goes bang! The fun begins.

Event after event is run off, but the finals are all down for the afternoon. Lunch hour passes and we listen to the band and rest. Most of the events were open; you entered on the spot. It was not uncommon to see a fine American, a strapping Frenchman, and a raw Highlander lined up for the '220 open to all'; it was great fun.

But the mule race! Gee! It was a shambles. Some of the jockeys had never sat on a mule before, you could tell that, and the roars from the crowds were terrific. How they laughed –

and cracked jokes at the expense of the officers. But it was a fine race and the winner came home with his arms around the mule's poor neck. He would be running yet only many hands grasped him to haul him off; his mule had run off to win by several streets. What a race! It was like the charge of the Light Brigade!

THE 100 IN MY SOCKS !

The officers' open 100 yards dash! On the spur of the moment I had made up my mind to run in it. I handed my starting gun to a brother lieutenant and strolled along to the starting post. Still as confident as in ye olden days I told Forrester to put his cash on ME. Knowing him as I did it was no surprise to me to learn, after the race, he had won a real packet. But wait! Off goes my jacket and pants and as I had got the loan of shorts I was ready in a few seconds, but had to run in my socks (this was a comedown); no spiked shoes here.

Lined up for the start, I was actually given some few yards of a start (my record was unknown); this was for size. Several long-legged starters were weighed up. These were worth watching? Blind! As usual I almost beat the pistol flash and skimmed out, down the straight. Could I stick it?

The breath is coming in short spasms and going fast. Thirty yards to go. Twenty. Ten. Five. I still lead. Forrester's Scottish voice won me the race.

'Come on Maulty! Come on One Six Nine!' I stagger past the tape. Done. Blown up, but happy. Maultsaid won the race. As in a dream I heard Forrester give all details then he hugged and pumped me. A flask is pressed to my lips – hot lemonade this; anyhow it revived me.

I had run my last race and WON.

the last Race

Never again since that day in 1919 did I don the racing gear – so I made a flying finish? They promised me a medal for winning but I'm still looking for it. But, after all, what's a medal? It's the race that counts!

So I ended my last sports meeting as a competitor. Captain Curtain said that night when we were celebrating on Forrester's, Simpson's and, on the quiet, Captain Curtain's winnings, 'Up Ireland', 'Ireland a Nation', 'Long Live Ulster' and 'Here's to 169 CLC – it lives for Evermore.' THE CURTAIN FALLS!

IN MY SOCKS YE GODS !

GOODBYE
TO MAJOR CURTAIN
"WELL BOYS........."
........GOODBYE!

His demob papers had at last arrived. We had come to the parting of the ways. Back to South Africa. Of course, he was pleased at the thought of getting clear of it all, and yet sorry to leave us all after years of struggle and strife together; but such was the soldier's life in these days. Here today – tomorrow, gone.

Before his departure he called me to the orderly room and handed me a sealed envelope which he said contained 'my character' and it was black (his little Irish joke to the end).

THIS SIDE OF JORDAN

'Maultsaid boy – if you ever feel like coming to South Africa, do let me know and I'll sure get you a job in the mines. You would be the man for overseeing the natives. I'm in real earnest – one of the best officers I ever had, thorough, painstaking, efficient and a grand Irish soldier. What more can I say?'

'Goodbye Maultsaid!' He finds trouble in speaking and we shake hands. 'Goodbye skipper.' My throat bothers me also, as I feel I'll never see the 'skipper' again, this side of Jordan.

'Look after 169 Company old man right to the end. You will now be second-in-command from this date. God bless you and keep you Maultsaid. G –o –o –d –b –y –e!'

Outside the Chinese boys were all lined up in a square. He moves forward and Mr Woo, our official interpreter, translates his final message to the Chinese boys. They nod and show much appreciation at his kind words. What praise he gave them, how pleased they all were; the best Chinese company in France, etc., etc.

BREAKING UP

He shakes hands with each white NCO and Chinese ganger, steps back a few paces and salutes. They return his salute in their own Chinese fashion and, somehow, HE IS GONE. And God bless him.

Gradually the 'old firm' is breaking up. The mess table that night was dull. His place was taken by Simpson, who was now OC Company and a full-blown captain. But it was not Simpson that I could see in the chair; it was the 'skipper' himself.

He had left several hundred francs for the Chinese, to let them have a feast in celebration of his departure; we could hear them making merry in the compound outside. I had an invitation to attend and, slipping out at the first opportunity, I made my way to the old huts and spent all the rest of the evening trying to sample their strange dishes, made in honour of their 'Big Captain'. 'Ding-hola.' He was good to all the Chinese boys.

for petrol were falling low – so the order came to demolish three of our depots, lock, stock, and supply. My No. 2 Depot was to be left in the meantime as the Army of Occupation on the Rhine had to be still supplied and mine was the supply centre. It was with sad hearts we lent a hand to put the other three out of commission, but sentiment meant nothing now– they had to disappear.

Gradually all the stocks were loaded up, thousands and still thousands of boxes packed into trucks for transport via ferry railway back to England. Then the sheds, little huts and various shelters were pulled down, the ground levelled out and all that was left to tell the story of the CLC was the railway lines. Remember please that we had actually built up all these store places and now had taken them to bits.

DEMOLISH.

Everything and everybody around me in these days seem to be going, going, going. Change and change. Most of the ROD boys had gone (the old hands) and the Army Service boys too that had worked with us in the days of hectic strife. Day after day, it was 'Goodbye, Mister Maultsaid!' And yet here I was, an old hand myself still in France.

The petrol depots Nos 1, 2 and 4 where 'no more' – shades and shadow only. Their commanders, Thompson (back home in Canada), Forrester (at headquarters) and Simpson (second-in-command, now OC Company) all gone, and here I was supervising the demolishing of all their work! Brand new second lieutenants had been sent to us to fill the gap; I cannot remember their names now, but most of them did not in any way appeal to the Chinese and, truth to tell, I was not too deeply interested myself as I was missing my old chums more each day – and just longed for 'the day' myself. Demolish! – Demob!

A NEW HOME

"HERE'S THE B –
PLACE "
AN OLD GERMAN P.O.W. CAMP

JIM. M. 1919

SHIFT CAMP "ORDER"

All is bustle. Camp is breaking up. Beds, baggage, equipment and all the thousands of all odds and ends that go to the making of home for five hundred Chinese plus some twenty whites is stacked up in readiness for the march. Our vast experience of moving out, gained in our old infantry days, stands in good stead. We know our business and see that the coolies carry out our orders. No band here to cheer us on – just hitch up the pack and 'quick march'.

Our new home is somewhere ahead but not too far; so we gathered from our maps. Down the road. I steal a last look at the remnants of the old Homestead. Regrets! Pat – pat – patter – patter. Shuffle is the word, not marching. They walk a few yards, then break into a dog trot. Funny!

Hearts in Bradford

As we hike along my mind goes back down the years. Somehow this was always a feeling of mine; I was marching again with the 'boys' – up the roads on the Somme. The Chinese were millions of miles away. Simpson by my side gives me a jolt: 'This is b***** awful, Maulty. Hell of a life this, and all the d***fighting over. What the h*** are we doing here?'

BY JIM. MAULTSAID

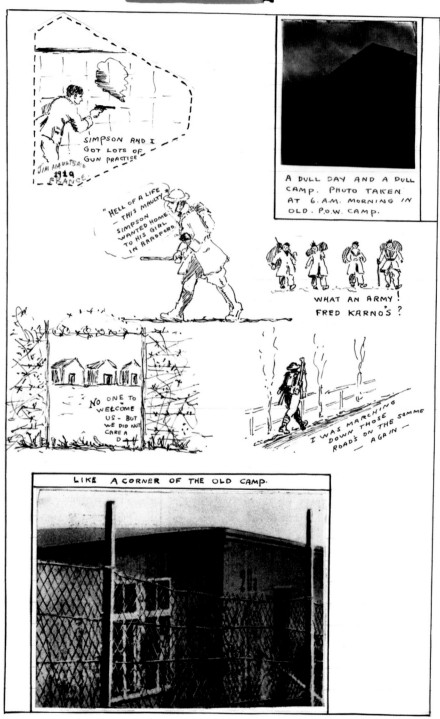

SIMPSON AND I GOT LOTS OF GUN PRACTICE

JIM MAULTSAID 1919 FRANCE

A DULL DAY AND A DULL CAMP. PHOTO TAKEN AT 6. A.M. MORNING IN OLD. P.O.W. CAMP.

"HELL OF A LIFE THIS MAULTY – SIMPSON WANTED HOME TO HIS GIRL IN BRADFORD"

WHAT AN ARMY! FRED KARNO'S?

NO ONE TO WELCOME US – BUT WE DID NOT CARE A D

I WAS MARCHING DOWN THOSE ROAD'S ON THE SOMME – AGAIN

LIKE A CORNER OF THE OLD CAMP.

He wanted home to his best girl in Bradford and was properly fed up I knew, but so was I – and yet what could we do? 'Cheer up old boy, the first seven are the worst – only two more to go!' We ease the pack straps and shuffle along. 'What an army! Fred Karno and George Robey's battalions.' Simpson is at it again. 'Halt! Sit down and have a rest.' No hurry, so we flop into the ditch. During this spell a big convoy of GS wagons pass us – down to the base for England. Smiles and happiness. How we envied them. Oh boy! Oh boy!

Not a living soul

'Here's the b***** place! Halt!' And, ye gods, it was an old German PoW camp, all wire and barricades, but the flowers were in full bloom. How those poor devils must have cared and loved these self-same flowers; they had somehow managed to plant and train them in great variety right up the barbed wire. This was the only redeeming feature about this depressing show. It was in the vicinity of a big railway depot and the usual canal was outside the camp. Railways again!

Not a single human being to meet or show us anything – but we did not care a d***. We simply took possession and no-one gave us even a single glance. What a rare life! Hard work squaring up – and chasing the rats (they were here in thousands to meet us). Simpson and I got some gun practice popping them off. How old Tommy Thompson would have enjoyed this. The day is done, we curl up on a cold and miserable floor and fall asleep. Let tomorrow look after itself. Let's sleep and dream of the demob papers. Home and civvies!

WHAT A JOB! Our new work was a sketch. Our job? Unloading big trucks of war refuse, German trains of rubbish, etc., etc.; we had to sort it all out. A sample truck contained machine guns, rifles, bayonets, equipment, boots, shovels, ammunition, old bloodstained uniforms, rolls of wire, hospital material, etc., etc., and very often a great amount of filth (from the Germans this).

Now we had to stack all the different articles in a dump by themselves. Pure and simple ragpicking. How we fell in our own estimation! What a life! But orders are orders and we had to make the best of a bad job. No pen could describe the stacks of material that grew up around us. Anything from a big battered filled gun down to a gas mask. Stacks, stacks, that covered many scores of square acres.

SKIPPER SIMPSON

How did the Chinese take to it? Slow at first and full of curiosity, many narrow escapes for them from violent death soon taught them to be careful and cautious. In a few weeks they were really skilled workers and certainly put in some fine work. I had a roving commission from 'Skipper' Simpson to go around all my 169 boys (all scattered over the place in small lots) and see that everything was sailing along properly. Salvage you might term this job, but I'm afraid John Chinaman scrounged quite a lot of useful stuff for gain (sale to French and Belgian civilians) and yet we did do wonderful work.

Trains and convoys poured in on top of us and we had to clear them full steam ahead to let the next day's lot into the sidings. It was interesting in a way this new business and such a change for us (the petrol kings) but sometimes the stench of the truck would almost make us sick. Quite a few of the boys turned green. Did the gas come down in trucks too?

DECAYED BODIES!

One day a big German 20-tonner simply oozed green slime and I was called to see it. Dripping out from every seam and crevice was some form of thick liquid that smelt like decayed flesh. Was this proof of the German dead body factory supposed to be an action during the war days? The smell was terrible – and the doors bulged outward. We could not approach within yards of this cargo.

Having a brainwave I sent a squad for gas masks and, instructing them how to use these (to the Chinese awful instruments of no understanding), I set them the task of pushing this dope factory on wheels well clear of the works into a disused siding. This to me was one of the funniest sights of the war – these twelve heroes in gas masks gasping and straining at a job they detested and feared. A day or two of this truck in our depot would have laid us all low with some awful disease I felt convinced.

I sent for our RE sergeant and told him to put a charge of explosive under it and below the d***thing to smithereens. He smiled and said, 'Leave it to us, Sir!'

276

JUST LIKE OURS

WAR-TIME ECONOMY
ON FRENCH BATTLE FRONT.

BRITISH ARMY'S SALVAGE SYSTEM.

About ten years ago, when the Great War struggle on the Western front was nearing its end, but still undecided, a Press Mission was permitted by the authorities to go out for the purpose of seeing with their own eyes what was being done in the way of administration. Much had been said about an enormous waste going on; and an entire day was devoted by the mission to the great Salvage Depot at Calais. A vivid description of his impressions on the occasion is given by that veteran journalist, Mr. Charles Baker, in the "Newspaper World," of which he is editor and proprietor.

Referring to the crossing to France Mr Baker says:—"We embarked at Dover on a dark and stormy night and sat below-deck, wearing inflated lifebelts and presenting much of the appearance of a school of porpoises. There was a destroyer on each side of us, but, with the exception of the pitching and tossing of the vessel, nothing happened, and Boulogne was reached in due course."

At the Salvage Depot in Calais he says:— "In the great workshops, each covering acres, all sorts of repairs and reconditioning were going on. On the back of every lorry that traversed the fields of military operations were printed in white capitals: 'What have YOU salved to-day?' and the idea was that anything found lying about during lulls in fighting should be added to one or other of the innumerable 'dumps' at road sides. These deposits were periodically removed by lorries to Calais, where they were sorted into their different denominations of metal, leather, fabrics, and what not, and afterwards into enormous heaps of identical things such as horseshoes, water flasks, helmets, rifles, bayonets, bandoleers, knapsacks, etc

HOW A HELMET WAS DEALT WITH.

Some of these heaps at the depôt were almost household, and they were dealt with in a way that was both interesting and surprising. A battered and war-stained helmet with dirty lining was taken in hand by girl No. 1, who removed its lining, passed it to No. 2, who put it on a rounded steel block and hammered it smooth, passed it to No. 3, who coated it, passed it to No. 4, who sprinkled it so that there should be no reflection from it of the sun's rays, and passed it to No. 5, who inserted the clean lining and added it to the store of renovated helmets that increased with each succeeding minute.

"With the battered water flasks the process was even quicker To these shape and symmetry were restored from within by compressed air under a pressure of 250 pounds to the square inch. One great factory was devoted to the repair of cycles —motor and pedal; another to the repair of boots; and a third to the conversion of mutilated haversacks and ambulance stretchers into horses' nose-bags and soldiers' gloves. The major—it was always a major who was at the head of each department—who showed us round the textile repair factory was enthusiastic about his

deputy, a young lieutenant, who had conceived and carried out these and other ingenious points of economy. Even the very rags left over were ground to furnish material for later remanufacture."

The great salvage organisations fascinated Mr. Baker more than anything else he saw. "From a horse-shoe nail to a 15-inch gun, everything that could be conserved from battlefield waste and reconditioned seemed to have its corner of the depot and a staff to deal with it."

UP THE LINE

THE desire to once again see some of the old battlefields possessed me and I took steps to get the necessary permission. This was easy as the authorities were actually running almost free trips down to Paris for the troops. As I had no desire to go on one of these joyrides it was simplicity itself getting a free hand to go the other way. Off I went on my own. I had no set objective. Just get out when I came to a railhead and wander around. France was all mine. I landed in Amiens and stayed there a night – and had my first sleep in a real bed for many, many months – or was it years? I was not quite sure. My mind and body was still weary from the strain of war. How I slept and slept – twelve or twenty-four hours.

A NEW WORLD

Sometime the next day I pushed off up towards Arras. A lift on an old French cart part of the way, then some kilos on foot, a turn in an old Ford car owned by a Belgian refugee, some more footwork and night has fallen.

I struck a tumbledown hut and spent the night in it all on my ownsome. It was not a pleasant experience, as the ghosts of many regiments marched past my hut that night, their equipment and entrenching tools rattling in that peculiar way they always did. Dreams of course, but even yet it comes back to me. This new strange world was so silent, just the mutterings of the breeze through the big wide cracks. And the guns? All quiet …

I woke up early in the dawn, and I'll confess I was frightened – of what? Lonely and sad and scared. A bar of chocolate, a hard biscuit and a drink of water comprised my breakfast and I up and away. I actually remember looking back at that hut by the end of a skeleton wood. 'Ugh! Get away. Jim!' I shook myself and 'vamoosed'.

WHAT MEMORIES!

Arras, Vimy Ridge, Givenchy, Neuville-St Vaast, Souchez, Roclincourt and even up to Lens all came under my survey. What names these were to conjure up, all the fierce fighting, all the horror, the heartbreaks, the pathos of it all. War's destruction still held it all in its awfulness. Ruined homes, furrowed fields from shell-holes, battered trenches and earthworks. The same scenes as around Ypres were being enacted daily. Lost and dazed

folk looking for homesteads. Starved cattle grazing by the roadside. Painfully thin children running here and there, dogs that looked like wolves and horses that could hardly stand up. But why repeat it all? You know it – or you should. War is Hell.

I wandered around. I sketched here and there. I explored little hamlets that were just piles of brick and rubbish. No nameplates, no anything. The war god came, looked, and then destroyed. Some of these villages I felt sure have never been rebuilt. Vimy Ridge (sacred to our glorious Canadians). I stayed on the breast of the hill, or mound I should say. I pictured it in my mind and let my imagination run riot. Oh for a camera. I would have paid £50 for one lens! The double of any industrial town in the North of England in or about Lancashire was laid to waste – almost.

Battered walls, evil and foul cellars that I did not venture to explore. Town of many terrific encounters and many despatches; it was a strange sight indeed, but I did not linger. It was brighter in the open country and I pushed on.

AMIENS AGAIN

Souchez, the home of many Lancashire troops for many weary months was explored and left by me in a hurry. It was no place for tourists in these days. No Sir!

I have no intention of boring you with all the sights and scenes I witnessed around these parts; suffice it to say I got weary of it, and sick, so 'pulled out,' as the Yankees say and beat it down the trail to home. Most of this journey back was completed in stages of footslogging down to the railhead of Amiens. The cathedral here I noticed had suffered quite a lot since my last look at it in 1915, but the life and bustle surprised me. Almost business as usual again. Wonderful! Wonderful! Dead tired, but happy and pleased with my experiences (and sketches) I once more reported to my CLC Company.

BARGE WORK

A new task fell to my lot – one we had never taken part in before and the job was loading up big barges with material for transport to England. What use half of it was ever put to I never found out. This canal with the barges was outside our new PoW compound and the goods for transhipment were from the big depot I told you about in my story 'Ragpickers'.

My Chinese boys did not fancy the new work a great deal, especially the ones down in the bowels of the old barges all day, looking at the sky only through the hatches, and half

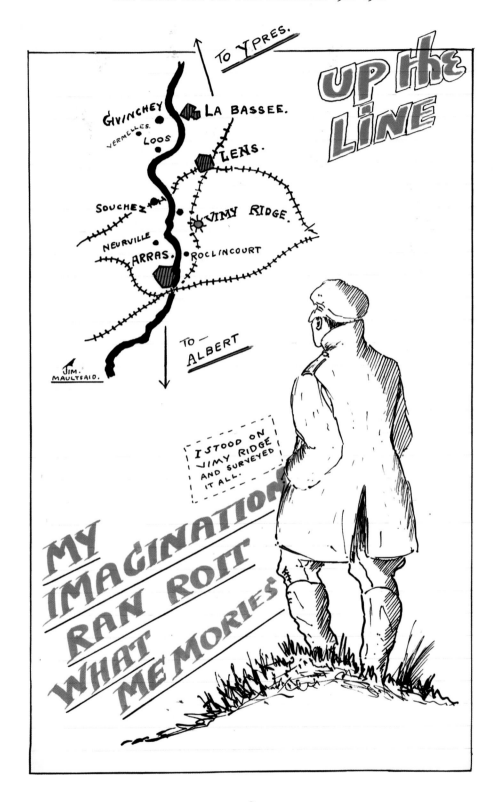

suffocated by dust plus thousands of microbes (you could almost see them through the fitful blasts of sunshine). These old barges were extremely dirty and evil smelling. I did not fancy this job one wee bit. We loaded up big bales of old clothes, bundles of equipment, rolls of blankets, rolls of horse covers, bags of old boots, bags of gas masks, bundles of greatcoats, puttees by the million, harness, etc., etc. – in fact the scrapings of the battlefield. When you picture most of this stuff covered with hard blood, mud and filth, not to mention the fleas and bugs in their billions, you get some idea of what our Chinese boys had to handle day and daily.

Was it any wonder we detested it all? Each day when their work was over they all had to wash themselves thoroughly and then get a dose of the spraying machine plus a dose of medicine. You get me? All the care and precautions we take; It was all needed. Our camp was 'walking away' with vermin and rats. It was one long battle against disease and sickness but, as usual in France, we surmounted all difficulties and carried out our work and loaded up our barges as they lay alongside the bank of the canal.

But truth to tell I had no heart in the business and did not unduly harass my boys. They also wanted back home now; the general opinion was their work was over and why keep them here? We filled up the barges, sealed down the hatches, and wished them 'bon voyage'.

As the camp had no space for any kind of recreation for our boys we had to more or less relax our strict 'pass out' methods and let them free from these surroundings on all possible opportunities. Each Saturday evening and all day Sunday found the surrounding districts swarming with Chinese out on pass. As a rule they were extremely well-behaved and seldom got into any trouble, faithfully returning to camp at the appointed hour. Most of our trouble was with French and Belgian toughs who took the Chinese for mugs and tried to put one across in a sharp deal of some kind and, if not successful, try to intimidate the yellow boys, but take it from me they often found their match.

When roused they can fight too and could use a knife with great skill, but a more peaceful people does not inhabit this globe. Drunken soldiers, including our own troops, sometimes caused trouble, but what most of these troublemakers overlooked, or did not know, was that these Chinese boys of ours in 169 Company were young and in a state of very fine physical fitness from hard work and could take care of themselves in a rough and tumble.

Almost murder

One very seedy underfed, underdeveloped foreign youth I remember tried the heavy stuff one day on the canal-bank and only my timely arrival saved his life. Several of my own gang had him battered to pulp almost and were on the verge of throwing his body into the canal when I turned up. When I had a look at him I almost let them carry out their intended deed, as I knew him for a thug and he well deserved all he got as I had noticed him staring and making obscene gestures on several occasions some time back and had myself told him to clear off to h★★ or I would shoot him. He had now got his desserts and I never set eyes on him again; his lesson had been a costly one, but effective.

Now we had to be on the alert for a different kind of peril and kept warning our troops against it, the peril of the 'loose woman'. These harpies we knew often tried to entice these units of ours into houses of ill-repute and downright rottenness.

the raid on the love nest

A place of this sort suspected by our higher command was raided once and all the occupiers scattered to the four winds of heaven in the night hours. I did not take part in the raid but knew it was coming off and it duly took place. Not a single member of 169 was caught but I'm sorry to say that quite a bunch of CLC members from China fell into the net and paid for their night's outing by long stretches in clink and deduction of pay. This more or less put *finis* to this kind of thing and we had little trouble afterwards. Midnight roll calls often took place. It was the Lord help any missing coolie when these spot checks were carried out, no matter what his excuse was.

So you see, even if the war was over, we still had our troubles and plenty. It was up to us to try and protect these boys of ours as well as we could from harm in a foreign land. I may say we were more than successful. No father or mother could have done more for them and indeed many parents in China often wrote to me and thanked me for my kindness.

Almost a trip to the Rhine

Falling in with an RAF lad one afternoon who was like myself still on 'the works', as he termed it, we had quite a long chat. The poor soul was lonesome for someone to yarn to and was glad to walk along and tell me all about his work. Of course I was interested to get an insight to keep my notes and sketches running smoothly (I was working hard on them in these days) and was always on the lookout for colourful material. Here was a real chance. I brought him to our mess and introduced him. He stayed for a cup of tea, then I explained all about our strange life. How his eyes opened. He did not know there was such a thing as the CLC.

Then I explained to him that we helped to keep him in the air as it were, by our supplies of petrol and oil. It was hard to get him started about his exploits in the skies but I gradually got it all from him. A mere boy even yet he had fought many battles 'upstairs' or on 'the roof' as we called it. I'm sorry now I did not record them, those stories of his; all true I knew, as his very bearing and uprightness would have convinced anyone.

nerves !

His job today? Carrying mail and urgent despatches to the Army on the Rhine in a big Handley-Page. No more bombs – just bundles of letters, etc. from sweethearts and wives. He thought it was dull work and could not settle down to it. Could you blame the youth? He said he always expected the 'archie'[10] batteries to open fire as he crossed the old battlegrounds and got a shock to know he was across and not a shot fired at him.

Of course it was nerves with the boy. From war to peace in a few short months and he had not yet got accustomed to peace. In fact he still scanned the heavens from force of habit – watching, watching, watching for the black cross of the Hun, but the Hun had gone.

Time up, I left him well on his journey to the aerodrome and gave him a promise to look him up on his return from Germany in a few days. Our meeting place duly arranged I was on the spot and of course so was he. His chums give me a great welcome to their mess. Tea over, and a drink declined, much to their astonishment, we wandered out to the big tarmac runway (or the plane parade ground) and I was explained all the inner workings of these flying kites, the 'old bus' he called it.

---

10. 'Archie' was a contemporary phonetic abbreviation for anti-aircraft defences which later became ack-ack.

The RHINE------- -

I climbed up into the control seat beside him and had my first lesson on how to fly. How my mind raced back to my boyhood days when I built a real flying model of the famous Wright machine and made it actually go up into the air, and now here I was sitting in a huge war bomber. How I enjoyed it! 'Would I like a trip to the Rhine?' 'You bet!' 'Well old man, I'll take you – but keep it quiet. Officially these joyrides are not allowed – but I'll smuggle you through without any trouble. Tomorrow week meet me here and you'll fly to Germany.' Was I not excited? Like a schoolboy all over again.

The day arrives. I'm here and so was my chum, but I knew before he spoke it was all 'napoo'. 'Sorry old bean. Got my demob ticket this morning and I'm finished. Can't touch the old bus any more.' There was sadness in his voice as he looked longingly at the joy of his heart sitting in the sunshine all ready to whirr into the heavens.

UNDERSTANDING

'I understand old man,' I whispered as his feelings were mine. I knew and understood.

We shook hands and said goodbye. The end of my RAF pal. I wonder what this boy turned to in civilian life? Another war friendship ended, but one I never forgot.

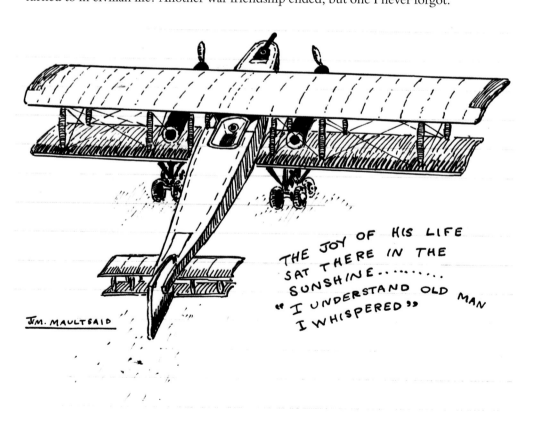

JM. MAULTSAID

THE JOY OF HIS LIFE SAT THERE IN THE SUNSHINE·······... " I UNDERSTAND OLD MAN I WHISPERED "

ROLL ON......
DURATION

RAINBOW HUT
NFND
JULY 9ᵗʰ 1919
ROLL ON DURATION
NPD

SOME OF THE A.S.C. BOY'S
WHO WERE NOT DEMOBBED.
NOTE THE DATE
JULY 9 th 1919.
STILL IN FRANCE.

OUR thoughts were all on the subject of the demobilization. Hundreds and hundreds of times it was discussed and talked about. All kinds of plans and plots hatched by officers and NCOs. Letters from firms at home to demand the immediate release of sergeant; letters from mothers, clergymen, from schoolmasters, aye from sweethearts, asking us to 'please' let him home, all to no avail. The War Office had their plans and they stuck to them.

MINERS FIRST

I remember it was the miners who got first preference. This cleared our company of a few fine fellows as we had many north countrymen on our rolls. Then the land workers came next – not our turn; our return was 'NIL' to this. Railwaymen soon loomed up and we lost some more. Gradually they disappeared; every single old-timer we had to be replaced with a new brand of NCO (Derby's men and NCOs) so we named them. Not much use to anyone and as little use to themselves. No heart for anything and not one in a dozen had heard a single shot fired in the Great War. Poor types indeed of British troops.

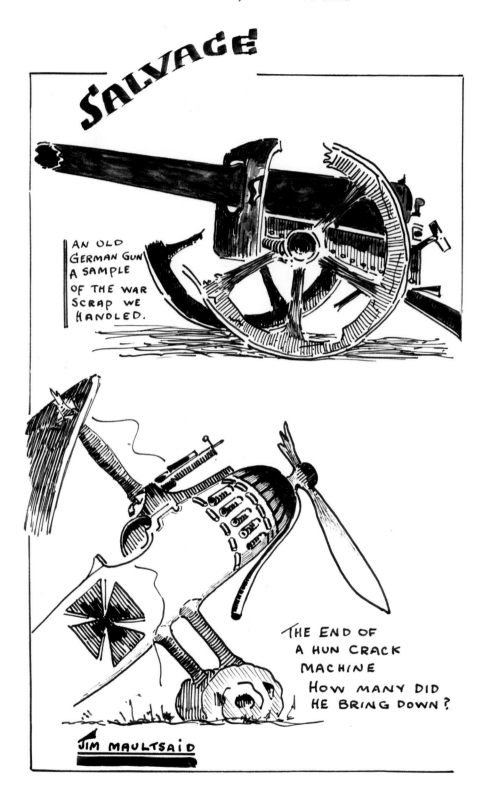

change change change

As for the officers, well, they were going too and being replaced by a brand that were never fitted for this position. At least most of them were not. Everything was change, change, change; and all the time it was getting worse.

MY THOUGHTS

I fretted a lot in these days and lost interest in my work to a great extent, but then made up my mind to stick to it and make the best of it as well as possible. There was nothing else for it.

What about my Job?

Would I get my back? Would my old firm understand that I could not get away from France? Or would my job be filled and no room for me? These thoughts ran through my mind a thousand times. A letter to the War Office brought me no hope. I was 'put', and stay 'put' I had to be. Why the devil was I picked? My records stated I had the longest service in the company. August 1914 – but it meant nothing apparently.

At this time I made up my mind to settle down and pick up the threads of civilian life once more. It would be a terrific task I knew, but the will to do means a lot in life and I was determined to make a new start all over again. Then thoughts of emigrating – or starting out in a new line came along. Yes! Why not? And yet! Home ties were strong and – and – you know the rest. It would be the old home for me again, when I got that length – when –!

Duration? What did this word mean? I thought it meant the last day of war – but oh dear NO.

CAMP LIFE (sometimes) IN 1919 WITH THE C.L.C.

TIME was not such a factor in these days and we did not unduly excite ourselves or the Chinese boys either on their tasks. I spent a great deal of my spare moments in SKETCHING.

It was as good to me as 'firewater' was to my brother officers in trying to drown your sorrows. When sad and longing fits took possession of my soul I sketched and sketched.

TYPES OF SCENE AND CHARACTER IN THE NATIVE THEATRE OF CHINA.

" In China (says a note supplied with these photographs) travelling theatre companies wander from place to place, and give shows where a certain sum can be guaranteed. If there is no permanent stage, a temporary stage is built in the middle of the main street. The theatre usually starts at sunrise and continues all day and all night, and sometimes for a week or more, the actors performing in relays. No seats are provided; the spectators come and go as they feel inclined. Sometimes two stories proceed at once on different parts of the stage, the orchestra doing its best to suit them both. The busiest man during the play is the director, who instructs the actors and explains the plot to the audience. The characters are generally a mandarin, a marriageable damsel and her lover, a soldier, a brigand, an executioner, and a villain. A good story ends with the execution of the villain and the marriage of the lovers. One actor usually represents the soldier, the brigand, and the executioner. The actors are nearly always men, women's parts being played by boys."

ON THE PETROL DEPÔT
LEFT TO RIGHT..........
J.A.B. MAULTSAID   1.
HEAD SANDOW.   2.
2ND SANDOW.   3.
LIEUT LA TOUCHE. 4.
AUGUST 1919.
FRANCE

FOUR OFFICER'S BOYS AND "YOURS TRULY" THE BOY DIRECTLY IN FRONT OF ME IS MINE YOU HAVE READ ABOUT HIM IN SEVERAL OF MY STORIES..........
AUGUST 1919.
FRANCE.

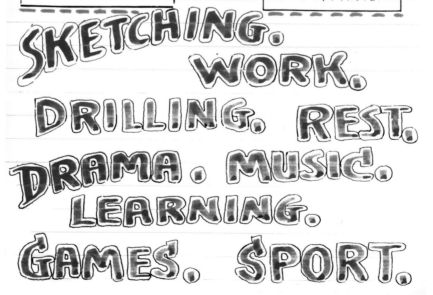

SKETCHING. WORK. DRILLING. REST. DRAMA. MUSIC. LEARNING. GAMES. SPORT.

That's one of the reasons you can now read this book and see my 'thoughts' in black and white.

Some of my old chums thought I was crazy, but far from it: it kept me from harm and harmful exploits; some of these carried out to kill time were of little credit to my chums, so my hobby was worth it all.

WORK and lots of it was still to be done. We were still on the rag picking end of it, dealing with mountains of traffic day and daily. Some very interesting cargos came our way and some very dud ones. As already explained, we handled everything under the sun, sorting out, putting into stacks, separating the good stuff from the rubbish, loading up the barges for England. Our depot was a regular scrapyard miles square.

We got spells down the docks shipping supplies back home. Life flowed past. It was interesting and instructive. Sometimes I felt like stepping on one of the departing cargo steamers and chucking it all but that could not be; I was still too much of a soldier. What would they ever do with all the big guns, all the aeroplanes, all the railway engines, rolling stock etc., etc. that we loaded up? The mind was staggered by it all. Yet we had to get rid of it somehow, as it came in from all the railheads and old battlefronts. Our Chinese companies were up there sending it down to us. Clearing up – cleaning up.

DRILLING the coolies was now a part of our programme. Of course this was always carried out more or less in our lot but now we gave them some fine spells of it. It helped to keep them fit and made them smart as well. They enjoyed it too and soon obtained a surprising degree of efficiency under our instructions. Most of our words of command were in English, some in French, and others in Chinese. Three languages rolled into one – and very effective too! But what an army as Simpson used to say!

DRAMA. Quite a few big stage stunts were carried out this year of grace 1919. We gave them every helpful encouragement as it occupied their minds and assisted us of course to keep things running smoothly. You must not forget that the Chinese boys also wanted home and asked again and again 'when plenty finished?'

These drama days I will not attempt to describe again as I have already given you a full description earlier in the book, but they were grander than ever and lasted several days. As usual, the officers were the guests of honour – ringside seats or boxes. I enjoyed it all. Some wonderful born actors (all so serious and not a smile). The star actors were as a rule the 'dud' workers in real life. They still 'acted' on their jobs? But, joking apart, it was fine.

All the costumes, the props and curtains made by themselves. My artist friend was in his element; this was his life now (a screen painter back in the land of dragons) and he simply excelled himself. Little Titch, Sandow, the acrobats all got a show and all the officers from miles around rated it first-class. Wonderful days!

MUSIC

Fiddles (one-string), trombones and other strange instruments got a run during these celebrations. It was earsplitting having to listen to this night after night getting all 'hetted up' for the big day. But we often cleared out from camp and let them hammer away.

FROM THE BOOK

Some curious musical instruments of torture.

Our newspapers were a source of great interest

I taught them by the aid of a large scale map. How interested they were.

Football

Cricket with home made bats.

Running

SPORTS OF ALL KINDS

East and west did I learn anything?

Then we rested.

BY JIMMAULTSAIO

This is the attempt to make our figures by my boy and the number shewn is his own. He spent hours learning to read and write our language. He was very fond of our newspapers and also my coloured inks and pens.

103701

Whether there was any music in it or not I cannot say, but it pleased the fans and, of course, that was all that was necessary.

LEARNING

A wave of the desire to learn swept through our 169 Company and I personally took a great interest in this. Securing a big map of the world I held a class once or twice a week and tried to teach them of other countries. This was voluntary of course but they turned up in scores to learn. I taught them quite a lot of our language, habits of life, about our machinery, how we build ships and various other things. The big blackboard (homemade) and some chalk came in useful. I sketched and explained. It was astounding how interested they were. Then I passed along all our newspapers, the *Daily Mail*, the *Express* and the *Pink*.[11] Of course the picture section was the main attraction. How they enjoyed it all. And I was the schoolmaster. What next?

GAMES & SPORT

This was my natural outlet and of course I had them 'into it'. Full steam ahead. All kinds of games (Chinese and British) we took part in. Football, rounders, cricket, shuttlecock, running, leapfrog – anything and everything I could think of came into the programme. Quick to learn, it was easy, once demonstrated, and to say they enjoyed it is putting it mildly. Then I offered prizes. The competition was fierce but my word was law and final. Some of my brother officers put me down as crazy. I did not care. It was all fun to me.

WAS THERE ?

Was there a company in all the CLC (100,000 coolies) as well versed and trained as ours? I don't think so! They came to us from the highways of China and went back home well-schooled citizens – first in many of the ways of civilisation and Western learning. No one took a deeper interest in them than me. I know they appreciated it all, as you will see later on in my story, and I was happy teaching them how to make good loyal citizens of their own land, with a very steep leaning to the old country.

I'm sure even to this day we have many, many friends in far-off China. And did I learn anything myself? I certainly did. It was East and West – different points of views and yet much to learn by all of us. When I look back on it all it was the experience of a lifetime crowded into a few short years. Years of joy, years of some sadness, and something that I'll never forget. I looked after these youths like a father and mother rolled into one, but they repaid me a thousand-fold, those boys of 169 Company Chinese Labour Corps in France.

---

11. The *Pink was Ireland's Saturday Night*, a now defunct sports paper and a sister paper of the *Belfast Telegraph*. It closed in 2008 after 114 years.

REPRODUCED

BY JIM MAOLTSAID

I SKETCHED ..... AND ...... SKETCHED.
YOU HAVE THESE PICTURES ....
ALL HERE IN THIS BOOK ....

THE MIND WAS STAGGERED WITH THE
VOLUME OF SCRAP WE HANDLED ....
HERE'S A PICTURE OF OUR DEPÔT ....

E ! ER ! SAN ! SIR ! .....

1 . 2 . 3 . 4 ....

WE DRILLED THEM ......

IN FRENCH, ENGLISH, & CHINESE

THEIR DRAMA WAS
WONDERFUL
SOME BORN ACTORS.

How we all longed for home – 'home, sweet home'. What made it so bad was our chums going each day almost. Then seeing the troop trains passing marked 'BLIGHTY', hearing the yells and the singing; it was hard to bear. I was very discontented indeed and you all know how an Irishman feels when he has a 'grievance'? Day follows day, week follows week, month follows month, and I'm still on Active Service. Somewhere – in – France.

Simpson had been on leave and left me in command. OC Company for a fortnight. Did I worry? I did not! All sailed along grand old style. The wheels went round, the good work was carried out, I did not hustle my troops and they worked like bricks for me. That was good enough for me. Now this gave me a brainwave and I chanced my arm (as per army slang) and put in an application for leave to HQ. Did I get that?

I almost collapsed when the news came through by phone to say I could have ten days all to myself – at home! Hurricane packing, grabbing my leave voucher (sent by special messenger) it was at the double I dashed to the railhead for a train to Calais. No need to describe this journey – it was so like the others, only one very big difference: there was no dark cloud of War away in the background; skies were blue, not black. Everybody was so light-hearted, but I noticed, at every point where my voucher was examined, the looks of surprise when it was noticed that my ticket was marked 'RETURN'.

A night club ....

'Going back – old man?' 'What's wrong?' Etc., etc.: such were the questions the RTO boys fired at me. Dover, London, Heysham, Belfast, all in a line. I'm on the Donegall Quay once more. How fine it feels! The ten days slip away into the past. I'm down at that dirty old Victoria Station once more asking the RTO for one more day in London.

I had looked up an old actor friend of mine from 1917 days at Chelsea Barracks and he had got around me to ask for an extension in my leave and come along to see 'our show'. The RTO captain was in good form (he was far from overworked now with outward passes) and endorsed my ticket for one more day. A seat in the stalls at night, then we all went along to a little place in the Strand (it was underground); supposed to be a nightclub of some sort, but to me a complete washout and I was far from sorry to get a breath of good pure air again.

Of course, it was all kindness on the part of my host and it cost him money in these days, but truth to tell I was sorry I did not go straight back. The 'twadyness', 'the tinsel', 'the veneer' of these night birds sickened me – what a life! Of course it was a novelty – but it did not impress me in the slightest.

Enough!

Back to 169 again. I was actually delighted to see the yellow faces once more. Here at least were honest men. Simple fellows perhaps – but true friends. More faces missing – and some new NCOs. What heart had I left? Very little now. This leave had left me more unhappy than ever – and unsettled to a far greater degree than I had been before it. Still a job to be done and I must do it.

Phew!

Summer days were now upon us. The old dumps of musty clothes, scrap and litter was hard to stand. Even the old canal stank. Everything around us was fusty – enough to drive you into ill health. We sweated, we cursed, and prayed for early deliverance. The smell left by the German prisoners of war still clung to everything around this old camp of theirs. The smell from the Chinese was bad enough, but the Germans? Phew!

Odd days down on the docks were eagerly looked forward to by Chinese and us as well. It was good pure air at least down there. At night we pinched bicycles or got a horse and cleared out miles away from it all. Enough! Enough!

I can smell it yet!

Did he whoop with joy? He was almost in a fit. 'Demobbed, Maultaid! Oh boy, I'm finished – Napoo!' My old heart sank like lead. He was 'all clear'. Although we had our arguments and very often disagreed, deep down I was fond of him, this old pal of mine – Simpson.

English to the backbone in all his ways, he and I were as poles apart but I knew he relied on me to a great extent and I never let him down. His discipline was strict – a good soldier without question; inclined to get fussy and a little excited when we others kept cool but at heart a good fellow – and now I was to lose him for ever. Well I was truly sad to say the least of it and felt as if there was a great blank somewhere.

The handing over business did not interest me very much. Orders from headquarters were to the effect that Lieutenant J.A.B MAULTSAID was to be ACTING CAPTAIN and take over command of 169 Company Chinese Labour Corps. My mind flashed back – away to Finner Camp 1914 – Private Jim Maultsaid – and now A/Capt. How life changes. Yet somehow I felt no great joy. I was pleased of course to advance, but losing old pal Simpson overshadowed it at the moment.

'You'll be good to the boys Maulty? Look after them as I do know you can. Sorry to leave you to it all, – but … .' This, and a great deal more, he said as we checked up his books, his cashbox and papers. I signed his clearance forms 'all correct', he reached me his keys, put the third star on my shoulder (as a joke of course) and we had settled up.

Never did a servant boy have to work as that boy of Simpson's had. He was hustled until the sweat broke from him. Poor soul, he was heartbroken too and was in a trance. He could not yet grasp the fact that 'his own officer' was going away – never to return.

"ALWAYS"

Again the full company of five hundred odd Chinese were mustered on parade, their last time for Captain Simpson. He made a short little speech in Chinese, French and English. Thanked them from his heart for all their great work. Told them he would always remember them. Asked them to keep up their famous record and work hard for Mister Maultsaid. Now he was leaving them forever – and hoped their Gods would take care of them all and bring them all back home safe and well. Farewell!

They bow low – and wonder at it all – why should their officers be taken away? They were visibly affected without a doubt – and takes deep emotion on the part of the Chinese man to make him show outward signs.

He shook hands with all that five hundred. I called them smartly to ATTENTION and gave the order SALUTE! Five hundred yellow hands touched their caps, and I gave mine as well; then we shook hands – a very tight grip. 'So long Maulty.' 'God be with you,' I managed to say. The tears were in my eyes and my throat was dry. He stepped back, saluted us all and so ended his career in the CLC. Dressed in full war kit, he left us; his yellow puttees and his light brown boots still shine in my eyes 'Goodbye Simpson!' 'Goodbye Maulty!' He waves his hand.

FAREWELL C.L.C.

THIS IS THE ORIGINAL SKETCH DRAWN IN FRANCE 1919

FRANCE

Jim Maultsaid 1919

SKETCHED BY HIS OLD CHUM JIM MAULTSAID

He was gifted this little man. Sent out from England representing the Anglo-American Oil Company (I think it was this firm) to take over the stocks of petrol in France, he had a great deal of time on his hands and seemed to spend quite a lot of it in and around our quarters. He was not a soldier but was glad of our company as it was hard to be always speaking French, so he said. Could he talk?

'Gifted', I said above and it is a word that suited him. His pet schemes on how to make money were many and varied. Oil, catering, stocks, transport, mines, gold, lead, silver, everything was a goldmine – to him. We listened and listened. He was plausible. He shared our mess table very often and took very freely to our hospitality and then talked, talked, talked.

I HAD MY DOUBTS

It was bound to have some effect. We fell, about five of us, and each subscribed a £5 note as a token of goodwill I suppose or, as he said, a deposit. The next item on the programme was a leave of 'special business requirements' and off he popped to London. What fun and kidding took place for several days after his departure. All the fivers had gone west; so we all agreed. The business you will be asking? It was a taxi business and he was over fixing the first deal for several cars. They were to cost four or five hundred pounds each. Brand new posh affairs etc., etc. I had my doubts!

Then a bombshell came from the most unlooked for quarter. Friend Simpson sent me a letter to say he had sunk about £100 in this self-same deal (on the quiet) with our little red-haired Londoner, then thought over it and demanded his money back. 'Get out Jim if you have fallen – get out at once. There are thousands of ex-officers running taxis in London and it's a complete washout.' This was a staggerer! We wired him to stop the deal – and return our cash.

"not today thank you"!

He never came back – and it was a long time before we got any kind of satisfaction for our good money. Then we all got a refund in part, it was about £4 each, the balance was deducted for expenses etc., etc. and the terrible slating for backing out. Now he was honest enough and convinced he was on a real good thing, but I was very pleased indeed to get clear of this taxi business. It would have taken us all the rest of our lives trying to pay the costs of them.

So ended our dreams of easy money and the life of a gentleman. The troops then invested in War Saving Certificates at 10 shillings 6d each – all the £4 from each of us – and lifted a load from our shoulders, through – per Cox and Co. (our bankers).

Every time in after life when I was accosted at the railway stations 'TAXI, SIR,' I started! 'Not today – thank you!'

The Last of the Big 5

As already explained, Captain Forrester was attached to headquarters group and we had lost him a long time back. This was a Scotch friend you read about earlier. A finer lad never donned a kilt. Generous to the last degree, he would have given away his last franc. And now? He was demobbed also. Just a flying visit to say his farewell piece, as he said. And this left me, the last of the Big Five in France. All my chums had now gone, leaving me as the one and only officer in 169 Company who took the Chinese in hand way back in '17 as they came down the gangways to face unknown dangers and a strange new world. Well! Well!

CAPT FORRESTER

Captain Forrester would not let me bring the boys on parade for him; he went around their huts one by one and said goodbye to his old yellow friends. His own platoon of course came in for a special leave-taking and he had great difficulty in wrenching himself free from these boys of his. They loved him yet, even after such a long absence. He was on the verge of taking his own boy home to Scotland with him, but I reasoned and pointed out how difficult this would be, also how lonely the little fellow would get in a strange country, so he at last agreed with me. His boy was simply prostrated and begged me to let him go to Scotland with Mister Forrester; but it could not be, we had to drag him away at last. This parting business was getting me down – down in the dumps. It was getting harder and harder to stick it. I felt like deserting, chucking it all. What use was I here anyhow? And yet ... .

303

"HERE HE IS"
"ALL SCOTCH"

"FORRESTER" "PURE" Scotch."

JIM
MAULTSAID
FRANCE
1919.

FROM THE
ORIGINAL
ABOVE.

JIM. MAULTSAID

·······CELEBRATIONS·······

This event was the excuse for a 'do' and of course I had to stand my footing and the celebrations lasted well into the wee small hours. Then we settled down and the 'old firm' sailed along – smoothly and well. The Chinese boys worked like a well-oiled machine and my troubles were small ones.

... SOMETIMES ...

Sometimes I sat back and thought over past events and thought of my old chums Captain Curtain, Lieutenant Simpson, Second lieutenant Tommy Thompson and Second Lieutenant Forrester – now ALL GONE. What a life! 'The Passing Show.'

... A PLEASURE ...

Needless to say I looked after the boys closer than ever and enjoyed it all – it was a real pleasure of course.

... CAPTAIN JAMES ...

In due course my term as OC came to an end and Captain James, a regular and a gentleman, took over. I was Lieutenant Jim Maultsaid again.

"PLENTY BIG OFFICER"

305

MAULTSAID —IN— COMMAND

"old COMPANY."

The command of 169 Company was handed over to me. I did not worry very much at this as by this time I was more or less case hardened and took it as part of the day's work. Orders came along to the effect that I was to hold the rank of acting captain with pay in accordance to rank etc. I was pleased of course to be in full control of all these boys of mine and they – well, they were delighted when the news leaked out. I was 'plenty big captain' then – plenty big!

TAKEN for a WALK !

BY. JIM .MAULTSAID

Swish! A million red lights seared the brain of Private W.........! The ground wobbled, buckled and swayed. His legs sagged at the knees, and almost without a sound his body sank to the ground, meeting the soft sand with a dull plop. Out to the world! Two shadow figures bent down and grasping the still form between them dragged it down a rough passage and, pulling aside the Army blanket that covered the doorway revealing a dugout that you would have found in or around the front line, dumped the body on the floor.

By the light of a candle stuck in the usual bottle neck a strange ritual then took place. The victim was stripped of his greatcoat, jacket, cap and pants, then his boots in quick order. These garments were carefully laid aside and very rough clothing was somehow put on Private W........s' body. Then he was again seized and carried back up the steps to be dumped behind a sand dune some distance away. His still form was brutally kicked as a final precaution by one of the toughs and the two figures slunk back into the mist – back to their hideout.

ALL THE NATIONS

The war was over some months ago, yet strange happenings still took place near the big French seaports almost daily. The British troops were going home in their thousands every day and these ports were seething with all the next troops from our far-flung empire, not to mention the French, Belgians, Americans, Poles, Russians, Italians, Indians, Africans, Chinese, and even lost and strayed German prisoners plus the surplus refugees. Truly an amazing array of humanity.

Big demobilisation camps cleared the various units day in and day out. Mixing with this vast cosmopolitan crowd was a sprinkling of toughs, deserters and men wanted even for murder and many other crimes. Men were posted as 'missing' from their regiments from the front line during the war days and now knew no regiment or unit. Outcasts from society and the friendship of fellow man – hunted like wild beasts with the constant dread and fear of sudden arrest by the military police. Some of these men if cornered would fight and kill again sooner than submit.

OVERFLOWING DRINKING DENS

The bars and drinking dens were overflowing. Thick heavy smoke and a laden atmosphere made it difficult even to see your next-door neighbour. A French automatic piano thumped out an air of some sort but the sound from this was almost overwhelmed by the rough shouts and loud laughter of the half-drunken soldiers who were packed like sardines around the space at the bar and the usual French tables. The clink of glasses and the popping of corks helped to swell the din. The scene was quite a common one in the byways and backways of dockland in the days following the Armistice in 1918.

The close observer would have noted the faces of some of these men, unshaven for weeks. Bloodshot eyes and a haunted look. Untidy uniforms; several had knives or bayonet wounds that in healing had left ugly scars: time is a great healer but these marks would never mend any more. No sergeant major had set eyes on these faces for many, many months. Of that you can be assured, yet here they were in uniform.

A party of three occupied a corner table, two of them rough specimens of British Tommies and the third almost stupid with drink, but a glance would have shown you that he had been neatly turned out earlier in the evening. He was a marked man. A signal passes and the two rough-looking fellows rise up, grasp his arms and all three stagger out through the swing doors, no one taking any particular notice. Seeing him to his camp? Not on your life! Instead of going for a ride as our American gangsters say he was going for a walk! Yes, a walk!

'LEAD SWINGING'

'We met in an estaminet, Sir. You know how it is, Sir!' My new-found friends seem to have lots of francs for drink. We came together as troops will. We told yarns and swapped stories of war fighting days as soldiers will, each of us blowing and 'swinging the lead' good and plenty about our own battalion and division. They stood me lots of drink and gradually I became half stupid until I had very little willpower left. My head burned. I think I was doped, then I find myself walking over the sand. The cold night air and the fog cleared my brain a little, but my companions still stuck to me, one on each side, and kept me moving. Then smash! Oh God! My very skull seemed to cave in. My head! Oh my poor head!

BATTERED AND ROBBED

Private W……… was found some days later wandering on the sand dunes, demented almost, half delirious, badly injured and beaten up. Brought to hospital, he told the story given above after recovering sufficiently to be able to talk. It was an eye-opener to the authorities who knew or suspected that gangs of desperate men were at large but these were put down as being French, Belgian or Chinese. Now here was proof that the 'bad men' were none other than our very own.

All his papers, paybook, travelling vouchers, and his clothing had been stripped from his body, even his watch, money and little keepsakes – cleaned out, then thrown to his fate after being sandbagged and beaten. The light of day filtered through the official mind. These robbers were deserters and formed part of the 'lost legion' who had banded themselves together and, travelling mostly by night, made their way down to the coast stage by stage, stealing, then hiding, robbing with violence and sometimes even murdering their victims. Arrived in the region by the seaports their biggest problem was to get past the embarkation authorities and on board the troopships for home that sailed from Calais or Boulogne.

Deserted sections of the sand dunes were used as hiding places by day, then they ventured into the city at nightfall. Dugouts were made and carefully covered up in the daylight hours and they hid in them, living the life of wanted men. Their plans were made, plots laid and thought out and then the victim was generally picked up in a drinking den, preferably one who was due to sail inside the next day or so. This man's complete identity was then taken over by one of these thugs when the body was safely in the dugout. The necessary details as to unit and battalion were carefully studied from the paybook and stolen papers etc. Don't you see it all?

---and disappear into the BLUE

BRASS NECK TO FREEDOM

A bold face, daring effort, lots of bluff and, of course, the necessary papers and pass-out form would give him a fair chance for a quick getaway to finally land at Dover, and disappear into the blue forever.

THE END

MY WORDS ARE CONFIRMED

Running through my last few stories you will no doubt have noticed an undercurrent of discontent more or less at our lot in being held on 'on army strength'. This feeling was very common in the ranks in 1920. I never really met open revolt, but on several occasions it came very near to it. Why? The main point was this: a man had joined up in 1914 and fought through the war; by some mistake he was still in France in 1920. You say what about that? Well! He stands and sees a very young soldier who has been conscripted in 1918-19 and landed in France as the 'ceasefire' was sounded being sent back home as a very much wanted man (so his papers say). It was enough to make the old soldier's blood cold. And it did! Did he see red? He did! And I did not find fault with his feelings. I had them too, but of course could not voice them to the men as you will no doubt understand.

REBELLION

No wonder they were bitter, as their innermost thoughts were. It was a terrible mistake on the part of the War Office. The old soldiers said these 'rookies' got all the good jobs and nothing but milk left for them. The cream was all gone. Now you get my point of argument? Of course we did not know or dream that some of the troops broke out in the actual revolt. That was all kept very quiet, and yet stray bits of news crept through to us. Rebellion at Dover! Bottomley only man could talk to the boys, etc., etc. Yes! We have got it.

Now, after all the years have passed, and these articles of mine were penned in 1920 (notes from the little book) every word I had written is confirmed up to the hilt by no less an authority than the Right Honourable Winston Churchill himself, fifteen years later, so you can see what I was telling you was all true. Every word this gentleman writes is also true about this matter and I tremble to think of what would have happened if the matter had not been speedily rectified.

OUR RETURN

169 COY C.L.C WILL DISBAND
CAMP AND PROCEED TO
GRAND NEWS !

Grand news indeed. Delighted to get clear away from this depressing spot, we made one of the quickest 'break camp' records on our books. Packing was swift and we took all the shortcuts that experience had taught us. You can study the little black-and-white sketches drawn by me after this march and almost picture the long column spread out by the roadside with your 'humble servant' at the head of affairs.

ORIGINAL SKETCH DRAWN IN FRANCE IN 1919

2 IN—1 OUT

Captain Simpson and I led them in, and here was I leading them out, the last remaining officer of the Big Original Five. Wonderful life! Away from the rubbish heap, and the smells, and disease. It gave us all new heart. Where were we going? Back to camp somewhere near the docks for a spell on the waterfront; that was pure air in store for us at any rate, if nothing else. And I was glad, glad for myself and the coolies too, as they (many of them) were far from well and I was worried a lot; so back to health and happiness.

The march was not a long one by any means and as the summer's day ended we were fairly well established in our new quarters. It was not a Chelsea Barracks by a long stretch, yet what a welcome change. A good hot meal had the boys in fine fettle, then I took a final walk round to see them all; 'plenty sleeper,' good night!

The work indent was before me for the morning's work and I soon had my four platoon officers and sergeants duly detailed for their various jobs. New work more or less this was to us, but nothing came amiss in these strange days, so I worked out my timetable and issued my orders. At dawn we paraded and, marching out at the head of the procession, the early French folk gave us a casual look and passed on. Our job was soon detailed to us by the RE officer and we were left to make the best of it. I noticed he was like all the rest of his tribe and no different from their 1915-16 days. He dried in! Did we worry? Not by a long shot. We knew our trade and carried on.

want a field gun?

All around stretched rows and rows of big guns. Hundreds of tanks, some new, some badly dented from battles of history now. Stacks of machine guns. Long lines of light filled artillery, limbers, GS wagons. Stacks of harness. But why go on? It was war material everywhere as far as the eye could reach and it was all to be loaded up for transhipment home. For scrap!

This stuff cost millions and now was not worth thousands. In fact we would have given you a fine bright sparkling field-gun for the taking away almost. It was all junk. War junk

Second Nature

The methods of loading soon gave little trouble and my boys enjoyed the novelty of hauling a big gun to the crane for hoisting aboard. It was more or less fun for them. They sang in chorus as they worked. This was a Chinese custom but had sound method at the back of it. Each note gave the sign 'altogether', 'pull', or 'ease off'. As the day wore on, the strange work became second nature to the coolies and I was well pleased.

no outsiders

In the course of several days they became experts in the art of loading cargo and it amused me to see all the tricks introduced to make things easier. It amused the RE boys too but they did not unduly interfere, having, I suppose, some previous experience of Chinese labour gangs and leaving the ordering about to my officers and NCOs.

The Chinese did not like outsiders butting in. All instructions had to come from their own leaders. Several times I had to tactfully explain to various majors etc. that any work to be done was to be explained to me and I would be responsible. It did not go down too well on occasions but had to be done to avoid a strike; then gradually these men found we were good workers, knew our work, could carry out their ideas (in our own way) and they left us alone.

The work sailed along. Guns and wagons were piled in. Tanks hauled on deck (these were hard to handle) and stacked side-by-side, and many big cargo boats soon sank to the watermark with the tremendous weight stowed down below. Our boys enjoyed it all and worked right merrily.

DID THEY see china?

Every day that passed brought new looks, new colour, new life to the coolies and the Medical Officer's duties became less and less. It lifted a load from my mind. The sea breezes were better than tons of medicine. This company of mine were all from a district near the sea, Wei-hi-Wei', and this was a touch of the home front for them.

JUNK

Day followed day, and week followed week. It found us still hauling, pushing, levering, jacking and lifting the war junk on board. By this time you would have almost thought we had been on this work all our lives. Adaptable by now, it was all child's play to 169 Company.

THE OLD DISEASE

As I watched the big cargo boats pull out and cast anchor, sometimes it caused me an attack of homesickness and I could see the yellow boys look with a faraway look on their passive faces too. Did they see China? Did they feel as I did? I'm almost certain we all felt the same – but our day had not yet arrived.

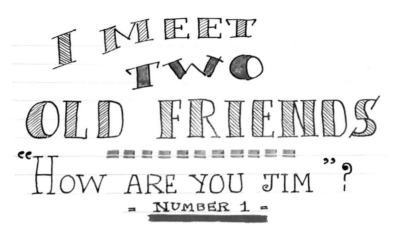

I MEET TWO OLD FRIENDS

"HOW ARE YOU JIM"?

= NUMBER 1 =

I got a surprise to hear a greeting like this at this stage of the Great War operations – and it came from a fine sun-bronzed upright officer leaning out of the railway carriage window. I had to look and look again. Then it flashed through my head, an old friend indeed who had not crossed my path since the days before the war.

Captain Johnston Jordan, from Belfast. The old Royal Irish Rifles badge on his cap. My, it was a treat to see that Harp and Crown. I dashed across the metals and climbed up the steps of the big French railway carriage to shake his hand. Boy! Oh boy! It's grand to meet an old friend these days. 'How goes it?' 'Demobbed?' 'So you got through safe and well old man?' We fired questions at each other like machine-gun bullets.

"HIS STORIES WOULD MAKE A WONDERFUL VOLUME'

314

THE OLD DIVISION

'Can you not jump out and have a few hours with me?' 'Yes! Why not, Jim. After all – the d★★★ war is over and no one cares. I have no troops to trouble me, so here goes.' Bag and baggage out he pops. We stroll out from the station yard and make our way to one of our Salvation Army huts. Sitting down at a little table made from chocolate boxes we had a cup of tea and swapped experiences.

He reviewed the history of the 10th Battalion Royal Irish Rifles (Ulster Division). How proud of his boys he was! And of course I was delighted to hear all the news. The battles! The raids! The misery! And all the rest. I was thrilled again. Good old Ulster Division. 'And you Jim?' My story was a revelation to him. 'The Chinese? What a rare mob, old boy.' He smiled and we both laughed heartily. It's a funny war. Yes! Sometimes.

Time was running short. We slowly made our way back to the dockside and, picking up his old kit (to show how casual we were in those days he had left his kit lying at the platform), we shook hands and I wished him all the best. I stood until the big transport faded out – into the mist.

= NUMBER 2 =

I had met him some years ago in Calais docks and we had developed a fine friendship. Master of several languages, his job was official interpreter for the troops. What his nationality was I cannot say but I think his father had been English and his mother French. A fine combination. I had no sooner turned around, sick at heart from my last view of the troopship, than I was surprised to feel a grip on my arm. Turning sharply we met again face-to-face. 'How are you, Mister Maultsaid?' 'My word old man – is that you? Where have you been all this time?' 'Everywhere. Paris! Le Havre! Dieppe! Ameins! Calais! etc.' 'Beaucoup promenade. And you , Lieutenant?' Confidences were swapped, old times reviewed, and the future discussed.

Nothing would satisfy him until we had a cup of coffee, fried potatoes, etc., etc. in a little French café. How I listened to him, his stories would have made a wonderful volume. He had met all the Allied generals, all the staffs, red caps, brass hats and all. This was a side of war I knew nothing about and of course I was deeply interested. What a book this fellow could write. The hour is late and it strikes me I have neglected my business today – but this did not worry me overmuch as my lieutenants could do some worrying now; it would do them good.

LIFE IS STRANGE

Midnight, almost, finds us saying goodnight outside his digs with the promise to meet again, but strange to say that meeting did not take place until three years later when I paid a return visit to the battlefields of France and Belgium in the summer of 1923. Life is strange! He was the first man I met on foreign soil. What a meeting!

My boy was almost frantic when I did not return with the squads, and no one could tell him anything. He thought I was drowned, or had gone home and left them all. How his eyes brightened up to see me again. Wonderful to have someone to worry about you like this! He was a loyal devoted kid – to his own officer.

Meeting these two old chums this day was a blessing to me and lifted my heart tremendously – like a drink of clear spring water out in the desert and yet it left me with a restless mind – a feeling that I could not explain. But I suppose it was war weariness and the desire to get clear of it all.

By this time almost all the troops were out of France, and I had watched the best part of them go – or so I imagined. Days followed each other down the quays and the troops sailed away in thousands, in great glee. Back to the homeland! But that was some months ago and now the rush was over. Old soldiers had all disappeared; they always do, somehow. Little odd parties drifted down from the lines somewhere – small details of RE or perhaps Ordnance Corps men.

Gradually, before our very eyes, the British army had 'faded away' and can you believe it I was now getting lonely, missing all the stir, all the hustle, all the boys in khaki, waves of that 'forsaken feeling' swept through me. We seemed to be the last of a mighty host. I had come in with the tide myself. The tide had gone out – and I felt as if I was left on the rocks, forgotten!

NOT QUITE ....

Would there be a boat left to take us home? Believe me reader when I say I felt downright lonely. It was the continual chatter-chatter in French and Belgian that got me down. Then I remembered our boys up on the Rhine and consoled myself with the thought: *'we are not just the last yet.'*

We were now practically our own masters and red tape was more or less absent. Of course our headquarters still held sway and controlled our movements, but did not unduly trouble us.

Still we slogged on at the loading up of war material. The dumps and stacks never seemed to get any smaller no matter how much we shoved down the holds, and yet it did grow less and less. The Chinese boys got weary themselves and so did we. Then the story got around that some of the Chinese Labour Companies had gone home, others were going, etc., etc. This did not help us much to be sure, but what could we do? Carry on! And we did!

BACK EAST WHISPERS BECAME REALITY!

They were going! Some had gone! At last the CLC had made a move. Back to China. As all the troops had now been returned to civilian life, except those who had volunteered to stay on at war graves work or other duties the transport department had found the necessary tonnage available to take the Chinese back home. Companies had disappeared almost overnight. Officers we had known came to bid us farewell, and then sailed away. Some of them went back with their charges but most of them did not. This looked good at last; but I was fated to spend many, many more weary months out here before my turn came.

318

a trip declined

I was asked to volunteer to take a trip to China to deliver my 169 Company back in Wei-hi-Wei, but declined the offer. I had been out here quite long enough; this would have at least meant another six months and I was hoping to get free any day. Of course, I wanted my work back and did not want to lose any time but, if I had only known then, I might as well have volunteered for China as I had to serve some six months longer roughly from this time, so the trip would have made very little difference after all. But we do not, or cannot, foresee all these things in this world. Anyhow, no China for me. I did not mention this to Mr Woo or any of our officer boys as they had a kind of an idea that I was taking them all back home, and I did not want to disappoint them – not just yet.

This time was rather difficult as the coolies now felt they should be going as well as their other brothers but I think it helped a great deal to see me still with them and I often talked to them in this strain. Peacefully quiet talk to keep them in good humour and get the work done.

HEARTBREAK!

On this work of salvage it almost broke my heart to see the waste. The wastage of war! Picture to yourself 'dumps' that stretched over many square miles of French soil and these contained everything from a needle to an anchor, almost! It was the big stacks of boxes containing tinned meat, tinned biscuits, tinned milk, tinned jam that worried me most. Then the stacks of hay, the hospital equipment, the blankets, sheets, stretchers, tents, and all the million and one articles pertaining to the upkeep of a huge army. Here it was – nearly all going to rot and ruin as we could not get it removed. Guards were placed to protect it of course but the guards were scarce and I'm afraid much pilfering took place.

We should have sold out to the French and Belgians lock, stock and barrel and cleared out as the Americans did. Even at tremendous loss we would have saved millions; but no, it was muddle! Muddle, muddle at home. I was on the verge of dropping into the London office of the *Daily Mail* or *Daily Sketch* and telling the truth when on leave – but I kept quiet.

About this time a circular reached us from the war office asking for volunteers for the Gold Coast. I took it the job would be in charge of the native police or black troops, a kind of District Inspector you would class it. I gave the proposition due consideration, but turned it down. Nothing doing! The home front would do me now. I had had enough of these wildcat ventures. You would be made use of so long as you were useful, but once this phase passed over, it would be 'get out now we have finished with you,' and then you were at a loose end, up in the air for a job! This is how I looked at it, and I did not make any mistake. I don't know if they got any volunteers, but I suppose as usual quite a few of the boys will be out for more adventure.

no Gold coast

The next stunt was the Indian Army. If we got a circular in this case I don't remember seeing but it was certainly a strong rumour and appeared to be quite genuine. Of course I thought of this too – and again I said NO to myself. Only too well I knew as soon our Regular Army would revert to all their old time pomp, style, appearance, upkeep etc., etc. It would take a small fortune to live as an officer in India. Your pay would not meet the mess bill even. I was having none of this business. Active service was my life – not regimental 'dope'.

Did any of the boys go? I cannot say. So no Gold Coast or India for me. Of course, we "kidded" each other in great style about it all but it was all only talk and nothing more. If it did not do anything else for us it gave us food for gossip and was a relief from Chinese, dumps, cargos and garlic.

"SPARE LIEUTENANTS."

Some months after the war was over I began to notice quite a few, in fact a great many, young officers 'floating around' and when you see officers from various regiments you naturally expect their own particular battalion to be somewhere in the offing. But no, they appeared to be somehow 'semi-detached' as it were. Who were they – and what did it mean? And it was mostly at night they appeared on the streets of the large French seaports. Do not misunderstand me. These boys were doing no harm to talk about and were never in any hurry – just making the most of things and having a bit of a spree.

DID NOT WANT TO GO

Eventually one of them confessed to me. They were supposed to report at a certain point for demobilisation, but did not trouble to do so – just took a different route and 'disappeared' or, in Army slang, 'dried in' – and strange to say still remained on the payroll through their bankers (Cox & Co.) Can you beat it? Of course the boys, as good soldiers, eventually did report.

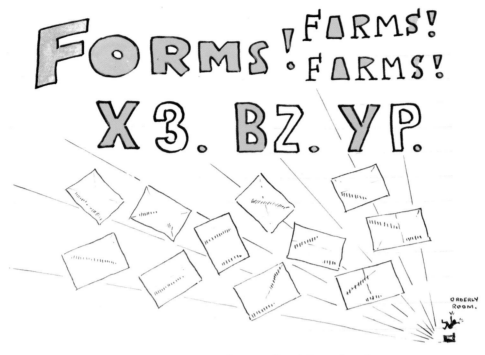

It was bewildering! It was enough to make you dizzy! Day after day new requests, new questions. How many? How much? When? Where? Have you? Did your company? Strength of coolies? White NCOs. Ages? Any deaths? Any? Any? Any? I could have employed a staff of clerks to cope with it all. My Quartermaster and his assistant had their hands full, and so had I in checking and signing all this stuff. This was all apart from the usual daily labour returns, reports and special forms.

It was bad in the days of war, but now a thousand times worse. What the devil half of them were wanted for baffled me. Making work for someone I suppose. I gave my platoon commanders all a turn in the orderly room, it was experience for them, and truth to tell it was an excuse on my part to get clear away, out to the works and good fresh air. Necessity only kept me in the OR. I never fancied this department.

streams of them

Our health return was now a real pleasure to make out. The general health had improved in fine style and was now back to the best 169 standard, thanks to the sea breezes and our new camp. Summer days and sunshine completed the good work. The MO grew fatter and fatter. Disease and sickness had all gone; it was a clean bill for good health and happiness in the summer of 1919. I was delighted.

This stream of buff slips never ceased all this summer. I was fed up with them and sometimes met them in my very sleep. A3, CZ, M6, H7, N4, YXZ, FORMS! FORMS! And FORMS AGAIN!

The Boys in Blue

I cannot bring my history to an end without a word about our 'boys in blue'. Every time I crossed the ocean it was in their care. How I watched the destroyer sneaking alongside our transport, cutting wide circles around us, watching, guarding, and mothering us, the 'landlubbers'. How proud I was of our wonderful Navy. Somehow I feel they never got half the praise they should have for all their magnificent work.

Not a single soldier was ever lost on the cross-channel route from England and France, not to mention the millions of troops escorted from all ends of the Earth. Night and day, duties were carried out in all kinds of weather, with very few of the big headlines in the newspapers and little of the limelight. Hats off to our Jack Tars. The best in the world.

SCROUNGING
—FOR CASH.——

Stores and dumps were everywhere. Valued at millions of pounds the only protection many of these terrific dumps had was a barbed-wire fence built around them that would have kept out no-one with intent on robbery. Of course we had armed guards on duty day and night, yet the goods simply 'walked' at an alarming pace and no trace could be found or no clue as to how it always happened. Personally my duties did not cover this department to any great extent but I came into close contact with it and formed my opinion on the matter and you will be surprised at my deductions. I suspected that some of my brother officers (not the boys in the Chinese Labour Corps) were in league with French and Belgian interests and were selling our stores for personal gain.

Now I also suspected some of our stores quartermasters, sergeants etc. were also in the swim. If they had given the stuff (foodstuffs) away to the starving civilians I could have forgiven them, but selling it! Yet it happened.

This was one of the 'hottest' corners I had found myself in for many years back. Out for a walk one night an ASC[12] private who knew me by sight gave me the warning that a small war had started in the cafe Rue-L -- ---- down near the docks and he thought some of my NCOs were mixed up in it. I broke into a trot and soon arrived at the corner of the street about fifty yards from this cafe. Pulling up for a few seconds I drew my six-shooter and rammed home six good bullets – in case; well I knew it was a bad grip and was taking no chances.

Here goes! A minute later I had reached the door and, gun-first, was pushing my way in. A dark-looking gentleman tried to stop me but, ramming the muzzle into his mid-section rather violently, he fell backwards more scared than hurt.

---

12. Army Service Corps. The ASC was awarded the prefix 'Royal' in 1918.

WHAT A PICTURE!

A long passage corridor was in front of me and the din coming from the end of it was terrific. No doubt about it – the 'war' was on alright. Several figures shot past at great speed. I did not pay much heed – I wanted to get to the heart of affairs.

A painted girl staggered into my path with blood streaming down her face and upper part of her body which was more or less in the undress stage. She was yelling like someone demented. What a picture! It was not pleasant. Curses! Screams of agony! Thudding blows! Bodies locked in death grips. All sorts and colours of men seemed to be involved. I found myself in the thick of it.

A solitary gas bracket lit up this grisly scene. The big central light had already been smashed to atoms. A lousy tout that I took to be a Belgian seaman made a kick at me but by good fortune I caught the movement in the nick of time and jumping aside drove my heavy field-boot into his stomach. He went down like a log!

On the matter and you will be surprised

TWO DOWN.......

My good Irish blood aflame, it was a case of 'to hell' with the 'afterwards' – here goes! Several boys in khaki seemed to be up against it, surrounded by half a dozen opponents of what nationality I could not fathom as the light was bad. Taking my gun by the muzzle to use as a club I sprang to their assistance. To this day I cannot exactly remember what happened and to this hour I'm sure those gentlemen still wonder where the 'whirlwind' came from. I simply sprang into the fray from the rear and slashed right and left. It was a shambles. Smash! Thud! Thud! Two of them were down. An undersized West African turned snarling at me while at the same time trying to draw a knife. Did I hesitate? No Sir!

Quick as a flash I shot out a right-hand punch, all my body behind it and caught him fair and square on the nose. Red hot pain shot up my arm, I thought my hand was smashed, he staggered back and I launched a powerful kick that caught his elbow and the crack was like a rifle shot. Poleaxed, he tumbled like a shot rabbit.

The British boys had now recovered their wind and crowded to my aid. It now dawned on me that not a single one of my own bright lads were in this affray at all – but no matter these were British troops and that was sufficient for me. 'Run for it boys,' I yelled, 'Run like merry hell, I'll cover your retreat.' As they dashed to the door I levelled my gun and shouted 'I'll b★★★★★ well drill the first man that moves a finger.' Backing slowly out I covered their retreat.

Crash! I'm down! Tripping over a body I fell backwards and at the same moment my gun flashed. A red flame, the smell of burnt powder and, believe it or not, that bullet ripped the solitary gas jet right out of its socket.

All is darkness. Scrambling up, I rush for the corridor and fate guided my footsteps. Now for a final dash. I bumped into several forms and imagined they were my friends the Tommies coming to my help again – so I shouted, 'For C★★★★★★ sake run boys!' 'Right, Sir!' We all rushed in a solid mass, crashed through the front door and found ourselves in a heap on the pavement. Good fresh air again. Did I stop to make any explanations? I did not.

we Beat it..........
Retreat

Picking our bodies up at a speed that was incredible we beat it up the dark street, down several more streets of the same brand and 'faded out' into the night air. I wanted no talk with the troops and gave them the slip. I'm sure they wanted none with me, so this was the easiest way out.

..........silence........

Quietly I slipped into camp. It was now about 2.00 in the morning. Dead tired, I lit a candle in my sleeping quarters and by the aid of a little piece of mirror was more or less startled to see my own face all covered with blood. 'Where the name of Jerusalem was I cut?' A wash convinced me that it was not my own good red blood, but someone else's. But Lord! How my head and body ached. Oh! oh! It was painful. Still I had indeed got off lightly and congratulated myself. Would I tell my brother officers about this adventure? No! Detesting all forms of enquiry or investigation, I made up my mind to let sleeping dogs lie. This is the story of that 'adventure' told for the first time. WHAT A NIGHT!

PETROL AGAIN

Back to our old love once more. Back to the petrol boxes and the oils. Our Army on the Rhine and on the lines of communication up to Germany through France and Belgium had run short of stock so we, 169 Company CLC had to replenish the dumps and railhead depots once more. It was like a page from past history somehow when we marched back to the scenes of our former triumphs and sorrows. Nevertheless, I knew and felt a wave of happiness sweep through the coolies. It was their true life. There would be little or no trouble now and it would keep them at ease, this return to the petrol job. I was still in command, of course, but my worries and small 'brothers' sat very lightly on my young shoulders.

LIEUTENANT LA TOUCHE

The petrol dump was now only a mere shadow of its former self. My old No.2 outfit was the one and only one left. All the other three had disappeared completely. Just the railway tracks left.

DUBLIN

The cargos were small, mere flea bites. Hundreds now where it used to be thousands, so you see we were far from being overworked. The work was carried out quietly, easily, efficiently and smoothly. Not the slightest cause for any worry. Half days for the coolies each week, sometimes two and three in the one week gave them time for a rest, for fun and walking-out passes.

I encouraged this for good work and good behaviour and was more than repaid. Lieutenant La Touche whose picture you can see standing beside me on the photograph in the story 'Camp Life in the CLC, I made my second in command. He claimed family ties with the City of Dublin dating back for hundreds and hundreds of years. This I could not verify of course but a more eager youngster to try and learn his work and do his very best I never met.[13]

"PLENTY MUCH" LITTLE CHILD!

A very likeable lad indeed, and of very fine breeding. How he loved to get me to tell the stories of my war days. My experiences, my escapes, battalion history and the tales of my bombing squads. He had not fought himself as he was far too young but I knew he envied me in his heart. And the tales of his 169 boys! Their magnificent work carried out in the hectic days before November 1918 simply thrilled him.

The life story of 'Tommy' Thompson was repeated to him a dozen times over. How his eyes grew bigger and bigger as he drank it all in. Did he ever write a book on it all? I would not be surprised if he had. And he spent hours looking over my numerous sketches and drawings books. A real little gentleman was Second Lieutenant La Touche, and the Chinese boys grew to love him too! So they told me, but added 'plenty much small child'; so there you are. My, those yellow boys could weigh you up to very last ounce. Readers of character – and seldom erred.

Life flowed on – on the petrol depot.

Lieutenant La Touche

---

13. Lieutenant La Touche's claim was correct. His family had produced many distinguished individuals, including soldiers.

CAPTAIN JAMES

Without warning he turned up, and took over the command of 169 from me. A regular officer who had to be placed somehow by the War Office, he was sent to take charge of my lot. A very nice officer; indeed it was a real pleasure to hand the reins of office to him and I had absolutely no regrets. Easy-going, he did not in any way excite himself, but for all that was a good soldier and knew his work. Furthermore he left all the details to me and did not on any occasion question any decision I made and signed the forms without a second glance. I never let him down in any way and he always stood loyally by me. What more can I say about a superior officer?

DID I MISS ....?

Always smiling, he looked on life as a joke. And again he took on with the Chinese; they liked him too. A dealer in some kind of Japanese fancy goods, he had had experience of Eastern people and understood their ways. What strange people I was now meeting. All kinds and manner of men. He still had a firm and his partner carried on the business in London. This was all explained to me in detail and would you believe that he wanted to make me a partner too! As I never did fancy the Japanese a great deal, I did not take up the proposition in thought or deed. Perhaps again I missed the boat? And perhaps not.

He had been out East a great deal and it was my turn to be deeply interested in his stories of travel and more adventure in foreign lands. Why did I not take a note of it all for future reference? What a book a real author could have put together in these days. His command of the Japanese language was fluent but he kept this to himself when dealing with the Chinese.

A GENTLEMAN

The thought of getting clear now grew stronger in my breast. Here was a good man in command, one who knew and understood the Eastern mind. My chance had surely come at last. But no. Not just yet. A visit to group headquarters brought me no nearer my ambition. Still too valuable to the CLC, so they said. And Captain James put no bones in it when he bluntly said he still required my services very much. I again gave up in despair.

LOYALTY

Under the command of our new 'Skipper' the company ran like clockwork. I was his understudy in name only; he treated me as his equal in every way. It was a pleasure to work under such an officer. He always had a word of praise for you. 'Well done Maultsaid!' 'Splendid old man!' Such were his expressions. I give him my full loyalty and did not slack a minute on any piece of work on hand. I was really glad to get clear of the orderly room detail, the Quartermaster and all that department! My heart was on 'the works' and I loved to be mixed up in the practical end of it.

Reflections

The summer was passing away and we were entering another winter. During these days I had time to 'reflect' on the years that had gone, and think of the ones to come. A great deal of my thoughts were taken up by this very book you have read. My original idea was something in the form of the scrapbook as I had hundreds of sketches on hand and wanted to paste them all in a book to keep and treasure in the years ahead.

Then my notes were numerous. These had to be all put against the little pictures; the job was a big one, but as life was still uncertain I put off the start of this self-imposed task until I was clear of Army life and had the opportunity of doing it properly. Of course I did do a big bit of spadework, planning and plotting the general layout of the work, so this book was born in 1919.

CAVALCADE of the CENTURY 1914. 1919. PASSED BY

worked, we loafed, we chatted, we made trips, we longed for home, we killed time, we watched the last remnants of a mighty army gradually fade away before our very eyes. We helped the destitute French and Belgian people in many ways to pick up the threads of life once more. We had helped to make history and were now unmaking it. We had handled all the machines of war and then disposed of them as scrap. We watched all the refugee soldiers, prisoners of war, lost and strayed, scrambling for the home stretch. In fact we had witnessed the 'Cavalcade of a Century' passing before our vision. And 1919 is drawing to a close.

The war was almost a year over. Here I was still in France. Can't you understand why I was unsettled? I'm sure you can! France itself had changed a great deal.

How DREARY

How dreary it all was. The troops all gone, the English voice seldom heard, all was foreign. A strange, very strange country indeed, outside the towns and villages. We missed the boys, the troops on the march, the sound of music. Oh, it was so different, and yet we soldiered on – duration! What did this mean? Every man-jack of my original bunch, officers and NCOs had all disappeared into the mists of time – all gone. Strangers all around me, good enough fellows in their own way but shades of the 'old-timers' kept looming up, often with startling suddenness, or so I sometimes thought in the long winter evenings.

Their voices, their very presence sometimes startled me: Simpson! Curtain! Forrester! Little wonder I sketched, wrote up my notes and more or less kept myself to myself. My Chinese boys came closer to me than ever; somehow I loved them more than ever and they understood my moods, as no white man did, and these youths also yearned for far-off China. I tried to ease their pain and ease my own as well – the pain of homesickness.

Not Good for me

Applications for demobilisation simply poured in to HQ from me, but all to no purpose: I was a fixture. I was now downright anxious about my position in the commercial world at home; we heard many stories of non-success, others of good jobs for the boys, and I did not know what to think but thought I would be left out in the cold in the scramble to earn a living when I did get back.

News from Simpson: he had got his job back and settled down now, in mufti. How strange he felt and all at sea. Thompson wrote from Canada; yes he was back at work once more. These letters did not do me any good but I sure was pleased to hear from them. Captain Curtain (now Major) back in the mines in South Africa. Would I not come out? He had a job for me! Forrester had never got the length of Scotland yet. He was held up in London. Why? I suspected a fair charmer, or perhaps business? Anyhow, all my old chums wrote me at least one letter and I was pleased to know they had at least attempted to settle down, as I had my secret doubts about some of them ever getting this length after four and a half years in this mad world.

Did time mean anything?

And 169 CLC? Still at it. Day after day. Here, there and everywhere. Loading up for the Rhine, taking up railways, Jack of all trades, and fairly proficient in most of them. Semi-skilled labour now and cheap. Yes! It was a grand brainwave on somebody's part to send the Chinese to France. Removals, flittings, shift camp were all in the day's routine. We worried about nothing in these days; it was all part of our life and accepted as such. At times I travelled far from camp. Little tours of inspection. Out into the country. Into the towns. Back to the war-scarred battlefields, and always my little sketchpad.

September, October, November 1919. We were encouraged to travel in these days. Trips to Paris for almost nothing. I did not go there, as I had little desire to see the gay city. Amiens, Ostende, etc., etc. was more to my liking and I took advantage of these opportunities, but with it all the pain in my heart still lingered.

Duration! What did this term really mean? Was it a lifetime? Was it any set time? Or did time mean anything?

AT the end of the road! A time of great uncertainty! The crossroads of life!

Readers, you can picture our young minds. Young boys when we joined up, now some five years older as age goes, but men and far beyond our age in life and its many complex problems – yet filled with great doubt and uncertainty as to what, or where, we should turn to start all over again. It was a real problem.

On top of all this, we had been used to the free and open spaces. Now it was back to the office, the workshop, the counter, or maybe back to nothing at all. Which way would

334

we turn? Canada was calling some, the USA appealed to others and our far-flung colonies were considered. Then again many of us had sweethearts who had waited and prayed for our safe return and the fulfilment of all our 'sweet nothings' that had been whispered on our leaves – so our minds were working overtime on all these matters.

We were now at the crossroads of life, looking at our new world from a new angle, and a world that somehow did not altogether want us. Most of the boys were more or less handicapped with wounds and various disabilities that would go hard in this civilian world. We had served our purpose and now these things can be so easily forgotten. 'It's Tommy this and Tommy that … when the guns begin to shoot' but when it's all over and the danger passed – well, that's a different matter. I made up my mind to grasp the threads of life firmly again. The first year was the hardest struggle of my life but I won through.

'To be demobbed as from ….' I read this brief notice several times before it dawned on me that my 'Day' had really dawned. At last! At last! Waves of great delight passed through my body. After all these years! Clear now. Finish-a-la! Then sadness came over me to think that it really meant parting from the staunch yellow boys who had worked so hard for 'their officer'. Everything must come to an end someday – and this was the very end of my Army career: 1914-1919.

It all passed before me in a flash. And now – goodbye to all that. This was the grand dismiss!

Captain James shook hands and congratulated me on my good fortune. 'Can I pack and clear out now, Sir?' 'Sure, Maultsaid – right now.' Hurried orders brought a scared boy to my side and the little soul knew there was something seriously wrong. 'Cheer up my buddy and pack your officer's kit – at once.'

FINISH-A-LA!

'Everything is finish-a-la! Your officer's going home.' The tears rolled down his cheeks and he could not speak. Turning away from me he dashed for the compound, yelling at the top of his voice: 'Mister Moorside finish-a-la! Finish-qua-qui!'

'San gowdy Officer going home.' In a few seconds hundreds had swarmed out in all sorts of dress and undress. Excited talk, looks of blank and utter amazement. 'Are you leaving, officer? Don't go. You please – stay with us.' Yellow faces, to me, had taken a lighter shade, and my head ganger had great trouble keeping them from mobbing me. I said a few simple words and told them to come out on parade in an hour's time and I would say farewell. Reluctantly they turned away. I went indoors.

It took threats almost to make my boy start packing. This was the first time he was ever disobedient and I pitied the kid. 'Will you take me, Mister Moorside? Please take me home with you. I'm going with you. Would you take me?' 'No! Sonny boy – I can't. Your mamma and dadda want you back home and would call me "plenty stealer".' But I thought it might be a hard task getting rid of him.

My mind was dazed. All my brother Officers crowded in to lend a hand in the packing. Regnets were numerous, expressions of downright goodwill very frequent and somehow a lump was in my throat. This parting business was h★★★, sad to go and leave them all – but such was a soldier's life in these days. Here today – tomorrow! Gone forever.

The head cook put his head in at the old canvas door and said he had a finish-a-la lunch spread out for us. Let's forget this part, readers. Speeches, compliments. I stood my last round of drinks (mine was a lemon soda). 'Long may One Six Nine live in our lives and memory. Long….' We clasped hands and sang 'Auld Lang Syne'. Goodbye. Goodbye. Five hundred yellow faces formed up in a big circle as I walked to the centre in full fighting war kit and took my stand at the trestle table spread over with a banner of some sort. *What's this*, I wondered? *What now?* Dead silence as I pulled myself together and tried to speak.

'Boys of One Six Nine Company … the best in France. Today I leave you with sorrow and sadness in my heart. I'm going back home … my work is finished. Big officer in London told me I must now leave you all. Before I go I want to thank you … for such glorious work … you helped to win the war. You never once failed me.' My throat is dry but I struggle on, slowly, in my own language mostly and little bits of Chinese. Mister Woo repeats it word for word but little real necessity for this; they understood me without his assistance.

'I'll take back with me a love for the Chinese people that will never fade from my heart until I reach my Great-Great-Grandfathers in the "Land of Many Shadows". I have loved you always, as a father, and try to give and get you a square deal in a strange land many thousands of miles from your own country. Sometimes I had to correct you (a few faint smiles here) for your own good. When you get back to Wei-hi-Wei in a few short weeks, be sure and remember your gallant brothers who died in France. They died for One Six Nine Company, and helped to save civilisation just as much as our own soldiers did. They now sleep their last long sleep in honoured graves.'

TELL YOUR FATHER'S

'I would counsel you to watch your hard-earned savings. Do not spend it in gambling or foolish ways. You will need every franc of it in your old age. Tell your fathers, your mothers, your brothers, and your sweethearts all about the wonderful times you had in France. And put in a kind word for me in case I should ever have to go to your land to earn my living.

Never forget our Great King and his people are now, and always have been, the friends of China. We shall always try to help your country. Let me say I never want to meet men of higher honesty, fair dealing, just staunch and true. The regard to the Chinese boy is deep and profound. In conclusion,. I'll never forget the One Six Nine Company of glorious, wonderful boys. I salute you – One and ALL.'

MOST WONDERFUL

Five hundred bodies bowed from the waist downwards in true Oriental fashion. Silence – deep and tense. The father of the flock as spokesman steps forward. He speaks for 169 Company. Mr Woo repeats it very slowly in English. Here it is word for word as written in the book next day.

'Most wonderful officer, how we worship you. A father to us in all our sorrows, we humble ourselves in your presence, we bow low indeed. Our hearts bleed with much sadness at your going away but we speed you on your journey wishing you well and many, many, many, many showers of blessings fall on you. An officer of very much knowledge and learning, you taught us many things. There is not a boy here today who would not lay down his life for you if you so commanded. Our judgement of you was "Ding-Ding-Hola". Good to work for. A bargain was a bargain always with you. Your love and care for us was as deep as the mighty ocean… Your foresight treasure in all our hearts. Your great English king had no officers in his service to compare with you.'

MY REWARD

'Always will our land be free to you. As this great honour has been thrust upon me, allow me to place in your hands a keepsake of our happy days, this banner (he unfolds a large banner in several sections and reaches it to me) has been held by us until this hour should strike. Every boy in One Six Nine has put a stitch of love in it. Yes, everyone, with much love, all for his officer.' My heart is filled to overflowing at this unique gift. A bowl of clear spring water stands on the table. He sprinkles some on the banner, dips his fingers in it (for purity, Chinese fashion). 'Farewell! Farewell! May the Gods care for you, and keep you.'

He salutes. Five hundred Chinese boys bend low. Can I ever forget? No! No! No!

Goodbye to 169 Company CLC.

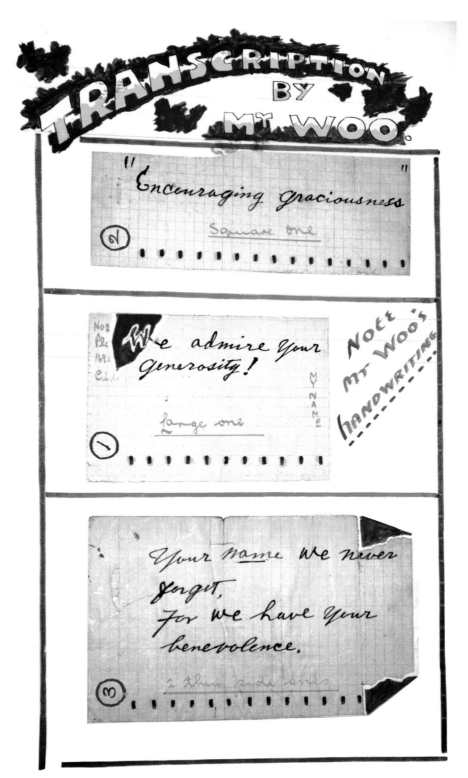

Did I merit all these quaint compliments? Be as it may, my method was to treat them as very honourable gentlemen always; and I can truthfully say never was I once let down and you must remember we were often in some very tight corners: only that loyalty to their officer pulled us through.

The banner is a work of Chinese art and each boy in the company, some five hundred strong, put a stitch in it – 'a stitch of love' – for ME.

It was a wonderful tribute indeed that I should have been chosen for this supreme mark of affection – marked out for special honour from all my brother officers. You will no doubt pardon my feelings of pride; my heart was filled with overflowing and great joy. What a keepsake? And a reminder of those glorious days spent with my Chinese boys on the Western Front, now fading into the realms of long-forgotten things, yet to me imprinted on my memory until the day comes that old soldiers sing about when my turn comes to 'Fade Away'.

JIM MAULTSAID

"THE END."

ORIGINAL
PICTURE
REDRAWN

JIM MAULTSAID
— 1920 —

PUFF!
PUFF!
PUFF!
MY LAST
WAR DAYS
JOURNEY
IN THE
LAND OF
SORROW
COMMENCES

SKETCHED
– BY –
JIM MAULTSAID

READ
the
STORY
"The End"

MY OWN BOY
IS the
LEADER
OF THIS MADNESS.

FROM
MY
NOTE
BOOK

— RE-DRAWN — BY. JM MAULTSAID
— 1920 —

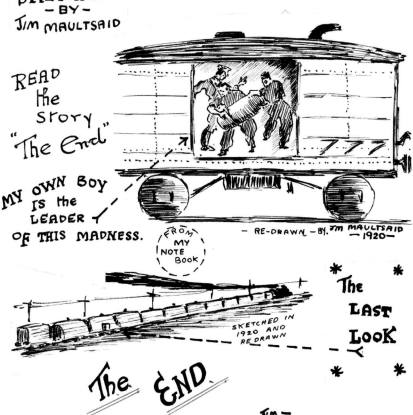

SKETCHED IN
1920 AND
REDRAWN

* The *
LAST
LOOK
*   *

The END.

JIM —
MAULTSAID
— 1920 —

The engine gives a shrill blast. Puff! Puff! Puff! My last war journey in the land of sorrow commences. As the long train gets under steam, I stand at the open door of a big open goods truck (still no carriage is available), my kit on the floor beside me. The last occupants must have been horses – my smelling sense tells me this. Lined up beside the track is every coolie of 169 Company.

Five hundred of them, all yellow solemn faces showing traces of the sadness in their usually placid countenances. Hands wave greetings. My own platoon start running beside the footboard. How childlike, how simple-minded they are, only children yet. Several catch up, clamber aboard. My own boy is the leader of this madness. I fear a serious accident and shout a warning that is ignored or not heard. My God! What's to happen now!? Desperately I reason, I curse, in Chinese, in English. It's all no use.

Into the truck several of them swarm and, grasping my kit hurl it from the truck. Heavens above, this is serious. Don't you see that idea at the back of it all? My kit outside and I must get out too. Therefore they will get me back. Simple fellows; they reason it like this. Frantically, I lean out from the door and wave a white handkerchief to the driver almost one hundred yards away.

The train is gathering speed. I sweat blood. What a mess! Would the driver see my signals? Bump! Bump! Bump! The usual French quick-time braking methods are brought into action and I'm almost thrown out on my head.

We pull up – slowly at first then to a dead stop. I'm speechless and unable to curse these boys of mine, some four in number. I stare at them. They blush and look downcast. Excited French voices outside jerk me back to reality again. The guard and his assistant clamber up and proceed to hustle these yellow laddies off in no ceremonious manner, cursing and swearing all the while.

My thoughts

Mad English, mad Chinese. We were all mad, then, noting my rank, they calmed a little and I tried to explain by signs and broken French my predicament. Compelled under force and by dire threats of violence, my bright young men had to double back alongside the track to recover my old kit, carry it back to the truck, hoist it aboard for the second time that day and then jump clear. Puff! Puff! Puff! Puff! Tut – tut – tut. Off once more. Tearing one of my badges from my greatcoat, I hurl it out to let them scramble like kiddies for the last memento of THEIR OFFICER.

The waves rush past. Homeward bound. Calais fades into the mist. I stare and stare. Can this really be the end? The end of that adventure started so long ago. How long ago? Five years and three months. Like the waves, my thoughts race in currents through my brain. Was I sad? Was I glad? Reader, I cannot tell.

ILL NEVER TIRE

Leaving my chums behind, the ones who would never call me Jim again, or Sergeant, their bones lay at Thiepval, at Ypres, Kemmell Hill, Cambrai, the Hindenburg line, and – and a sob shakes my body. Good G★★, it's awful, just awful. What a memory! A glorious memory! And God had spared me, spared me to live and tell the story you have read, and the story I'll never, never tire in telling of that Army of mere boys that halted, held, fought, beat back to the Rhine, the most terrible war machine this world has ever known. 'Glorious and immortal memory.

WHAT A MEMORY!

THIS IS RE SKETCHED FROM A ROUGH DRAWING OF TOMMY "ROONEY" – ONE OF D COY'S BEST – AND A GREAT SOLDIER

AS I write these last few words in completion of my self-imposed task embodied in *Star Shell Reflections* a tear drops from my eye, a sob is in my heart as the mists of time fade away. Tis as yesterday. Memories keep crowding back. I can hear the tramp! tramp! tramp! of marching men on the cobblestones of that old French highway; like a ripple on the sea it travels down the ranks. 'There's a long, long trail a-winding … into the land of my dreams.' We pick up the chorus, and sing as only D Company could sing. And I'm marching, towards that blood-red horizon, on the Western Front with

Jim Maultsaid

THE END

.......and I'm ━━━━
.......marching ━━━━
......towards ━━━━ THAT BLOOD RED HORIZON,

JIM MAULTSAID